Reason without Freedom

D0165759

'David Owens's book is an original and important contribution to the emerging literature of "virtue epistemology" and deserves to be widely read: it could help jar epistemological debate out of its well-worn grooves.'

Michael J. Williams, *Northwestern University*

'Owens engages with extremely basic questions about belief and knowledge in novel and suggestive ways. . . . An original and liberating contribution to epistemology.'

Adam Morton, *University of Bristol*

We call beliefs reasonable or unreasonable, justified or unjustified. What does this indicate about belief? Does this imply that we are responsible for our beliefs and that we should be blamed for our unreasonable convictions? And does it imply that we are in control of our beliefs, that what we believe is up to us?

Reason without Freedom argues that the major problems of epistemology have their roots in concerns about our control over and responsibility for our beliefs. The founders of modern epistemology – Descartes, Locke and Hume – addressed these issues but they have been largely neglected by contemporary epistemology. Yet the issues we confront today – scepticism, the analysis of knowledge, and the debates about epistemic justification – can be tackled only once we have understood the moral psychology of belief. David Owens argues that we do not control our beliefs, either by means of the will or through reflection. Nevertheless, we are responsible for our beliefs since responsibility does not require control. Thus, we can see where the truth lies in the debate between Descartes, Locke and Hume over whether belief is governed by reason.

Reason without Freedom also explores how memory and testimony can preserve justified belief without preserving the evidence which originally justified it. This book will be essential reading for all those interested in contemporary epistemology, philosophy of mind and action, ethics and the history of seventeenth and eighteenth century philosophy.

David Owens is a Lecturer in Philosophy at the University of Sheffield.

International Library of Philosophy

Edited by José Bermúdez, Tim Crane and Peter Sullivan

Recent titles in the ILP:

Personal Identity and Self-Consciousness
Brian Garrett

The Sceptical Challenge
Ruth Weintraub

Dispositions: A Debate
D. M. Armstrong, C. B. Martin and U. T. Place
Edited by Tim Crane

Psychology from an Empirical Standpoint
Franz Brentano

G. E. Moore: Selected Writings
G. E. Moore
Edited by Thomas Baldwin

The Facts of Causation
D. H. Mellor

Real Time II
D. H. Mellor

The Conceptual Roots of Mathematics
J. R. Lucas

Stream of Consciousness
Barry Dainton

Knowledge and Reference in Empirical Science
Jody Azzouni

Reason without Freedom

The problem of epistemic normativity

David Owens

London and New York

First published 2000 by Routledge
11 New Fetter Lane, London EC4P 4EE

Simultaneously published in the USA and Canada
by Routledge
29 West 35th Street, New York, NY 10001

Routledge is an imprint of the Taylor & Francis Group

© 2000 David Owens

Typeset in Times by
BC Typesetting, Bristol
Printed and bound in Great Britain by
St Edmundsbury Press, Bury St Edmunds, Suffolk

British Library Cataloguing in Publication Data
A catalogue record for this book is available from the British Library

Library of Congress Cataloging in Publication Data
Owens, David (David J.)
    Reason without freedom: the problem of epistemic normativity/David Owens.
        p.   cm. – (International library of philosophy)
    Includes bibliographical references and index.
    ISBN 0–415–22388–1 (hardcover) – ISBN 0–415–22389–X (pbk.)
    1. Belief and doubt. 2. Free will and determinism. 3. Reason. I. Title. II. Series.
    BD215.O94 2000   99-087518
    121′.6–dc21

Contents

Preface

An author decides, not discerns, that their book is finished. This book is no exception. There are points that could be made more clearly, issues that ought to be settled more definitively and opponents who should be refuted more decisively. Readers will discover these flaws for themselves; but I can't resist entering two pre-emptive caveats.

First, *Reason without Freedom* focuses on an epistemic notion of belief rather than on the action-explanatory notion that you find in, say, decision theory. I explain why in the Appendix to Part 1 but this material is confined to an appendix precisely because of its provisional character and limited scope. An adequate treatment would involve a long excursion into the philosophy of mind and perhaps the philosophy of science as well.

Second, if I am right, many of the issues confronting epistemologists turn on a question which (at least nowadays) very few of them consider at all: whether responsibility requires control. In Chapter 8 I argue that it does not, but the matter needs a much deeper treatment than I give it there. Despite this, I hope to have said enough to bring out the huge importance of the issue and to establish that my rather unorthodox response to it is at least defensible.

Many people have helped me with this book. I am particularly grateful to a current colleague, Chris Hookway, and a former colleague, Tom Pink. Conversations with Tom were a major source of inspiration in the early stages of this project, while Chris provided generous criticism and sage advice during its later stages. Michael Huema and Robert Hopkins read large parts of the manuscript, and their responses occasioned substantial revisions. In 1998 I gave a series of talks at the University of Birmingham, and the audience there helped me to clarify my ideas on a number of issues. I also benefited from comments provided by Michael Martin, Johannes Roessler, Helen Steward, Richard Holton, Paul Noordhof, Jody Azzouni, Jonathan Adler, Peter Carruthers, Robert Stern, Leif Wenar, Jennifer Saul, Michael Smith and Keith Frankish. Writing a book can be a desiccating experience; without Sam Gonzales it would have been.

The first complete draft of this book was written during the academic year 1996–7 while I was a visiting scholar at the Graduate Centre of the City University of New York. I am grateful to the Graduate Centre for having me, to the Fulbright Commission for granting me a senior scholarship and to Steven Stich for arranging the visit. The University of Sheffield granted me one semester's sabbatical leave and the British Academy funded a second semester.

The majority of Chapter 10 is taken from 'The Authority of Memory', which was published in the *European Journal of Philosophy* 7(3) in December 1999.

Introduction
Rationality, responsibility and control

Two views of belief

Is belief governed by reason? Here is McDowell:

> Judging, making up our minds what to think, is something for which we are, in principle, responsible – something we freely do, as opposed to something that merely happens in our lives. Of course, a belief is not always, or even typically, a result of our exercising this freedom to decide what to think. But even when a belief is not freely adopted, it is an actualisation of capacities of a kind, the conceptual, whose paradigmatic mode of actualisation is in the exercise of freedom that judging is. This freedom, exemplified in responsible acts of judging, is essentially a matter of being answerable to criticism in the light of rationally relevant considerations. So the realm of freedom, at least the realm of the freedom of judging, can be identified with the space of reasons.
>
> (McDowell 1998a: 434)

McDowell takes his cue from Kant, but he might equally have invoked Descartes or Locke. In recent years, similar sentiments have been expressed by Burge and Korsgaard, among others. All these writers take it that beliefs are subject to reason, that we are responsible for them in being aware of what would (and would not) justify them, that belief formation is something we do, not something which happens to us – and that this implies the existence of intellectual freedom.

But not every Enlightenment thinker followed Locke and Descartes. Hume observed that belief 'depends not on the will, nor can be commanded at pleasure' (Hume 1975: 48). Rather 'nature, by an absolute and uncontroulable necessity has determined us to judge as well as to breath or feel'; for Hume, 'belief is more properly an act of the sensitive, than of the cogitative part of our natures' (Hume 1978: 183). Does this mean that belief is not governed by reason? If we like we can *call* the psychological laws that govern the formation of belief 'laws of reason', but in that case 'beasts are endowed with thought and reason as well as men' (ibid.: 176). A dog learns how to please its master; it believes, on the basis of experience, that running when summoned will bring reward and avoid punishment. Such 'experimental reasoning' is something we have 'in common with beasts' and 'is nothing but a species of instinct or mechanical power, that acts in us unknown to ourselves' (Hume 1975: 108). It sounds as if Hume places belief, not in McDowell's space of reasons, but in the naturalist's space of causes.

Hume and his opponents sharply disagree about whether belief is subject to reason. But underlying this is some measure of agreement over what would have to be the case for belief to be subject to reason. Believing would have to be a form of agency that is free in a sense strong enough to ensure that we can be held responsible for our beliefs. Without such accountability, how can there be such a thing as epistemic rationality? And what is the point of calling beliefs 'justified' or 'unjustified' if the believer cannot be held responsible for them? In denying the existence of epistemic agency, doxastic responsibility and intellectual freedom, Hume means to reject the idea that belief is subject to reason. He allows that beliefs are governed by the sort of biological norms that apply to the process of breathing, or the workings of the human heart, but no one thinks us responsible for non-compliance with such norms.[1]

Two views of freedom

I think both Hume and his opponents would accept the connections diagrammed in Figure 1.

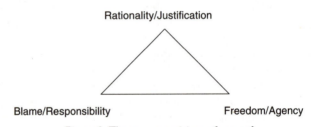

Figure I The presuppositions of reason?

But they don't think alike about either agency or freedom. Hume observes that belief is not subject to the will – I can't form a belief at will as I can move my arm at will – and this seems a pertinent observation in that those bodily movements which are our paradigms of free agency are indeed subject to the will. On the other hand, Hume's opponents will insist that there is a broader notion of agency (and of freedom), not equivalent to being subject to the will, which applies to anything governed by reason and which underwrites the Kantian idea that the realm of reason is co-extensive with that of freedom.[2] Surprisingly little effort has been put into saying exactly what this broader notion of control amounts to, but we can start by picking up some hints from McDowell.

When we are told that beliefs are freely formed, or are under our control, we are being told something which is meant to *explain* why they are subject to reason, why the norms which apply to belief formation are not of the same sort as those which govern heart-beats, and so forth. For the notion of freedom to help here, we must be able to say something more about what it involves than merely that it applies just to those states which are subject to reason; otherwise calling something 'free' would be just another way of saying that it is subject to reason. It is not that the philosophers who deploy this broad notion of freedom have altogether ignored this requirement. They tell us that freedom arises when reasons can influence us by means of a certain mechanism, the mechanism of *reflection* on our reasons.

We can see this idea coming through in the passage quoted from McDowell. McDowell acknowledges that belief is not always, or even usually, the result of 'judgement': we don't habitually exercise our power of control over belief. But belief is subject to reason only because we have such control, a control we exercise by forming a view about what we ought to believe. I dub this form of freedom *reflective control*. McDowell *et al.* think that wherever a subject's psychological states are governed by reason, they are under his or her reflective control; so intention and action, as well as belief (and perhaps certain desires and emotions), must be under our reflective control. But these writers should allow, as McDowell implicitly does, that many states which perfectly reflect the subject's reasons, are not a product of *actual* reflection on those reasons.

Let us try to explain, along these lines, what it is for a state like belief to be governed by reason. We start out from the idea that a belief is justified if it adequately reflects those reasons available to the subject: a justified belief in *p* is produced by the operation of the subject's experiences and other beliefs, states which combine to provide a rational motivation for the belief that *p*. None of this need involve reflection; rather it requires a *responsiveness to reasons*, reasons of which the subject is non-reflectively aware. Now how do we make room for an element of agency, freedom or control? If anything is in control of the belief-forming process here, it looks to be the beliefs and experiences that motivate belief in *p* rather than the subject who enjoys these beliefs and experiences.

McDowell tells us that responsiveness to reasons requires that the subject be *able* to do something which he does not usually do, that is make a judgement about what he ought to think. A rational subject must be able to influence the process of belief formation by reflecting on the quality of the reasons for and against belief in *p*. In so doing, the subject takes control: he assumes responsibility for his belief. Now we have put freedom, agency and control back into the picture; now we have an account of what governance by reason involves: governance by reason exists where we can take responsibility by exercising reflective control.

Three of the notions I've just deployed will reappear regularly in what follows, so it is worth defining them:

- A state is *subject to reason* (or *governed by reason*) when we can assess it as justified or unjustified, rational or irrational.
- A state is *responsive to reasons* when it can be motivated by an awareness of reasons which would justify that state.
- A state is *under reflective control* when it can be motivated by higher order judgements about the probative force of the reasons for it.

These definitions are provisional, but I have said enough to distinguish the three notions and set up the issue that interests me.

In what follows, I shall assume that 'subject to reason' and 'responsive to reasons' are *a priori* co-extensive. Take beliefs. If *internalism* about epistemic justification is the doctrine that a subject's beliefs are to be justified (or not) by considerations of which she is aware, then (throughout Parts 1 and 2 of this book) I embrace internalism. A rational believer is precisely a person whose beliefs are motivated by an awareness of considerations which justify them. There may be a reason for my heart to beat at a certain rate (to ensure the proper circulation of blood), and I might be aware of this reason, but this reason doesn't justify my heart-beat since my awareness of it does nothing to make my heart beat. Similarly, a reason of which I am unaware, or which leaves me unmoved, for me to believe that p does nothing to justify my belief in p. Much the same is true of desires, emotions and actions: they are subject to reason only in so far as they are responsive to reasons.

What remains an open question is whether 'under reflective control' and 'responsive to reasons' also are co-extensive: our beliefs, desires and emotions are responsive to reasons, and are thus subject to reason; but are they under our reflective control? This seems to be a substantive issue and that alone shows that 'under reflective control' and 'responsive to reasons' cannot be synonymous. The fact that 'under reflective control' and 'responsive to reasons' are distinct concepts means that McDowell *et al.* must work to link them; but it also gives them an opportunity: as a distinct concept, reflective control can be used to provide a substantive account of what it is to be responsive to reasons (or subject to reason) and, in particular, of what it is for epistemic norms to apply.

One might think reflective control intrinsically unsuited to this task because this notion cannot itself be elucidated without an implicit reliance on the idea that certain mental states are subject to (epistemic) norms. The instrument of reflective control is a higher order judgement, a judgement about whether epistemic norms are satisfied: how could we understand the distinctive content of such a judgement without already grasping the idea that certain states are subject to epistemic norms? This objection would be well taken were we seeking a reductive account of what it is to be subject to reason. But a substantive account need not be reductive: it need only be capable of falsehood and, I'll argue, this non-reductive account is indeed false. It is interesting because it purports to tell us how the notion of freedom gets a grip in the realm of belief; and its failure shows that such intellectual freedom is a mirage.

Reason without freedom

I agree with internalists that talk of justification or rationality is in place only where we are willing to impute responsibility, and a subject can be held responsible for thinking in accordance with reason only in so far as he is aware of the promptings of reason. I diverge from Enlightenment rationalism in rejecting the idea that such responsibility requires control. Philosophers from Locke and Descartes through to contemporaries like Burge and Korsgaard insist that we are responsible to epistemic norms only if we are free to conform our beliefs to the demands of reason. These philosophers adopt what I call a *juridical theory of responsibility*: for them, normativity implies responsibility and responsibility requires control. I argue that this commitment to control is both unnecessary and impossible to fulfil: an internalist must renounce it.

Those hostile to internalism, as well as some internalists themselves (including Descartes, but not Locke) have tended to assume that 'under our control' must mean 'subject to the will' and since we clearly cannot believe things at will, internalism begins to look untenable.[3] But I agree with McDowell *et al.* that there is another notion of control available to us, namely reflective control. When properly elaborated, it is a notion of control which can do some very important work for us, providing us with a theory of freedom of the will. As I argue in Part 2, the will is not itself subject to the will and so freedom of the will cannot be explained in terms of the will. Rather our capacity to make practical decisions freely involves a form of control exercised by the judgement rather than the will, namely reflective control.

Anyone who thinks that rationality and responsibility presuppose some form of freedom will hope that such freedom extends beyond the will to belief, desire and all those other things which are governed by reason. In Part 1, I argue that this hope will remain unfulfilled, at least for belief. The demand for reflective control in the epistemic sphere leads ultimately to scepticism: as Hume (1978: 184) puts it, reason 'must infallibly destroy itself' when applied to belief.[4] This leaves us with two options: either we follow Hume and abandon the internalist idea that we are responsible for our beliefs, that we can be held to epistemic norms; or else we reject the juridical theory of responsibility, the assumption that responsibility requires control.

Externalist epistemologists embrace the first option by breaking the connection between justification and responsibility (Goldman 1986: 384) and sacrificing the idea that justification must be based on reasons of which the subject is aware (Goldman 1979: 2).[5] For them, a justified belief is a belief which is the product of a process that reliably forms true beliefs, whether or not it involves awareness of reasons. Such a thin conception of justification could hardly support the sort of normative assessments that exercise the internalist. I recommend the second option, retaining the internalist link between justification and responsibility while rejecting the juridical theory of responsibility: we should detach responsiveness to reasons from reflective control.

I defend internalism, the idea that a subject's beliefs are to be justified (or not) by considerations of which he is aware, through Parts 1 and 2; but in Part 3 internalism receives an important qualification. No workable model of either memory or testimony can be constructed unless we acknowledge that a subject's beliefs can be justified by considerations of which *he himself* is not *currently* aware. I allow that our beliefs can be justified by reasons of which we are aware no longer, and by reasons of which someone other than ourselves is aware. This is hardly to concede the externalist's point that facts unknown to anyone can justify our beliefs. It simply allows us, in certain circumstances, to transfer our epistemic responsibilities on to someone else (or on to our earlier selves), someone who has evidence unavailable to us. As the internalist insists, justification requires awareness of reasons.

Part 1
Belief and reason

Chapter 1

Reflection and rationality

For Descartes and Locke the very idea that belief formation can be rational requires that it be governable by reflection. Both sought to guide the conduct of our understanding, to persuade us to regulate our thinking by reference to the natural light of reason. Both thought that to be free to conform one's thinking to the philosopher's recipe for correct reasoning one must be able to control one's beliefs by reflection on whether they do so conform. Both moreover held us fully responsible for any lapse from cognitive propriety and neither shrank from using words like 'duty' and 'obligation' in this connection.

Before I criticise this line of thought, it requires much further articulation: a fair amount of work on the opposition's behalf has to be done. Chapter 1 is devoted to this task. In particular, two questions arise. First, what is reflection? What is the instrument by which we are meant to exercise control over our mental lives? Second, given that each of us can reflect on our mental life, what is required for that reflection to be an instrument by which we can exercise control over it? What sort of impact must our reflective judgements have on thought and action for us to be in control of these phenomena?

Reflective control

Korsgaard links reflection and rationality in the following passage:

> A lower animal's attention is fixed on the world. Its perceptions are its beliefs and its desires are its will. It is engaged in conscious activities but it is not conscious *of* them. That is, they are not the objects of its attention. But we human animals turn our attention onto our perceptions and desires themselves, onto our own mental activities, and we are conscious *of* them. That is why we can think *about* them.
>
> And this sets us a problem no other animal has. It is the problem of the normative. For our capacity to turn our attention onto our own mental activities is also a capacity to distance ourselves from them, and to call them into question. I perceive, and I find myself with a

powerful impulse to believe. But I back up and bring that impulse into view and then I have a certain distance. Now the impulse doesn't dominate me and now I have a problem. Shall I believe? Is this perception really a *reason* to believe? I desire and I find myself with a powerful impulse to act. But I back up and bring that impulse into view and then I have a certain distance. Now the impulse doesn't dominate me and now I have a problem. Shall I act? Is this desire really a *reason* to act? The reflective mind cannot settle for perception and desire, not just as such. It needs a *reason*. Otherwise, at least as long as it reflects, it cannot commit itself or go forward.

(Korsgaard 1996a: 92–3)

There is something very attractive about this picture of human life. It connects up freedom, rationality and self-consciousness in a most satisfying fashion by suggesting that these constitutive features of our personhood stem from a common source. It also makes no distinction between practical and theoretical cognition. Korsgaard denies that our beliefs need be dominated by evidence any more than our actions are dominated by desire. She thereby secures the autonomy and dignity of our mental life as a whole.

We might put Korsgaard's point as follows: *my* reasons must be reasons *for me*, reasons in my eyes, reasons whose force I can appreciate and then implement in belief and action. Were perception to determine belief, and desire to motivate action, without (the possibility of) intervention by 'the reflective mind', these perceptions would not be my reasons for belief and these desires would not be my reasons for action. These are my reasons only in so far as I am disposed to endorse them. By endorsing them, I make them my own and I commit myself to the line of thought or the course of action which they recommend. And this commitment has a motivational impact: without it, I cannot 'go forward'.

Here reflection sounds like a form of judgement. To reflect on our perceptions and desires is to think about them, to make them the objects of cognition. Reflective judgement is a psychological state which refers to other psychological states, a state with a *second-order content*. Furthermore, it is a judgement with a *normative* content, a judgement about what justifies what. But is this correct? Why can't the instrument of reflective control be a desire (perhaps a desire with a second-order content[1]) or, more plausibly, an act of will? Perhaps I exercise control in deciding what I *shall* think or do, rather than in merely deciding what I *should* think or do.

In Part 2, I argue that practical judgement, and not the will, is the instrument of control over our own agency. I can fail to endorse my intentions, I can think that I ought not to act on them. Were I unable to stop myself acting on them, I would no longer be in control of what I do. For those who extend reflective control to our convictions, the same will be true of belief: someone who can't stop thinking ill of racial groups whom he realises he knows nothing about, has lost control over his beliefs. We lose control when our mental life is not as we think it should be and we can't put it right: normative judgement is the locus of control. True, I can think that my judgements about what I should believe and do are themselves unreasonable, but to think this is precisely to *judge* those states. So we have an answer to our first question: the instrument of reflective control is a normative higher order judgement.

Less clear is what influence these judgements are meant to have on our mental lives. Surely rationality does not require continuous reflective inter-vention; rather it implies the capacity to control what happens by means of reflection. But what exactly does this control, when exercised, involve? Sometimes we exercise control by endorsing (or rejecting) beliefs we have already formed, or decisions we have already taken. Korsgaard calls belief or action 'rational' when reflection *would have* endorsed it. But such retro-spective endorsement can't be the only form reflective control takes. For retrospective judgement to be a form of control at all, it must have some effect on whether we hold the belief (or implement the decision) in question. And if we can influence our beliefs in this way, surely this is because we have a general capacity for epistemic control, one which also enables us to deter-mine our beliefs in prospect: control can't be purely retrospective. Korsgaard appears to acknowledge this when she speaks of us standing back from the impulses of perception (and desire) and assessing them *before* committing ourselves to belief (or action).

Metaphysical libertarians will be unimpressed by this picture of freedom. If our judgements as to what we should believe (or do) are themselves deter-mined by factors beyond our control, be they evidential or non-evidential, how, the libertarian will ask, can our capacity to make such judgements set us free? But the assumption lying behind this question, that true control must be total and unconditional, is unwarranted: control can emerge from a psychological background which we do not control. Korsgaard is trying to articulate a modest compatibilist notion of freedom, one which applies to both belief and action. For her, human beings have reflective control over their actions, have freedom of the will, precisely because we can form a view of what we ought to do and implement our practical judgement in action. My interest is in whether this modest conception of freedom can also be applied to belief, as Korsgaard clearly thinks it can.

Deliberation and reflection

How can we hope to gain reflective control over belief? As Hume insisted, we can't expect belief to be subject to the will in just the way that action is: if we do direct belief, this control must be exercised through our judgement rather than by means of our will. Now we often decide how things are by thinking about evidence. One determines whether John is the murderer by attending to indications of his guilt. Contemplating his bloody clothes and unexplained absence from work, we are convinced that he is the murderer, while if we paid no attention to these things and went by his pleasant demeanour alone we might have let him off. But we did attend to these things, and they determined our view. Can this fact alone give us some sense of control over what we believe?

Here what directly determines how we think about John are his bloody shirt and absence from work. I do decide to attend to these things, but once that decision is made, the evidence takes over and I lose control. It might be argued that I held off from forming a view on the basis of his pleasant demeanour alone and waited for more evidence. Doesn't this amount to an exercise of control over what I believe? But all that occurred was that his agreeable countenance proved insufficient to close my mind on the matter, to eliminate doubt about his innocence, and so I set off once more in search of evidence. In the end, it is *the world* which determines what (and whether) I believe, not *me*. When I reach a conclusion by means of evidence, one external fact is convincing me of another: the bloody shirt establishes John's guilt, as ice on the sidewalk indicates snowfall. Where is *my* input at this final stage? Indeed I must be aware of these facts if they are to move me, but why should that give me any sense of controlling my convictions, as opposed to my beliefs being controlled by manifest features of my environment? Rational control requires more than responsiveness to reasons.

It seems that *first-order* deliberation cannot be the instrument of epistemic self-control. Reflection involves *higher order* judgements about our cognitive states, about their probative force and their ability to establish the desired conclusion. To determine whether John is guilty by such means is to reflect not on the bloody shirt but on my beliefs about the shirt, on the grounds for these beliefs and on their evidential significance. Reflective judgement concerns itself with the evidential relations between normatively constrained states, not objective statistical (or causal) relations between external facts. In second-order deliberation, I ask not whether the blood on John's shirt was the effect of him committing the murder but rather whether my evidence on this point would justify a belief in his guilt.

Now suppose the judgements which result from such a normative ascent determine what we think: that they compel conviction. Suppose it is *my judgement* that there is sufficient evidence of John's guilt which determines whether I think him guilty, not just the evidence (experience and testimony) itself. Then belief is no longer being determined solely by the impression the world makes on us: our view of the quality of our reasons, our judgement of the normative significance of our psychological situation, is what commands conviction. Wouldn't this constitute a capacity to exercise reflective control over belief?

The epistemic aspect of control

We now know that higher order judgement must be the instrument of reflective control. But how must our higher order judgements connect up with the rest of our mental life for them to play this role? My higher order judgement could hardly be an instrument of rational self-control unless my view of what I ought to think and do accurately reflects my reasons, both practical and theoretical. So reflective control has an *epistemic* aspect. Furthermore, these higher order judgements must have an influence on what I actually think or do. So reflective control has a *motivational* aspect, too.

According to the view under discussion, rationality presupposes reflective control: only someone whose mental life is under their reflective control can be rational. Since the rational person does what she has reason to do and thinks what she has reason to think, it is a requirement of rationality that reflective judgement correctly register the person's reasons and implement them in thought and action. In this section, I attend to the epistemic aspect of this requirement – the idea that a rational person's reflective judgements must correctly register her reasons – leaving the motivational efficacy of higher order judgement until later.

Non-reflective awareness

The internalist's central claim is that a subject's beliefs are justified only by considerations of which that subject is aware. To put it another way, if something is to be a reason for me, it must be something of which I am conscious. We shouldn't confuse such awareness, or consciousness, with being the object of higher order cognition.

As my discussion of first-order deliberation showed, responsiveness to reasons does not require actual reflection on reasons: I can form a rational belief in p based on evidence e without forming either the belief that I have that evidence, or the belief that e suffices to justify p. For example, an experience as of a black swan can move me to believe in black swans without the mediation of the thought that I am having such an experience. (The retort, 'But what if one didn't believe one was having such an experience? Surely then the experience couldn't serve as evidence for belief?', is unimpressive once we distinguish not believing one is having an experience as of p from positively believing one is not having such an experience.) Coherentists have a problem with the idea that sensory experience might justify belief, but the point I am making is not confined to the rational role of experience. If, by putting together various facts, I decide that Sarah is dishonest, I don't need to reflect on my various beliefs about Sarah in order for my conclusion to be rationally responsive to these beliefs: I normally reach such conclusions without any recourse to deliberation about the inferential significance, or well-groundedness, of the supporting beliefs.

McGinn appears to suggest that reflection is implicit in rational belief formation as such:

> the very possession of propositional attitudes requires self-consciousness: for the possession of propositional attitudes requires sensitivity to principles of rationality, and such sensitivity in turn depends upon awareness of one's attitudes. . . . [I]f a person were not aware of his beliefs, then he could not be aware of their inconsistency; but awareness of inconsistency is (primarily) what allows normative considerations to get purchase on beliefs; so the rational adjustment of beliefs one to another seems to involve self-consciousness, that is, knowledge of what you believe.
>
> (McGinn 1982: 20)

How are we to read 'awareness of', 'knowledge of', 'sensitivity to' as they occur in these remarks? On one interpretation, they imply that when a subject is reasoning about what he should believe, what moves him directly are not his thoughts about how the world might be but rather his beliefs about his own beliefs and other mental states. On this view, to comply with epistemic norms, our subject must engage states with a second-order content: he must concern himself first and foremost with his beliefs and whether they measure up to the epistemic mark and only indirectly with what the world itself is like (Shoemaker 1988: 190–2). In other words, a subject is responsive to reasons only when he is reflecting on those reasons. So construed, this picture of belief formation is phenomenologically off-key: we usually form beliefs by asking ourselves how the world is. Even when engaged in abstract reasoning, our attention is not focused on our psychological states: one infers q from p without first forming the belief that one believes p and the belief that one believes that p entails q.

But perhaps my reading of McGinn's remarks has been rather uncharitable. McGinn could endorse a weaker and more plausible thesis: that the subject must be *capable* of ratifying at the reflective level any belief he forms without reflection. On this view, someone who believes that there are black swans because he seemed to see a black swan but without forming the belief that he has this experiential evidence and so forth, must be capable of forming these higher order judgements and of finding in them a compelling reason to think that there are black swans. He need not actually exercise this capability for his belief to be rational.

This idea sets reasonable limits to rationality and responsibility. When I glimpse a truck bearing down on me, I am automatically convinced that my life is in danger; there is no opportunity to exercise reflective control over this conviction. I have no time even to judge that I am having such an experience. Precisely for this reason, many will feel that blame is out of place here: where freedom and control are absent, responsibility cannot exist and without the possibility of our being held to account, assessments of rationality lose their point. There are epistemic norms only because there are many occasions when we can exercise reflective control over what we believe.

A creature who altogether lacks the concepts of 'belief', 'reason' and 'evidence' will not satisfy McGinn's condition. Such a creature may well process information about the world but it is not subject to reason because it has no awareness of the normative constraints on belief formation. It is tempting to move from this thought to the view that the process of rational belief formation must always engage these conceptual capacities, must always involve beliefs about what is a good reason for what, what contradicts what and so forth, that the notion of a belief must itself enter into the content of the states which motivate rational belief. But this temptation both can and should be resisted by the advocates of reflective control. To be responsive to reasons, the subject must have a *non-reflective awareness* of the considerations that move him, and this non-reflective awareness gives him the ability to reflect on them. But the actual formation of mental states with a second-order content is unnecessary.

Reflection and self-knowledge

For the advocate of reflective control, the ability to exercise rational control over belief is implicit in the very idea of a rational believer. Clearly, this cannot entail that we are continuously reflecting on our reasons, but it does entail something about the sort of epistemic access we have to our reasons. It implies that a rational subject must be in a position to know her own reasons.

Since we can exercise rational control over a belief only if we are in a position to motivate it by reflection on the quality of the reasons for it, if rationality presupposes reflective control then a believer's rationality alone must guarantee that she can make higher order judgements which correctly represent her reasons. Someone who is wrong about the character of her experiences or beliefs is hardly in a position to assess the rationality of those beliefs which depend upon them. So if a rational subject could be wrong about their reasons, then she could, without compromising her rationality, be unable to exercise reflective control over her thought. But it is supposed to be a requirement of rationality that we are in a position to exercise such control: therefore, our rationality alone must guarantee that we can know our own reasons (Burge 1996: 98–116).[2]

If rationality alone guarantees such self-knowledge, our access to our own reasons must have a non-observational character. When I come to know of *your* reasons by observing your behaviour and listening to what you say, these indications may mislead me about your reasons without compromising my own rationality. But I have a quite different way of knowing my mind. Not that we are infallible when it comes to the character of our own reasons.[3]

For instance, I may wrongly think I modestly believe that I will lose the race and I imagine this because I would very much like to be less prone to foolish optimism than I am. Here my erroneous view of my own beliefs is a symptom of wishful thinking. What is excluded by the idea of reflective control are *brute* first-person errors, errors about the reasons I now have that do not compromise my rationality: if I am fully rational and I form a view about my reasons, then that view must be right.[4]

Note that the claim here is about the epistemology of *reasons*, not the epistemology of *mind* as such. There may be all sorts of mental states – subpersonal, subconscious – for which brute error is a possibility. I am no more of an authority about the 'inferences' which, many perceptual psychologists tell us, are the precursors of my visual experiences than you are about mine. I, too, can be brutely incorrect about the explanation of my behaviour where the correct explanation does not invoke my reasons. Nor am I an authority about whether a particular instance of my behaviour is motivated by reasons or not (I may mistake a reflex for a bit of intentional behaviour). Reflective control requires only that I can know the reasons which actually do motivate me.

It is worth emphasising the individualistic character of the notion of reflective control. The advocates of reflective control think that we each have a responsibility for our own beliefs which we don't have for the beliefs of others. They think this because, in their view, I have a control over my own beliefs which I don't have over the beliefs of others. True, I can exercise a certain influence over another's beliefs, by reasoning with him or her (and other more surreptitious methods), but this influence is indirect: if anyone is directly responsible for this belief, it is the believer. We certainly think each individual has a special responsibility for his or her own deeds precisely because we all have direct control over much of what we do; the advocate of reflective control says the same for belief.

One might explain this first-person–third-person asymmetry of control by reference to an epistemic asymmetry: I directly control and am thus directly responsible for the rationality of my own mental life because rationality alone ensures that I get my reasons right. In contrast, I can be wrong about your reasons without irrationality. So reason gives me a control over my mental life which I do not have over yours. But this can't be the whole story – control has a motivational aspect also. If rationality requires that our beliefs and actions be under the control of reflective judgement then rationality must guarantee not only that I can judge my reasons correctly but also that this judgement can motivate compliance.[5]

This book is largely about the motivational aspect of reflective control. My contention is that belief escapes our control because of a motivational failure, and I leave it open whether we have that authoritative knowledge of our epistemic reasons which reflective control requires.

The motivational aspect of control

For us to exercise reflective control over belief, our views about what we should believe on the evidence before us must have an influence over what we actually do believe. I'll put this point by saying that these normative judgements must be capable of *rationally motivating* belief. The word 'motivating' here is not meant to imply some sordid, illicit influence on belief. It is used simply to register the fact that reasons for belief produce belief, as reasons for action produce action, by explaining their product in a way that makes sense of it.

Scanlon affirms the motivational efficacy of higher order judgements and uses it to mark out those psychological states that are subject to reason:

> The class of attitudes for which reasons in the sense I have in mind can sensibly be asked for or offered can be characterised, with apparent but I think innocent circularity, as the class of 'judgement-sensitive attitudes'. These are attitudes that an ideally rational person would come to have whenever that person judged there to be sufficient reason for them and that would, in an ideally rational person, 'extinguish' when that person judged them not to be supported by reasons of the appropriate kind.[6]
>
> (Scanlon 1998: 20)

Because such attitudes are judgement-sensitive, Scanlon goes on, they are 'up to us' and we can properly be held responsible for them, even though they are not under our 'voluntary control' (i.e. are not subject to the will) (Scanlon 1998: 22 and 400 n.13). Note that, on Scanlon's account, the mere fact that we can causally influence a psychological state by judging it would not make that state 'judgement-sensitive'. We can see this by considering a type of psychological state *not* governed by reason: perceptual experience.

Many perceptual psychologists (Descartes and Locke included) have noted that one's expectations may influence the content of one's sensory experience: expecting a friend to emerge out of the fog in the next few minutes, I am much more disposed to see a swirl in the mist as his silhouette. Now if such first-order beliefs can exercise a causal influence over experience, the higher order judgement that I ought to see my friend coming though the mist in the next few minutes could surely exercise a similar influence. But that would not show that sensory experience is responsive to reason, that we can fix our sensory experiences by reason alone. Clearly sensory experience is not subject to reason and, on a Scanlonesque view, this is because it is not 'judgement-sensitive': someone without such a capacity to influence their experience may still be ideally rational. If human sensory experience is completely impervious to belief (as some psychologists of perception insist), our rationality is not thereby compromised.

Scanlon offers us an account of responsiveness to reasons along the lines suggested in the passage quoted from McDowell (1998a) with which I opened the book: responsiveness to reasons presupposes reflective control because it requires possession of the capacity to motivate beliefs, desires, emotions, actions, etc., by making higher order judgements about the quality of our reasons for them. To make this account work we must allow Scanlon (as I did McDowell) the circularity involved in specifying the demands of reason as those reflection on which necessarily has motivational impact on a rational person, otherwise sensory experience might be subject to reason. But even granting this, an important question remains unanswered: how can such higher order judgements exercise any motivational influence at all on the rational subject *over and above that already exercised by the subject's non-reflective awareness of her first-order reasons*?

Scanlon observes that 'judgement-sensitive attitudes can arise spontaneously, without judgement or reflection' (Scanlon 1998: 22), so there must be a way in which reasons can fix our attitudes without our needing to reflect on those reasons. Someone can be responsive to reasons without actually seeking to exercise reflective control over his mental life. So when one does form a view about one's reasons, and thereby seeks to exercise reflective control, exactly how can this judgement exert a rational influence on one's mental life? How does it strengthen the motivational force of one's reasons? After all, to have arrived at the reflective judgement in the first place, one must have been (non-reflectively) aware of the reasons on which the judgement is based; and if that awareness was insufficient to motivate a reasonable thought or action by itself, how can the higher order judgement do any better?

Of course, Scanlon is right to observe that an ideally rational person will form a correct view of what she ought to think or do and that her beliefs, actions, etc., will conform to that view, simply in virtue of her rationality. But such conformance doesn't give the judgement a motivational role of its own unless we also suppose that the rational person's thoughts and actions conform to her higher order judgement *because* she makes the judgement, rather than simply because the judgement correctly reflects the reasons that actually motivate her. If you already have a non-reflective awareness of the reasons which ought to motivate you, how does the judgement that you ought to be moved by them help to ensure that you are so moved? Such judgements look like an idle wheel in our motivational economy, whether we are perfectly rational or not.

Judgement versus inquiry

One can miss this point quite easily because of an ambiguity, already noted, in the words 'reflection' and 'judgement'. On the one hand, these words may refer to first-order deliberation, a process of looking for new evidence, sifting and weighing it, and generally seeking out grounds for belief in a certain proposition. It is undeniable that such inquiry often does affect what we believe (and do), and it has an impact precisely because it expands the range of considerations of which we are aware *tout court*. But to exercise reflective control, as I am using the term, is not to engage in an activity intended to uncover new first-order reasons: rather it is to attempt to get yourself to be reasonable by explicitly acknowledging (by means of higher order judgement) the normative force of those reasons you already have.

Might the advocates of reflective control duck the issue I have just raised by re-defining the notion of reflective control? When they say that we have reflective control over belief, perhaps all they really intend is that we can influence our beliefs by means of inquiry, by means of activities (like evidence gathering) intended to get at the truth. There is indeed such a view abroad but, seeing no sign of it in the authors under discussion, I postpone a detailed examination of it until Chapter 5. Nevertheless, it is worth pausing to indicate why such 'reflective control' cannot serve their purposes, cannot explain why our beliefs are answerable to epistemic norms. Again, perceptual experience can be used to make the point.

Perceptual experience is not subject to reason: sensory experience can be veridical or illusory, but it cannot be justified or unjustified, rational or irrational. As we have seen, Scanlon may offer to explain this difference between belief and experience by asserting that we have reflective control over the former and not over the latter: if a rational person judges that one of his beliefs is false, this motivates the abandonment of that belief but the judgement that an experience is illusory need not extinguish this experience. Take the Muller–Lyer illusion. If I learn that one parallel line looks longer than the other only because of the misleading depth cues provided by the arrows at the end of the lines, I will cease to believe they are different lengths on pain of irrationality. But the illusory experience may still persist without any irrationality on my part. For Scanlon, belief, and not experience, is subject to reason because belief, but not experience, is under our reflective control.

Now Scanlon's account works only if we understand reflective control as involving higher order judgement and not first-order inquiry. For it is perfectly possible to remove a sensory illusion by doing something to expose the source of the illusion to view (e.g. ignoring the misleading arrows and concentrating on the relative length of the lines). Searching with our sensory organs, the perceptual scrutiny of a surprising phenomenon, are activities intended to get at the truth, activities which can transform an illusory into a veridical experience. If the only control we had over belief was by means of first-order activities intended to gather evidence and reveal the truth, belief and perceptual experience would be on a par: the one would be no less under our control than the other. Clearly our control over our beliefs is supposed by Scanlon to be more direct than that, as is our responsibility for them, and so reflective control cannot be understood in this fashion.

There is more to epistemic control than simply causation of belief by first-order inquiry: higher order judgement must be a source of rational motivation for belief. But the problem remains – how can such judgements be a source of reasons, even for me, over and above those provided by the first-order reasons they concern? In Chapter 7 I provide an answer to this question, but it is an answer which applies only to judgements about what we ought to do and not to judgements about what we ought to believe.

Reason and motivation

Let us now isolate and highlight the target at which I'll direct my fire throughout Parts 1 and 2:

> *Reflective Motivation*: if R is a *prima facie* reason to believe that p, reflection on R provides the rational subject with a motive to believe that p.

Reflective Motivation claims that reflection on *prima facie* reasons for a certain belief is a source of motivation for that belief: such reflection provides a subject with a way of exercising rational control over his beliefs. And rational subjects necessarily possess this source of higher order motivation. Reflective Motivation says nothing about the motivational powers of reflection on other topics. I might, for example, contemplate how nice it would be if I acquired a certain desirable belief, but since the desirability of that belief is not even a *prima facie* reason for it, Reflection Motivation says nothing about whether that reflection will move me.

So understood, Reflective Motivation can be passed off as mere common sense: after all, if R is a reason to believe that p and you judge that you have reason R, surely that reflection ought to incline you to believe that p, at least in so far as you are rational? To dispel this air of banality, it will be helpful to distinguish two different claims which, taken together, imply Reflective Motivation:

> *Rational Motivation*: If a rational subject is aware of something R which provides them with a reason for belief, it also provides them with a motive for belief.

> *Reflective Rationalisation*: If R provides this subject with a reason for belief, the judgement that they have reason R also provides them with a reason for belief.

Taken together, these claims imply that if R furnishes a rational subject with a reason for belief, then reflection on R must furnish him with a motive for belief, just as Reflective Motivation says. So if evidence e provides the rational subject with a reason to believe that p, the reflection that he has evidence e must provide him with a motive to believe p.

Now Rational Motivation is true simply by virtue of the meaning of the word 'rational'. But to pass from Rational Motivation to Reflective Motivation, we need Reflective Rationalisation and that is where I baulk. My own view is that while both Reflective Rationalisation and Reflective Motivation may be commonsensical when applied to action and the will, neither carries over to belief. Reflection on the quality of our reasons for taking a certain practical decision may rationally motivate that decision but, perhaps surprisingly, reflection on the reasons for belief in a proposition cannot, in the same way, convince us of its truth. A *non-reflective* awareness of the considerations in favour of believing p is what rationally motivates belief in p. Rationality alone does not give the subject any capacity to influence his beliefs simply by reflecting on the quality of his reasons for them. In Chapters 2 and 3 I'll argue that Reflective Motivation fails and then, in Chapter 7, I'll trace its collapse to the failure of Reflective Rationalisation.

The juridical theory of responsibility

I take it that human belief is under the discipline of reason in a way that animal belief and the machinations of the sub-personal are not. People are held to account for what they believe because their beliefs should be based on a (perhaps non-reflective) awareness of something which would justify that belief. Reflective Motivation links the discipline of reason with control by reflection: we are responsible for our beliefs because we have the capacity to determine what we believe by reflecting on our reasons. This demand for reflective control goes a step beyond what I would accept, namely that we can be held responsible for our beliefs only because our beliefs are responsive to reasons. As we have seen, what drives this further demand is the thought that responsibility requires freedom and control: *nothing is down to you unless it is also up to you.*

I have called the last claim the *juridical theory of responsibility*. I chose this label because, in law, one is held responsible only for that over which one has control and, in this respect, the juridical theory seeks to assimilate all responsibility to legal responsibility.[7] But there are other aspects of legal responsibility with which I do not wish to burden adherents of the juridical theory. The law is a set of explicitly formulated (and published) rules. We all have an obligation to learn what these rules are and to apply them to our own situation. Someone over-impressed by the legal analogy might think that correct reasoning involves applying explicitly formulated rules to derive theoretical and practical conclusions. The exercise of reflective control will then be a matter of consulting these rules and asking what beliefs and actions they require of us.[8]

Now Reflective Motivation makes no mention of rules. It assumes that we are capable, by reflecting on reasons, of forming judgements about what we should believe (or do) but it says nothing about how such reflection should be conducted. Reflection might, on occasion, involve consulting principles of evidence or decision-theoretic maxims but we usually form judgements about what we ought to think (or do) intuitively, by weighing those considerations that strike us as relevant. Rule consultation happens only in quite special circumstances (e.g. when one is trying to identify a fallacy in reasoning). Nor do we rely on intuition only to save time. In Chapter 3, I urge that there are no rules which could always tell us what to believe.

Many writers insist that the formation of a belief can be justified without any explicit inference from or reflection on rules of reasoning (Van Cleve 1979: Part 2; Pollock 1986: 124–32; Burge 1993: 476–7; Brandom 1994: 18–30). For example, one does not come to believe that *p* by judging that one is enjoying an experience as of *p* and then invoking the principle that one is (*ceteris paribus*) entitled to accept the content of one's experience: rather the experience makes one feel entitled to the belief and, since there are no obvious grounds for doubting it, one believes. But this concession represents no retreat from Reflective Motivation. The sensible advocate of reflective control will admit that even when we do form a view as to whether a belief is justified, we are no more likely to consult a rule than we are when judging what we ought to do. Reflection (theoretical and practical) need not be a matter of consulting rules.

In Part 2, I argue that what drives the juridical theory is a practical analogy: we are responsible for our practical decisions because we have reflective control over them; and, the juridical theorist supposes, responsibility for belief must be rooted in control also. Clearly one can press this point without foisting upon theoretical deliberation an over-intellectualised model of practical deliberation. But, as we will see, the analogy is in any case misleading and the juridical theory misguided.

Chapter 2

Motivating belief

Before striking a blow against Reflective Motivation, I must first consider a widely held assumption about beliefs – evidentialism. Evidentialism is the thesis that what justifies belief in p is just evidence in p's favour. Nothing else is relevant to belief justification. Now evidentialism, far from being a support of Reflective Motivation, might appear to be in tension with it. After all, Reflective Motivation is there to articulate a claim to control belief, and what evidentialism seems to tell us is that (rational) beliefs are entirely constrained by how the world is (or appears to be). But the tension is only apparent. Many evidentialists wish to hold on to the idea that our (better) convictions are under rational control without claiming that they are somehow subject to the will. Reflective Motivation offers them a form of control that resides in our ability to influence what we believe by reflecting on the quality of the evidence for and against the proposition in question. According to them, this capacity to decide what is true by considering evidence is what gives us control over, and responsibility for, our beliefs.

However, there is a serious problem with this account of how we control belief: evidence alone cannot motivate the formation of a rational belief. When we assess how sensible a belief would be, we must ask ourselves whether there is *sufficient* evidence to justify that belief, and it is impossible to determine how much evidence we should require to convince us of the point without considering the importance of the issue, the cognitive resources available to resolve it, and so forth. These considerations are non-evidential and yet essential to the justification of belief. Therefore evidentialism must be rejected.

Can we dump evidentialism while adhering to Reflective Motivation? In fact, the whole idea of reflective control over belief is under threat once we acknowledge that such non-evidential considerations are needed to motivate rational belief. I can get myself to make a decision or perform an action by reflecting that time is running out, but I can't convince myself of p, even if p is favoured by the evidence, simply by judging that the time for a decision has arrived. Though pragmatic considerations are needed to rationalise belief, our rationality alone won't ensure that reflection on them can compel belief. Belief cannot be justified without considering pragmatic constraints, but reflection on these constraints is not a source of rational motivation for belief. It looks as though Reflective Motivation must be abandoned along with evidentialism: our substitute for the will, namely the power of reflection, will not secure us control over belief once we allow that non-evidential factors are needed to motivate belief.

Before getting down to business, some terminological preliminaries. I shall call the norms governing belief *epistemic* norms. In determining the rationality of belief, epistemic norms invoke both evidential and non-evidential considerations. The non-evidential considerations relevant to belief I shall call *pragmatic* considerations. I shall call the norms governing action *practical* norms. Practical norms include that of prudence, but I don't want to stipulate that the rationality of an action is determined solely by prudence. Instead, I shall assume that an action is rational just if the occurrence of that action (together with its consequences) would be desirable. The desirability of an action may be determined by all sorts of things, including ethical considerations (or even norms of etiquette).

Evidentialism is the doctrine that epistemic norms invoke only evidential considerations. Pragmatism (as I shall use that word) is the doctrine that epistemic norms invoke *practical* considerations, either as well as or instead of evidential considerations. In this chapter, I shall reject both of these doctrines, maintaining that epistemic norms invoke *pragmatic* (as well as evidential) considerations, but also that belief is not governed by the norms of practical reason. To put the point in a nutshell, while the rationality of an action is determined by the (apparent) desirability of that action, the rationality of a belief is not determined by the (apparent) desirability of that belief. Since I distinguish pragmatic considerations on the one hand from practical considerations on the other, it would be better for me if pragmatism had not been called pragmatism but, on that point, the history of the subject is against me.

Evidentialism

The evidentialist insists that evidential considerations alone are relevant to the fixation of rational belief. The function of a belief is to represent how things are in the world and therefore a reason to believe one thing rather than another must be a reason to think that the world is a certain way: a reason for belief must be a piece of evidence for the truth of the proposition believed. The evidentialist doesn't deny that non-evidential considerations do sometimes affect what we believe – we are prone to wishful thinking, self-deception and other such failings – but their influence is not a rational one. The fact that it would be beneficial to have a certain belief is no evidence for the truth of the believed proposition and therefore no reason for belief in it.

To get the evidentialist view exactly right, we must distinguish the rationality of beliefs themselves from the rationality of actions intended to induce belief. It may be rational to induce a false belief in oneself if one can't live with the truth, but the belief thereby induced remains irrational: the practical rationality of the belief-inducing action does not affect the theoretical irrationality of the induced belief. For example, the evidentialist can perfectly well admit that it is reasonable for me to visit the hypnotist in order to ensure that I think well of my boss and thereby improve my promotion prospects, regardless of how little there is to be said in his favour. And because this action is reasonable, a rational person can get herself to visit the hypnotist simply by reflecting on how desirable it would be to have this opinion. What the evidentialist will deny is that the belief induced by the hypnotist is reasonable: my desire to please my boss can provide no justification for this belief.

Given Reflective Motivation, the evidentialist can draw some conclusions about the motivational psychology of a rational believer from these normative facts. Since evidence justifies belief, we may infer that reflection on evidence should be able to motivate belief in a rational person, while our rationality gives us no similar capacity to motivate a belief by reflecting on its desirability. We might be able to cause this belief in ourselves by contemplating its desirability but such contemplation won't be a source of rational motivation for the belief. That is why a rational subject usually needs to visit the hypnotist (or engage in some other self-manipulative activity) in order to induce it (Williams 1973a: 148–51).

A problem for evidentialism

Unfortunately for the evidentialist, the mere fact that I am confronted with evidence for p can never, by itself, convince me of p: the evidence before me may not be enough to make belief reasonable. A reasonable belief will be forthcoming only when I have *sufficient* evidence in p's favour to warrant belief in p. And how are evidential considerations alone to determine when I have sufficient evidence? (De Sousa 1980: 136; Foley 1993: 198–201; Pollock 1995: 48–9). Perhaps if I had conclusive reason to believe that p were true, that would suffice but, the evidentialist will admit, I almost never have conclusive evidence. The amount of evidential support required for belief must be set at some level which allows that the belief may yet turn out to be false. And how are we to determine what the appropriate level is? Clifford's much-quoted evidentialist slogan – 'it is wrong, always, everywhere, and for anyone to believe anything upon insufficient evidence' (Clifford 1879: 183) – begs this question magnificently.

At this point, an externalist about justification can wave his hands and say that contextual factors determine what level of evidence counts as sufficient for rational belief: it is quite unnecessary for the subject to be conscious of this threshold, or of the facts which determine it. But someone of an internalist frame of mind should insist that a rational belief be motivated by factors of which the subject is aware, factors sufficient to justify the belief. So if evidence alone cannot determine when a belief is justified, the internalist evidentialist is going to have to find something else to complete the justification. This must be something the subject is apprised of and which is capable of moving him, if rational belief is to be possible. How could this something be anything other than the (perceived) needs and interests of the believer? I'll give some examples intended to illustrate this point, but my case against evidentialism does not rest on these particular examples. It can be made simply by asking: how are you going to tell us, in purely evidential terms, what level of evidence is needed to justify belief? Unless this question can be answered, evidentialism (internalist and externalist) must be abandoned.

I am wondering whether to purchase a house this year and that decision depends largely on whether I think prices will rise. I carefully read the property pages, listen to the pundits on television, determine that the house market will remain flat and plan an expensive holiday instead of a house purchase. Just before I form this view, a newspaper article by a respected economist appears which purports to show that house prices will rise. I don't read the article, and I don't let it worry me. Having insufficient time to try to assimilate and weigh his testimony against that of other experts, I stick to my view that prices will not rise. And this, we may suppose, is a perfectly reasonable line for me to take and one that I can explicitly avow to myself or to others.[1] Were I an economist specialising in the housing market and about to give a paper on future price movements to a conference of estate agents, I probably wouldn't be entitled to have a belief on the matter that did not take account of this article.

In this example, the belief I form is of some practical importance, but this feature is inessential. However abstruse the issues, however remote from everyday concerns the arena of inquiry, each of us must strike a balance between believing truths and avoiding falsehoods (James 1956: 17–19). How much risk of error are we willing to run in order to relieve ourselves of the burdens of agnosticism? The curiosity of an amateur astronomer about the origins of the universe will not be assuaged until he has a view on that question. Of course, he might not be able to form a view – the state of the evidence might be such that he remains agnostic – but such enforced doubtfulness will be a source of discontent (while to a professional astronomer, the frustration of curiosity may be less important than the risk of making a mistake). Here the amateur has no practical interest in the origin of the universe, but we can still determine when he has sufficient evidence to form a view.

These examples are not intended to illustrate some clash between evidential and pragmatic constraints on belief formation, rather they show how purely evidential considerations *underdetermine* what we ought to believe until they receive pragmatic supplementation. The evidentialist may be right to insist that whether I believe p rather than not-p is something that should be fixed purely by the balance of evidence for and against p. But where and when I form a view as to whether p is true will be determined by my sense of how important the issue is, what the consequences of having a certain belief on the matter would be and how much of my limited cognitive resources I ought to devote to it before reaching a conclusion. I can't spend my life assimilating evidence for and against all the propositions which interest me; and, even if I could, I would have no way of retaining it all for future consultation. At some stage I must form a (revocable) view on them; once I have done so I can cease to deliberate about them, throw away the evidence both for and against, and think and act on the assumption that they are true (or false).[2]

Perhaps the evidentialist can accommodate at least some of these points by distinguishing two issues: first, that of when we ought to engage in theoretical inquiry (i.e. collect, deliberate about and retain evidence) and, second, that of whether we ought to form a belief on the basis of the evidence before us. The evidentialist can happily concede that practical considerations have a bearing on the former issue; the collection, assimilation and retention of evidence is an activity which we can choose to perform or not as we please. Inquiry and deliberation are rationally motivated by practical considerations. Nevertheless, the evidentialist insists, whether a belief gets formed or not once deliberation begins is (or should be) determined entirely by the balance of the evidence considered. Evidence is the only thing that should motivate the formation of a rational belief.

But the above examples are aimed precisely at this evidentialist claim. Non-evidential considerations are relevant not only to the justification of further inquiry but to the justification of the result of inquiry. I don't just decide to ignore the economist's article, I make up my mind about whether house prices will rise without considering it, given the shortage of time and so forth. Whether it is rational to make up one's mind without this evidence or else to suspend judgement is determined by how much the issue matters to us, how difficult it would be to resolve, how much time we have to spend on it, what the consequences of forming a view would be and so forth. And it is the subject's (non-reflective) awareness of such non-evidential constraints that moves him to doubt or decision (Locke 1975: 659).

Renouncing belief?

The only way out for the evidentialist is to abandon belief altogether. Given that we can never have conclusive evidence about matters of empirical fact, might it not be best to refrain from forming beliefs about the empirical world and confine ourselves to registering the balance of evidence for and against the propositions which interest us? Of course, we must act but action does not require belief: we can act on the assumption that a certain proposition is true and our propensity to act on that assumption may be sensitive to the amount of evidence we have in its favour without our needing to determine its truth value. On this view, what is at stake in the examples sketched above is not whether there is evidence sufficient to underwrite a belief but rather whether enough evidence is available to justify action.[3]

In the house purchase example, the importance of the belief is largely practical. Perhaps belief could, for these purposes, be replaced by a behavioural disposition attuned to the strength of the evidence. But often we want to believe the truth for its own sake: we are interested in crossing the line between having the truth and not having it. Passing that evidential threshold, I think I know the truth. This may generate pride at an epistemic achievement, or pleasure in the satisfaction of curiosity, or simple relief that I now know how things are. Until I know whether John stole the bike, my emotional life is in turmoil: anger, sorrow, forgiveness all require *knowledge* of what John did (Unger 1975: 183–96). Once the matter is settled, my emotions are baffled no longer. How are we to account for all this without invoking the idea that evidence often suffices to move us across a threshold into a new state?

The evidentialist might hope to gratify at least some of our doxastic needs simply by informing us how much evidence there is in favour of any proposition which interests us. But often we think we know how it is with the world, not merely how likely the evidence makes it. And even if we are content to know only how much evidence there is in favour of various propositions, this is still something we wish to *know*, and the question arises once more: when are there sufficient grounds for claiming to know this? Either the evidentialist must maintain that this question somehow doesn't arise for claims about the balance of evidence or he must take the Pyrrhonian route and deny that we should believe, that we should claim to know, anything at all.[4]

But perhaps there is a middle way here. Perhaps the evidentialist can reconstitute the ordinary notion of belief – that tied to knowledge claims – by factoring the process of belief formation once more. Rather than dividing the activities of inquiry from the evidence which they generate, the evidentialist now makes the cut at a later stage, after all the evidence has already been collected. On this picture, one element of the belief forming process is our 'level of confidence' in the proposition – a quantitative sense of conviction tied to evidence. The other component is a commitment to the truth of the proposition, made in the light of the evidence and other practical considerations. By adding this element of commitment, we could arrive at the 'all-out' sort of belief tied to knowledge claims. Commitment sounds like an action motivated by practical considerations. At this point, evidentialism shades into pragmatism, and I will consider this proposal once pragmatism has been introduced.

Pragmatism

Non-evidential considerations are needed to motivate and justify action. We have seen that non-evidential considerations are needed also to motivate and justify belief, so it is natural to wonder whether the norms which govern agency also govern the formation of belief. Pragmatists say 'yes'. Pragmatism is the hypothesis that believing in p can be justified by reference to the desirable consequences of belief in p, just as raising one's arm can be justified by reference to the desirable consequences of one's arm rising. And if beliefs are governed by the same practical norms as actions, surely they are actions?

Were pragmatism correct, the prospects for Reflective Motivation would be bright. As rational people, we surely can move ourselves to act by reflecting on the desirable consequences of so acting. Practical norms seem to be norms we can enforce by means of reflection. So if beliefs are governed by practical norms, reflection is, on the face of it, a source of rational motivation for belief. In Part 2, I endorse the idea that action is under our reflective control and agree that this fact is the origin of our practical freedom. What I can't endorse is the suggestion that beliefs are under our reflective control because they are governed by the very norms that regulate rational agency. Epistemic norms are not practical norms, and the amenability of the latter to reflective enforcement gives us no reason to believe that the former are enforceable at the level of reflection.

One might object to the pragmatist view that beliefs are governed by practical norms on the grounds that practical rationality presupposes theoretical rationality. Any practical deliberation must employ beliefs about the consequences of various actions (including acts of belief formation). It can be rational to act in a certain way only if the beliefs on which we act are themselves rational, and so the rationality of action needs to be explained in terms of the rationality of belief. But the pragmatist could simply bite the bullet and insist that the rationality of these background beliefs is itself to be assessed by practical criteria. True, one could then ask how we know that these background beliefs are prudent if not by means of further beliefs, but the pragmatist might reply that his hypothesis creates no difficulties for theoretical reasoning which theoretical reasoning does not face already. If I believe p on the basis of evidence for p alone, it is a question how I justify the belief that I have evidence for p. This regress is not avoided just by making the rationality of belief a function purely of my evidence.

Yet such crude pragmatism remains indefensible: if there is little evidence for p, it is irrational for me to believe that p, however desirable belief in p may be. As already noted, we must distinguish the rationality of a belief from the rationality of an action designed to induce that belief. Suppose the parents of a boy reported killed in action would be far better off were they to believe that their son is still alive, in the teeth of all the evidence. They might well take measures to induce this belief in themselves, measures which would make them forget or ignore countervailing indications. But though it may be perfectly rational for them to do this, the belief thereby induced would not be rational. Our parents might have good reason to do things that would induce this conviction in themselves but these reasons do nothing to justify the conviction.[5]

Some philosophers have thought that a certain special class of beliefs – self-fulfilling expectations – are governed by practical norms.[6] A stunt man has decided to jump a row of twenty double-decker buses on his motorbike and, as things stand, he has an even chance of success. However, if he believes he will succeed, this tips the balance by making him approach the ramp with confidence while pessimism renders it likely that he will falter at the last moment and crash. The stuntman knows all this, and wants a successful stunt. Can a belief that he is likely to succeed be justified by the fact that this belief makes success more likely than failure?

If the answer to this question is 'yes' (and Reflective Motivation is true), the rational stuntman ought to be able to get himself to believe that he will clear the buses simply by reflecting on the advantages of having this belief, and on the fact that the formation of the belief will tip the evidential balance in its favour. But rationality alone hardly guarantees that he can do this. Try it yourself. Suppose there is strong evidence that believing one is attractive to others will be enough to tip the balance and make one attractive to others; could you go ahead and command belief on that basis? And if not, would that be a failure of rationality on your part, a doxastic analogue of weakness of will? Surely not.

As many writers have observed, we cannot reasonably form a belief simply to break an evidential tie.[7] Forming an intention to eat one of two equally desirable meals is a perfectly reasonable way of ensuring that you eat something and don't starve, and so the rational subject can get himself to form such an intention simply by reflecting on the need to take a decision. Yet so long as the evidence seems evenly balanced between p and not-p, the rational subject can only suspend belief, however much she might wish the matter resolved. And this is so even if she knows that belief in p would itself tip the evidential balance in p's favour. Of course, it may be rational for our stunt man to do something to induce optimism (drink a stiff gin), and once he has done it, optimism may become rational. But that is quite another matter.

Pragmatism reformulated

In the last section I argued that our needs and interests can influence the formation of a rational belief, so why exactly are the boy's parents being irrational? Suppose that instead of denying his death, they simply suspend judgement on the matter beyond the point at which a disinterested bystander could reasonably conclude that their son was dead. Since it matters so much to them to be right about whether their son is dead, are they not entitled to ask for more evidence than the disinterested bystander before coming to a conclusion? Such suspension of belief is not just understandable but epistemically unexceptionable. The parents fall into irrationality only when their needs and interests determine what conclusion they arrive at, rather than whether they draw a conclusion at all.[8]

In the light of this the pragmatist might qualify his claim as follows: practical considerations determine whether we should form a view about the truth of p but given that we want a belief on the matter, evidence alone determines whether we ought to believe p or believe not-p. Here the pragmatist is claiming that we should form a belief about whether p just in case the costs of having such a belief are outweighed by the benefits. On this view, belief formation is an activity constrained by the state of the evidence – it wouldn't count as an act of belief formation unless it reflected how we perceive the balance of evidence (just as saying certain words won't count as a sincere assertion that p unless p is believed) but, being governed by practical norms, it is something we do nonetheless (Heil 1984: 63; Nozick 1993: 85–9).[9]

The pragmatist, like the evidentialist before him, is attempting to factor the constraints on belief formation into a purely evidential and a practical component. But he is doing so in order to defend the idea that belief formation is subject to practical norms. Now I agree with the pragmatist that non-evidential considerations are needed to rationalise and motivate belief formation. But I don't agree that this makes believing subject to practical norms: the non-evidential considerations which help to fix the rationality of belief are not the practical considerations which govern the rationality of action. So there is no room in our cognitive lives for an act of belief formation, an act which is under our reflective control.

Say it would be very convenient for me to have an opinion about whether house prices will rise next year: perhaps I have to address that conference of estate agents and the way to create a good impression is to arrive at some definite conclusion, whether or not I turn out to be right in the end. On balance the evidence favours a flat market but really there is very little to go on. Can I reasonably believe in a flat market on this basis just to ensure that I speak with conviction and put in a bravura performance? I doubt it. One can't reasonably believe a conclusion favoured by the evidence before one, simply because it would be convenient to have a view on the matter and regardless of how little evidence there is (Nozick 1993: 88–9 and 96–8). That is why I could not get myself to believe in a flat housing market by contemplating the practical advantages of this belief: to induce it, I would have to visit the hypnotist, or whatever. But were the pragmatist correct and were Reflective Motivation to hold, a rational person ought to be able to motivate such a belief just by reflecting on the need to make a convincing speech.

The pragmatist might try to avoid this difficulty by tightening up the evidential constraint which must be satisfied before the act of belief formation takes place, before practical considerations are allowed to operate. Obviously what is required is *sufficient* evidence for *p*, not just that the balance of evidence should tip in *p*'s favour, and, as we now know, a certain quantity of evidence counts as sufficient evidence for *p* only against a background of pragmatic constraints. But we have yet to be given any reason to think that these pragmatic constraints are practical, that whether we should form a belief about whether *p* on certain evidence is a function of how desirable the belief that we would have to form on that evidence would be. On the contrary, it seems clear that at least some beliefs which are reasonable in the light of our evidence are also highly undesirable. Belief is governed by pragmatic considerations in a way very different from action.

This is hardly a surprising anomaly: many states are governed by norms which are neither practical nor purely evidential. For example, at least some emotions are subject to reason and it is quite obvious that both evidential and non-evidential considerations are needed to determine when gratitude, hope and joy are appropriate. Yet emotions are not governed by the norms of practical reason: if I need to make a rousing political speech, it is greatly to my advantage to be angry about something, even if there is nothing that I ought to be angry about. In this situation, I may quite reasonably get myself worked up without the resulting anger being at all reasonable. And because the anger's desirability does not make that anger reasonable, I can't get myself to be angry by reflecting on the advantages of anger. Anger is not, in that way, under my reflective control; and neither is belief.

The impotence of reflection

I have argued that pragmatic (but not practical) considerations are essential to the justification of belief. Were Reflective Motivation correct, it would immediately follow that reflection on these pragmatic considerations is a source of rational motivation for belief. But can we really exercise reflective control over belief by thinking about such things? No. Reflection on the pragmatic considerations which do determine the rationality of belief is no more efficacious than reflection on the desirability of the belief.

We deliberate about whether to believe that *p* just by deliberating about whether *p* (Heal 1990: 108–11). Ask yourself whether it is raining; what comes to mind is evidence for and against rainfall – the sunshine outside versus the watery blobs on the window pane. You don't decide that it is raining after contemplating how little time you've got to decide, how much the issue matters, what the consequences of making up your mind are, and so forth. Even if you do happen to reflect that time is running out, this reflection does not move you to belief in a way that it might move you to act. And you don't feel that your rationality is at all compromised by this fact.

Under pressure to leave the house, you can *act on the assumption* that it is raining (and take an umbrella): reflection on pragmatic factors can motivate activity. But contemplation of these time constraints, etc., cannot get you to believe that it is raining; only something which you take to establish that rain is falling can do that. Once you are convinced, all sorts of pragmatic considerations may be brought forward to justify the formation of this belief (on the evidence before you). And they justify the belief only on the assumption that it was indeed responsive to those reasons. But reflection on such pragmatic considerations does nothing, in a rational person, to motivate either the acquisition or the retention of the belief.

Wondering about this second-hand car, what is at the front of my mind is the evidence which the salesman brings forward to convince me and the signs of decay which I observe. But whichever way the balance tips, neither sort of evidence resolves the matter by itself. What makes up my mind is a *non-reflective appreciation* of the fact that I have other things to do, that it would be too much trouble to check up on everything I am being told, given the price of the car, and so forth. These considerations usually remain in the background, and for good reason: I could not force the epistemic issue by bringing them to the foreground, by reflecting that now is the time to form a view, that it would be best to believe that the car works. The case is quite unlike one where I remain agnostic about whether it will work or not but decide to buy the car anyway because I judge that I don't have time to think about the matter any more. Here I take a practical decision, I don't form a conviction, and I take that decision because I reflect that time is pressing, etc. Reflection on the limitations under which my practical deliberation labours can motivate action in a way that reflection on the limits of feasible theoretical deliberation cannot motivate forming a belief.

Action is under our reflective control. But what about practical decisions? Are they reflectively controlled? Surely they are. Say I decide now whether to ϕ because I reflect that later I won't have time to think about the matter, I want to avoid making an ill-considered choice in the heat of the moment and so I ought to settle things well in advance. Such reflections can rationally motivate the formation of an intention. It isn't true that to deliberate about whether to decide to ϕ is simply to deliberate about whether to ϕ – the merits of deciding whether to ϕ as well as the merits of ϕ-ing are food for motivationally efficacious reflection. So intention formation is under our reflective control, whilst belief formation is not.[10]

The role of deliberation

In Chapter 1, I articulated a notion of reflective control which was meant to underwrite our responsibility for the rationality of our beliefs. Any threat to such epistemic control appears to undermine the idea that we can be held to account for the rationality of our beliefs: responsiveness to reasons gives

us responsibility for belief only in so far as it gives us control over belief. Or so my opponents say. We can now see why the claim that pragmatic considerations are needed to motivate the formation of rational belief encounters such resistance, its extreme plausibility notwithstanding; we can now appreciate evidentialism's appeal.

Reflective Motivation implies that, if pragmatic considerations provide reasons for belief in *p*, reflection on these considerations must be capable of convincing us of *p*'s truth, at least in so far as we are rational. Obviously, we can't make explicit everything relevant to the justification of either belief or action. But to the extent that our reasons can be made explicit, Reflective Motivation guarantees that reflection on them can assuage doubt, or persuade us to believe and act. Now many of the pragmatic constraints on belief formation undoubtedly can be made available to reflection, yet I have denied that reflection on them is liable to convince us of anything simply in virtue of our rationality. Such reflection might cause a conviction but, then again, anything *might* cause a conviction. The point is that our rationality alone will not guarantee that such reflections have any motivational influence. We just do not have that sort of control over belief.

Does this assertion fly in the face of obvious facts? We sometimes engage in internal ratiocination about whether we ought to believe what we do, confident that such ratiocination may have some effect on us. And this internal ratiocination often has a pragmatic aspect ('I have not thought enough about this. . . . I made up my mind too quickly'). Similar assumptions underlie social ratiocination: we talk to one another about whether our beliefs are sensible given the importance of the issues before us, hopeful that the probity of our reasoning will have a sobering effect on our interlocutor (Pettit and Smith 1996: 429–36).

But we can account for such facts without supposing that my views as to whether either you or I should believe that *p* normally have any direct influence over whether we do believe that *p*. If I judge that we shouldn't believe that *p*, this may motivate first-order inquiry into whether *p*, and the considerations which inquiry unearths may get us to abandon our belief in *p*. But, as I urged in Chapter 1, such indirect control over belief is not sufficient to underwrite rational responsibility for belief. According to my opponents, rational responsibility requires reflective control, and to determine whether we have reflective control over our belief we must ask whether we can get ourselves to believe not-*p* simply by judging that we have sufficient reason to believe not-*p*, as I can get myself to raise my arm simply by judging that I have sufficient reason to raise my arm. This we cannot do.

Conclusion

On the one hand, evidence alone can never convince a reasonable person of anything (*pace* evidentialism) because evidence alone can never determine when he has sufficient evidence to form a belief; other non-evidential factors are essential to reasonable belief. On the other hand, it seems equally clear that our needs and interests cannot motivate belief as the pragmatist supposes: reflection on these concerns might stimulate various epistemic activities – the collection of evidence, a certain amount of deliberation – but it cannot move us to belief. Reflective Motivation must be abandoned: we must acknowledge that there are reasons to which rational believers are responsive, reflection on which could not rationally motivate belief.

But don't we end up with a rather messy account of theoretical deliberation? There are now two kinds of reason at work in the epistemic realm, each with a quite different mode of operation: first, the evidence which naturally comes to mind when we think about what we should believe; and, second, the pragmatic constraints which operate in a more 'subterranean' way to produce belief in a proposition, given the evidence for it. How, one wonders, can they interact to produce a belief? A desire for theoretical simplicity tempts one to look for a psychological state which is produced by the evidence alone, whose strength is proportional to the evidence and which can stand in for full-blown belief. At least this would provide a unitary account of how epistemic reasons motivate belief formation.

But this disparity between evidential and non-evidential reasons for belief is illusory. As I shall argue in Chapter 3, belief can no more be motivated by reflection on inconclusive evidence for the proposition believed than by contemplation of the limitations on our cognitive resources. To believe that p, I must be under the impression that I have a conclusive reason to think p true: reflection on inconclusive evidence is quite inadequate. Nevertheless, my awareness of inconclusive evidence plays an essential non-reflective role: it combines with a sense of the constraints on my cognitive resources to produce the impression of a conclusive reason. And all this happens beneath the level of reflection: evidential and non-evidential motives for adopting the belief operate in an exactly similar fashion.

It is a commonplace that belief aims at truth. One might imagine that belief aims at truth in the way that a shot aims at a target. In the case of an ordinary target, there is some point short of the target at which we calculate we are sufficiently close to risk a shot at it, given how important it is for us not to miss, etc. It is not like that with belief – to believe is already to be sure that you have hit the target. We can't get ourselves to believe, to shoot, simply by reflecting that it is sufficiently likely that we will be on target. In belief, what we claim is *knowledge* of the truth, not just a sporting chance of being right. Believing is not an action with truth as its goal, which is why it is not under our reflective control in the way action is. Pursuing truth in belief is nothing like seeking the good through action.

Chapter 3

Knowledge and conclusive grounds

In Chapter 2, I argued that reflection on inconclusive evidence for p alone could never move us to belief in p because a certain body of inconclusive evidence will appear sufficient to justify belief only against a certain pragmatic background and this background must exercise its rational influence beneath the level of reflection. But why can't reflection on the pragmatic sufficiency of a certain quantity of inconclusive evidence move us to belief by virtue of our rationality? Is this just a brute fact or is there something about the nature of belief which explains why this should be so?

To see a way forward here, we must acknowledge a link between belief and knowledge – to think yourself justified in believing that p is to think you know that p. Now suppose that knowing p involves more than having inconclusive evidence for p (and p's being true). Suppose it requires that we have a conclusive ground for p. Then it would be clear why reflection on inconclusive evidence, however adequate, could never move a rational person to belief in p. For to think yourself entitled to believe that p is to think you know that p, and to think you know that p is to think you have a conclusive ground (not inconclusive evidence) for p. To clinch this point, I must begin by re-establishing the connection, recently lost from sight, between knowledge and justification.

Knowledge and justification

Epistemology is the theory of knowledge, but much recent epistemological writing concerns not knowledge but justified belief. This change of focus reflects a widespread conviction that producing an analysis of knowledge and producing a theory of epistemic justification are two quite separate tasks. The connection between knowledge and justified belief once seemed very simple – to know that p was to have justified belief in p which was true – and so, provided we had an account of justification in hand, knowledge would pose no problem. But Gettier's counterexamples to the true-justified-belief analysis of knowledge convinced the philosophical community that there was more to knowing than having a true (internally) justified belief;

knowledge requires an extra element which is, like truth, external to the mind (Gettier 1963).

Philosophers reacted in rather different ways to this result. Those sympathetic to internalism about epistemic justification tended to see Gettier as dealing a death blow to any internalist account of knowledge. In a defensive manoeuvre, they sloughed off the project of analysing knowledge while insisting that no external element need enter our analysis of justification (Pollock 1986: Appendix and Foley 1993: 54–9). Some internalists went even further by suggesting that knowledge is simply unimportant: justification is what matters (Kaplan 1985).

But it is a grave error to divorce knowledge from belief justification: belief implies the claim to know. Knowledge (and not just truth) is the aim of belief. Once the connection with knowledge is broken, the whole idea of belief as involving a certain 'yes or no' commitment to the truth of propositions is undermined; it becomes unclear why we don't just replace our all-out notion of belief with that of a state which reflects the subject's degree of confidence in a proposition, one which implies no claim to knowledge. I think we can weld knowledge and belief justification back together and thereby defend the ordinary notion of belief without falling into externalism about justification.

Two models of knowledge

The pressure to divorce justification from knowledge does not come solely from the demise of the true-justified-belief analysis of knowledge. There is a far older and perhaps deeper tension between two different views of knowledge. When I claim to know something, I may be asked how I know this, and it is by answering the question correctly that I sustain my claim to knowledge. So if I claim to know that there is snow on the ground, it may be that I can see the snow or it may be that I infer this from the people I see entering the office in snow-covered boots; both answers would establish my title to knowledge. But how exactly do they support my knowledge claim?

According to one model of knowledge, these answers cite the inconclusive evidence on which I base my claim to know. My experience of the snow and my experience of the dirty boots are just different forms of evidence. Evidence for snow is a state of the world which does not involve snow but which indicates that snow is present, which makes snow likely. Either of these sensory experiences may serve as evidence in this sense: both can exist without there being any snow but both give us grounds for believing that snow is around. I can never have absolutely conclusive grounds for such a belief; nevertheless some level of evidence entitles me to claim to know.

But there is another picture of knowledge which requires that my reasons be conclusive. On this view, to say how I know that *p* is not to note something which makes it more or less likely that *p* is true but is to describe how the truth of *p* manifested itself to me: either I perceived the snow, or I learnt of it from the boots. Each state requires the presence of snow: snow is necessarily implicated in the perception of snow and in any process of learning about it. I could neither perceive nor learn of snow unless snow was indeed present; neither is mere evidence of snow. Indeed, according to this picture of knowledge, no knowledge claim could be based on evidence for snow because mere evidence could not ground the certainty required for knowledge.

Each of these models of knowledge has some appeal. When we inquire whether it was reasonable of someone to claim knowledge of *p*, inconclusive evidence for *p* together with the constraints on their cognitive resources seem quite sufficient to underwrite an affirmative answer. But once we assume the deliberative standpoint and ask ourselves whether *p* is true, to answer with inconclusive evidence seems quite insufficient: at best that can tell us whether *p* is likely to be true. To motivate a claim to knowledge we feel the need for something which establishes *p*'s truth: a conclusive reason. Knowledge both does and does not require conclusive grounds.

One obvious way to resolve this tension is to claim that the two models are modelling different things. The evidential model concerns the *internal* justification component of knowledge – our reasons for belief – while the conclusive reasons model focuses on the *external* connections which must be present for me to know; thus, we divorce our account of justification from our analysis of knowledge. But, in fact, the tension arises within the internal standpoint itself – the need for conclusive grounds is felt by the epistemic subject and not just by the analyst of knowledge. Over the next two chapters, I intend to resolve the quandary from that internal standpoint and thereby defend internalism without divorcing knowledge from justification.

To prepare the way, I adopt a terminological convention. I'll speak of inconclusive evidence and inconclusive reasons for belief but not of 'conclusive evidence' or 'conclusive reasons' for belief; rather I'll use the terms 'conclusive grounds'. Reasons are what motivate and justify the subject's belief; grounds are what the subject needs in order to have knowledge. My contention is that the subject can believe he has conclusive grounds for *p* and yet be perfectly well aware that his evidence for *p*, the reasons which motivate his belief in *p*, are inconclusive. The key to resolving the apparent contradiction is to allow that knowledge claims are rationally motivated by considerations reflection on which could not rationally motivate a knowledge claim. Rejection of Reflective Motivation is required.

The evidential model

Gettier's problem

Textbook discussions of knowledge usually start from the true-justified-belief analysis but they rarely try to *motivate* that analysis. Rather they assume its attractions are sufficiently obvious to make their demolition of it an event of some intellectual consequence. I agree that this account of knowledge does look extremely plausible; it is plausible, not because of its simplicity (or venerability) but because it forges an intuitive link between belief and knowledge. It explains why one is not justified in believing that *p* unless one is entitled to claim to know it. On the true-justified-belief analysis, someone who feels justified in believing *p* will feel entitled to claim to know *p*, for (on this analysis) the only thing knowledge of *p* requires, over and above a justified belief in *p*, is *p*'s truth and someone who believes *p* is already committed to *p*'s being true and thus to their knowing *p*. So the connection between belief and the claim to know on which I have just insisted falls straight out of the true-justified-belief analysis.

Furthermore, rejection of the true-justified-belief analysis threatens to break this natural connection. Suppose there were more to knowing that *p* than having a true and justified belief in *p*. Call that extra requirement *X*. Then in order to claim knowledge of *p*, one would have to have grounds for thinking that *X* was satisfied. Yet (we are supposing), one might have a justification for *p* even if *X* were not satisfied. It seems to follow that one is not committed to believing that *X* is satisfied simply by virtue of thinking one has a justified true belief in p: one could think oneself justified in believing that *p* without thinking one knew that *p*. But this is surely absurd. To think of oneself as being in a position to believe that *p* *is* to think oneself justified in claiming to know that *p*. One might believe *p* without claiming to know that *p* if one thought one's belief in *p* unjustified, but how could one think it right to believe *p* without thinking one knew *p* to be true? Hence the true-justified-belief analysis of knowledge must be sound.

But is this apparent consequence of rejecting the true-justified-belief analysis really so absurd? Having heard the weather forecast, I declare that I believe it is going to rain tomorrow but refrain from claiming to know this. Here I say that I believe *p* because I have evidence which favours *p* more than it favours not-*p*, but I am not yet in a position to declare for *p* outright and so deny that I know it. This suggests that belief sometimes aims for truth rather than knowledge: we are justified in believing that *p* where we are justified in thinking *p* true, and we can feel justified in thinking *p* true without claiming to know that p.

The words 'believe' and 'know' are indeed used in this way, as more or less emphatic modes of assertion. But I am interested in a different use of these words – one which dominates the literature on the analysis of knowledge –

on which they denote two interconnected states. Nothing less than thinking that you know could be the psychological state which, together with justification and truth (and perhaps something else), ensures that you do know. And so the beliefs which interest me imply claims to knowledge. Of course, one's beliefs can be more or less well justified, but someone who thinks she has a certain level of justification for belief in p will, to exactly that extent, feel justified in claiming to know p. Using this epistemic notion of belief, we can express the state of mind of someone who is willing to say only that she believes (and not that she knows) it will rain tomorrow as follows: she believes rain tomorrow is more likely than not (where this is something she would claim also to know).

Having grasped the point of the true-justified-belief analysis, we are ready to confront Gettier's counter-examples to it. Take the case of a plausible liar who tells me that the Queen is dead. I have every reason to trust him so I acquire the belief that the Queen is dead: if any belief acquired by testimony is ever justified, surely this belief is. Suppose further that, unbeknown to the liar, the Queen has in fact died. Here I have a true and justified belief but I could hardly be said to know that the Queen is dead. My belief was based on excellent evidence; nevertheless my belief is true by sheer fluke, and that is not good enough for knowledge. Condition X is, it seems, the requirement that it be no accident (in a sense yet to be elucidated) that my belief is true given the evidence I have for it.

Gettier's counter-examples leave the true-justified-belief theory stone dead, but any replacement for the theory must respect the motivation behind it. An acceptable analysis of knowledge must ensure that we are justified in believing p only where we are entitled to claim to know it. The way to secure this result is to find a condition, X, to complete the analysis which is such that any evidence sufficient to justify belief in p will be sufficient to justify also the belief that X obtains (and therefore p is known).

Harman's (first) solution

Harman is one internalist who seeks to accommodate Gettier's point within an evidentialist model of knowledge while remaining true to the spirit of the true-justified-belief analysis. He argues that what goes wrong in the Gettier cases is that there is some proposition q, essential to our justification of p, which we (justifiably) believe but which is false (Harman 1973: 120). For example, we justifiably believe that the liar is a reliable informant and we accept that the Queen is dead because we have this false belief. But knowledge cannot be based on a false belief, so whilst we are justified in believing that the Queen is dead we don't know that she is dead. In Harman's view, there really is no more to knowledge than justified true belief but what has to be true (and justified) are all the beliefs relevant to the belief that p and not just the belief that p itself. Since to be justified in believing p is to be justified in thinking that p, and all the propositions which I would use as evidence for p, are true, it is clear why, if I am justified in believing that p is true, I am justified in claiming to know p.

Now one might wonder whether there will always be a false background belief in any Gettier example to pin the blame on, especially where the justified belief in question has been acquired without inference. But even if this question is answered in the affirmative, Harman's proposal can't prevail. Take the set of all my beliefs and suppose they are all both true and fully justified. Since there is now no question of a false belief in the background, it should simply follow that my beliefs constitute knowledge. Yet *ex hypothesi* the evidence I have for each of my beliefs is inconclusive – the propositions I would invoke to support them do not guarantee their truth – so each of them can be false, my evidence notwithstanding. But if they can be false, given my evidence, why can't they also be true by accident, given my evidence? Therefore justified true belief is still insufficient for knowledge.

To illustrate this point, suppose my informant is not a liar and is in fact reliable. Then the relevant beliefs of mine will be true and, on Harman's account, I should have knowledge. But if the belief that he is reliable is to constitute inconclusive evidence for the belief that the Queen is dead, its truth cannot (when taken together with the truth of whatever else I believe) *entail* that the Queen is dead. Even reliable people can be wrong on occasion. But if reliable people can get things wrong, why can't they also be right by accident? We could try to rule this out by stipulating that I must have a further (true) belief that this has not happened but such a belief won't solve the problem. Either this further belief will (taken together with what I already believe) entail that the Queen is dead, or else it will be possible to construct an example in which it is a fluke that the Queen is dead, even given the truth of that belief.

The problem is not confined to Harman's proposal. Any analysis of knowledge (internalist or externalist) whose fourth condition, X, does not actually entail the truth of p will face exactly the same objection. For if X does not entail the truth of p, then p can be false even though X obtains and if p can be false even though X obtains, why can't p be true by accident even in the presence of X (Zagzebski 1994: 69; McDowell 1998c: 403–4)? It looks as if knowledge requires conclusive grounds.

The conclusive grounds model

I have been examining an evidential model of knowledge according to which we support a claim to knowledge by citing evidence for the proposition we claim to know. Evidence for p will never guarantee p's truth, at most it renders p likely. An advocate of the opposing conclusive grounds model will be unsurprised that this produces trouble. How, he will ask, can one claim to know that *p* if all one really knows is that *p* is likely to be true? On his view, the real moral of Gettier's examples is that we can't make a belief supported by inconclusive evidence into knowledge simply by supposing it to be true. One can truly believe that *p* and have plenty of evidence for *p*, yet fail to know that *p*. Knowledge requires conclusive grounds (Dretske 1978).

According to the conclusive grounds model, we went wrong in equating justification for belief with possession of evidence for the proposition believed, where this evidence is consistent with that proposition's falsehood. To perceive or learn of *p* is to be justified in believing that *p* in a way which really does suffice for knowledge of p: it is to have a conclusive ground for *p*. Such a ground would simply be unavailable unless *p* were true: we can hardly perceive or learn of something which isn't so. Furthermore, because these knowledge-constituting states cannot be factored into an internal evidential and an external truth component which might be accidentally conjoined, there is no way of constructing a Gettier example. To have a veridical hallucination as of *p* is not to perceive that *p*; to hear some lie which is coincidentally true is not to learn that p: one perceives and learns of *p* only if one thereby acquires knowledge of *p*. On this view, the analyses of knowledge spawned by the Gettier problem are best seen as attempts to explain what it is to have such a conclusive ground, i.e. what it is to perceive, learn, etc.[1]

Internalist worries

Many will feel that a verbal trick is being played on them here. Such conclusive grounds are reasons only in the extended (externalist) sense of the word in which the fact that it is raining can be my 'reason' for believing that it is raining. Surely the rain must register with me before I feel entitled to believe anything: my belief is motivated by a state of mine which registers the rain, not by the rain itself. True, my perception of rain informs me of it but, to those inclined towards internalism, this state looks like a combination of a state of the world (light from the rain hitting my eyes or whatever) and a state of me – an experience or some sort of belief – which registers the rain and which alone is my real reason for belief in it.

As formulated, this worry contrasts states of the world with states of the subject, but it would be a mistake to search for some physical or metaphysical boundary here: the point at issue is a normative one about what can serve as my reason. Say that I seem to be perceiving rainfall, but in fact I am enjoying an illusory experience, an experience whose veracity I have no grounds to doubt and take for a perception. If my sole reason for thinking it is raining is that I perceive this and in fact I don't perceive it, then it looks as if I believe in rainfall while lacking any reason so to do. And to believe without reason is surely irrational. Yet is it not grossly unfair to accuse me of irrationality just because I have been taken in by an illusory experience? To require that knowledge claims be based on conclusive grounds is, it seems, to expose ourselves to allegations of intellectual irresponsibility every time we believe a falsehood.[2]

The internalist's insistence that sensory knowledge must be based on inconclusive evidence derives from the need to cover us against the possibility of illusion. When the subject discovers his experience as of p to be illusory, he has to admit that he fails to perceive that p, and therefore does not know that p. Once apprised of the situation, he should be willing to admit his ignorance; but must he also concede that his claim to know was groundless? Can't he draw our attention to some mental state which justifies his previous claim to know that p? Since he never perceived that p, he won't appeal to that mental state. So, the internalist infers, inconclusive experiential evidence, so conceived, must be capable of motivating a claim to knowledge. But this sits ill with the moral I drew from the Gettier examples that knowledge requires conclusive grounds.

Worries resolved

In fact the tension between the internalist's plausible claim and the thesis that knowledge requires conclusive grounds is merely apparent. To think I am justified in believing that p is to think I know that p and to think I know that p is to think I have a conclusive ground for believing p. So far so good. Why does this conclusion make trouble for the idea that inconclusive evidence can rationally motivate belief? Suppose we assumed Reflective Motivation. Then from the proposition that inconclusive evidence can rationally motivate belief we could infer that reflection on inconclusive evidence for p can also rationally motivate belief, something I would deny. But this untoward result follows only given Reflective Motivation.

Once the assumption about rationality embodied in Reflective Motivation has been abandoned we can do justice to both models of knowledge. On the one hand, it seems that the evidential model must be right because our knowledge claims are invariably based on inconclusive evidence. On the other hand, it seems the conclusive grounds model must be correct because we could never convince ourselves of something simply by reflecting on inconclusive evidence for it. The answer is that the evidential model is right in that beliefs (and so knowledge claims) are rationally supported by a *non-reflective* appreciation of inconclusive evidence, but the conclusive grounds model is right in that one can claim to know something only in so far as one thinks one has conclusive grounds for it. Inconclusive evidence makes you confident that you know that p precisely by making you believe that you have perceived (or in some other way learned of) p. And you do know that p just when this belief is true.

Note I am not saying that the thought of a conclusive ground for *p* can motivate belief in *p*. It is not the *belief* that I am perceiving (or learning) that *p* which moves me to belief in *p*. Rather the belief that *p* and the belief that I am perceiving that *p* are coeval, each motivated by a non-reflective appreciation of the evidence for *p* (and relevant pragmatic considerations). The belief that I am perceiving that *p* (if true) registers the fact that I have a conclusive ground and it is this fact, not the belief in it, which enables me to know. When I am asked how I know that *p* and I reply that I have seen that *p*, I am not citing an element in some deliberative process which led me to form the belief in *p*; I am simply explaining (in a third-person sort of a way) how *p*'s truth manifested itself. The psychological situation in a case of knowledge based on perception is illustrated in Figure 2.

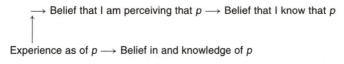

Figure 2 Perceptual knowledge

Two quick questions. First, couldn't we concede that a claim to know requires the thought of a conclusive ground while insisting that this thought may be motivated by reflection on inconclusive evidence? If inconclusive evidence is sufficient to justify a belief in *p*'s truth, why isn't inconclusive evidence sufficient to justify the belief that there is a conclusive ground for *p*? Indeed it is, but one can't get oneself to believe that one has a conclusive ground for *p* by reflecting on inconclusive evidence for *p*, any more than one can get oneself to believe *p* by reflecting on inconclusive evidence for *p*. To believe that one has a conclusive ground is to claim to know this and, like all knowledge claims, this cannot be motivated by reflection on inconclusive evidence.

Second, anyone with her wits about her will realise that her beliefs are based on inconclusive evidence. Shouldn't this reflection undermine these beliefs if they do indeed require a conclusive ground? No. Such reflections can neither motivate nor undermine belief. When I reflect that there is no way of making sense of my beliefs unless I suppose that they are motivated by non-evidential considerations like the importance of getting things right, that reflection does nothing to motivate the belief but equally it does nothing to undermine it. And it is precisely such pragmatic factors that move me to regard some inconclusive evidence as establishing the presence of a conclusive ground.

Summary

I have relied on two premisses:

(1) To think that I have a rational belief in *p* is to think that I know that *p*.
(2) To think *x* knows that *p* is to think *x* has a conclusive ground for *p*.

Premiss (2) is the idea that knowledge requires conclusive grounds – which is, in my view, established by Gettier's examples. Premiss (1) is a truth expressed from the first-person present tense standpoint. Note that the impersonal analogue of (1) –

(1*) To think *x* has a rational belief in *p* is to think *x* knows that *p*

is false. One can easily think of someone else (or of one's past self) that he or she (or oneself) has a rational belief which is not knowledge.
  Now from (1) and (2) we can infer

(3) I can think that I have a rational belief in *p* only if I think I have a conclusive ground for *p*

which is perfectly consistent with the fact that one can have a rational belief in *p* even if one lacks a conclusive ground for *p*. The troublesome analogue –

(3*) To think *x* has a rational belief in *p* is to think *x* has a conclusive ground for *p*

which prevents us from recognising the possibility of rational error, follows only given (1*). (3*) would prevent you judging of yourself that what you once reasonably believed was not known. What is impossible is not this but rather the judgement, ruled out by (3), that what you now reasonably believe is not known.

Knowledge unanalysed and rationality uncodified

To know that *p* is to have a conclusive ground for *p*. Does this constitute an analysis of knowledge? I fear not. I gave some examples of conclusive grounds and said enough to distinguish them from inconclusive evidence, but I didn't say what a conclusive ground was. And since I didn't tell you what a conclusive ground was, neither did I tell you what knowledge was. For example, a veridical hallucination as of *p* might furnish me with evidence sufficient to justify belief in *p*, provided I have no reason to suspect that it was an hallucination. And if I enjoy a veridical hallucination as of *p*, I am in a state which I couldn't be in unless *p* were true. But such an experience neither provides me with a conclusive ground for believing that p, nor gives me knowledge of p. A proper analysis of knowledge should explain the difference between sources of knowledge like perception and states like veridical hallucination.

Anyone familiar with the epistemological literature of the last thirty-five years would rightly shudder should I now propose to analyse knowledge: evidence we do not possess, deviant causal chains, pre-emptive, over-determining or fail-safe mechanisms, bizarre but close possible worlds, all conspire to frustrate analyses of knowledge in general and of perception and memory in particular. Fortunately, my purposes in this book do not require a reductive analysis of knowledge, or even the assurance that such an analysis is possible.[3] But they do require me to point out a certain consequence of a failure to analyse knowledge.

If I am right, the unanalysability of knowledge has an interesting corollary: the uncodifiability of rationality. I insisted that you are entitled to believe that p just when you are in a position to claim to know it; from the inside, knowledge and justification cannot come apart. Given this, were it impossible to say what it is to know that p, what it is to be a conclusive ground for p, we should encounter similar difficulties in saying what it is to be entitled to believe that p. And so we do. The fact that rational belief implies the claim to know explains the link between knowledge's unanalysability and reason's uncodifiability.

This connection is somewhat obscured in the extensive literature on the analysis of knowledge. Gettier focused our attention on hypothetical situations where a belief is both true and justified but fails to constitute knowledge. This made it look as if the hard task for an analyst of knowledge was to say exactly what, over and above mere justification, is required to turn a true belief into knowledge. But why take the justification component for granted and problematise only the elusive 'fourth condition' (X)? After all, to be justified in believing that p is to be entitled to claim knowledge of p (and *vice versa*), so if it is impossible to say what constitutes knowledge of p, how can it be any easier to say what constitutes a justification for p? The fact that you can have justification without actually having knowledge, that you can perfectly reasonably think the conditions for knowing obtain without their actually obtaining, is beside the present point.

Harman for one is sensitive to this connection between knowledge and justification. He suggests that we 'turn scepticism on its head and use intuitive judgements about when people know things to discover when reasoning occurs and what its principles are' (Harman 1973: 112). We'll discover that, though knowledge requires conclusive grounds, any attempt to explain what a conclusive ground is will invoke pragmatic considerations of the same sort as those needed to explain the rationality of belief. And we'll also discover that there is no obvious way of codifying these pragmatic constraints. Applying Harman's method, this suggests that our intuitive judgements of belief rationality may escape capture in a normative theory. The unanalysability of knowledge and the uncodifiability of rationality go together.

Externalism

To begin with an externalist account of knowledge, suppose we say that my belief that p is knowledge of p just if my belief is produced by a mechanism which reliably produces true beliefs. This immediately suggests an explanation of why perception, memory, etc., provide conclusive grounds, are sources of knowledge, while veridical hallucination, for example, is not. Hallucination may occasionally be veridical, but depending on it is hardly a reliable way of learning about the world, while perception and memory surely are. The notion of a reliable mechanism seems to be just what we need here but perhaps it is so well suited to our purposes only because neither 'reliability' nor 'mechanism' can be understood independently of the intuitions about belief and knowledge which these words are being introduced to elucidate.

Take 'reliability': under what conditions should a mechanism work successfully for it to be a reliable mechanism? Hallucination will mirror reality in some narrow range of circumstances, and we don't want to count hallucinations as reliable just because one of these circumstances actually obtains. On the other hand, virtually any information-gathering mechanism will play us false on occasion, and we don't wish that fact to disqualify it from ever giving us knowledge. Armstrong acknowledges this difficulty and responds in a revealing manner (Armstrong 1973: 171–5). For him, reliability must be a pragmatic matter. A reliable thermometer is one that will yield correct readings in just those circumstances in which we are likely to want to use it. The network of nomological connections between ourselves and our environment underlies but also underdetermines our knowledge of it and the pragmatic constraints needed to settle what we know resist exact formulation. As a result, it may not be possible to specify the range of circumstances in which a reliable thermometer delivers the right result in any precise fashion; but, as Armstrong remarks, that hardly renders the notion of reliability useless. No more exact analysis is required.

Observations I made in Chapter 2 about the need for non-evidential considerations to fix what counts as sufficient evidence for belief are just the same point seen from an internal perspective. The more evidence we have, the wider the range of epistemically unfavourable circumstances which can be ruled out – if you've checked that the room isn't de-pressurised before reading the barometer, your opinion of the likely weather is more secure than if you've just read the barometer – and the level of evidence required for belief just reflects the range of such circumstances which we need to eliminate for our purposes. But our purposes may not yield any very precise requirement.[4]

Internalism: Harman's second solution

To see how these points apply to an internalist model of knowledge, consider a proposal Harman offers in place of the one I discussed earlier. He suggests that we can know that *p* only if a consideration of all the available evidence on the matter would not undermine this belief (Harman 1980).[5] If I correctly and on good grounds believe my friend is in Italy, but an untruthful letter lies unopened on my desk telling me that he has moved unexpectedly to France, I don't actually know that he is in Italy if I would change my mind upon reading the letter. Here, Harman concludes, I fail to know *p*, even though I have what would otherwise be sufficient grounds for *p*, because there is a misleading piece of evidence available to me, sufficient to undermine my belief in *p*, which I have yet to consider. It is reasonable for me to form this belief (to claim knowledge of my friend's whereabouts) without considering the letter only because it is reasonable for me to assume (falsely) that the letter contains nothing which would undermine the belief.

Obviously, not every piece of misleading evidence is relevant to a knowledge claim, hence the qualification 'available evidence'. But what is availability? Again, this is determined by all sorts of pragmatic considerations. An unopened letter on my desk does seem relevant but not so if it were lost in the post and is now in a dustbin in Tangiers. It would be too much to expect the rational believer to worry about the contents of lost mail but not too much to expect him to take his own mail into account. In forming a belief about his friend's location, the rational subject is making assumptions about the one and not the other.

We have the same pattern once more. You won't believe unless you are satisfied that you know. You won't feel entitled to claim to know unless you think you have considered enough of the available evidence. But there is a vagueness about what constitutes 'available evidence'. Therefore there is a vagueness about what you are claiming when you claim to know. It is impossible to capture our epistemic norms in some precise formula – perhaps a few rules of thumb are all we can manage – and that is why our attempts to analyse knowledge have so consistently failed.

Should this failure worry us? Should we pine for a codification of our epistemic norms? Some writers with internalist sympathies argue that if epistemology has any purpose at all it is to provide us with methodological precepts which we can use to regulate and improve our cognitive lives (Kaplan 1991). And the founders of the internalist tradition, Descartes and Locke, appear to have shared this methodological ambition. But in Chapter 2, I argued that even rational believers can't hope to exercise control over their cognitive lives simply by assessing the normative quality of their beliefs. Therefore, they can't hope to enforce the internalist's methodological precepts by reflection alone. So we lose nothing in the way of doxastic control by admitting that there is in fact no manual for believers, no code of epistemic norms which provides a blueprint for our cognitive lives. Of course, if we had such a blueprint, we might choose to enforce it by means of action (undertaking epistemic training and so forth) but rationality does not require this of us: action is properly governed by practical and not by epistemic norms.[6]

To abandon the desire for control over beliefs is not to cease to evaluate them. What the epistemologist does is to describe, as best she can, the principles underlying our practices of evaluation. In Chapter 9, I lay down some principles of evaluation, each qualified by *ceteris paribus* clauses which it is probably impossible to cash out. We can use these principles to address certain theoretical questions (e.g. does the epistemic authority of memory and/or testimony derive from that of perception and induction, or do they have an independent epistemic role to play?), questions which are properly epistemological and which can be answered without producing a fully articulated code of epistemic norms.

Conclusion

Chapter 2 was predicated on the assumption that evidence (at least for any empirical proposition) is always inconclusive and so we constantly face the question of how much evidence is needed before belief can be justified; any answer inevitably alludes to pragmatic considerations. The conclusive grounds model might appear to offer us a way out here: insist that inconclusive evidence in any quantity will not do and so the question 'exactly how much?' does not even arise. We feel entitled to believe only where we think we have a conclusive ground. So while the conclusive grounds model may conflict with the letter of evidentialism about knowledge, it does capture the spirit of it by preventing the intrusion of pragmatic considerations into our assessment of the rationality of belief.

But far from being a saviour of evidentialism about belief, the conclusive grounds model reinforces my critique of it. Indeed, we can believe only where we think we have a conclusive ground – but what makes it rational to think you have a conclusive ground? Inconclusive evidence, of course, supplemented by a non-reflective awareness of the limitations on your cognitive resources. True, reflection on inconclusive evidence could never move you to belief, even when reinforced by thoughts about how little time you've got to consider the matter (and so forth). But a non-reflective awareness of these considerations can so move you by convincing you that there is a conclusive ground for belief.

If reflection on inconclusive evidence could help to motivate belief, it would follow that reflection on the pragmatic considerations which determine whether a given quantity of evidence is sufficient to make belief reasonable must also be capable of motivating belief. But when one realises that belief requires the thought of a conclusive ground it becomes quite obvious why such pragmatic considerations could never play this role. We can reflect on them, as we can reflect on our inconclusive evidence, to determine whether a belief is reasonable, but never to command belief.

Chapter 4

Scepticism, certainty and control

Scepticism arises from the demand for reflective control over belief. Behind this demand lies the juridical theory of responsibility: our beliefs being governed by reason, we are responsible for them; and, since we can be held to account only for that which is within our control, we must have control over belief. Beliefs are not subject to the will, so this control must take the form of reflective control. True, neither reflection nor control appears in the textbook statements (or diagnoses) of scepticism; rather one hears of the demand for certainty or the search for an infallible criterion of truth. But, I'll argue, the sceptic feels entitled to demand conclusive grounds for belief precisely because it seems the only way to retain reflective control over belief.

For many philosophers, past and present, the reference to certainty indicates that the sceptic is operating with a factitious conception of knowledge: as usually understood, knowledge requires neither certainty nor an infallible criterion of truth. If so, the sceptic can be turned away simply by observing that his arguments pose no threat to ordinary knowledge-claims. Nor can the sceptic make his point by refocusing on the justification of belief: our epistemic norms tell us that we are perfectly entitled to base beliefs on inconclusive evidence; and what grounds have we been given for querying these norms? But this diagnosis of scepticism is shallow. Sure enough, the sceptic demands certainty, but this demand arises from a deep worry about rationality and intellectual freedom.

In Chapter 2, I argued, first, that inconclusive evidence can rationalise belief only in conjunction with non-evidential factors, factors which determine when we have *sufficient* evidence to justify belief; and, second, that we cannot motivate (and thus control) belief by reflecting on such considerations. Sceptics (along with many others) think that normative assessment is in place only where we have reflective control: to make belief subject to reason, we must regain control over belief by excluding such pragmatic factors from epistemology. This can be done only when the troublesome question – what level of (inconclusive) evidence is sufficient for belief? – no longer arises. In the sceptic's eyes, the demand for certainty is what rules this question out of court and secures our intellectual freedom.

Why certainty?

The scepticism of Descartes' *First Meditation* was clearly rooted in the demand for certainty:

> Reason now leads me to think that I should hold back my assent from opinions which are not completely certain and indubitable just as carefully as I do from those which are patently false. So, for the purpose of rejecting all my opinions, it will be enough if I find in each of them at least some reason for doubt.
>
> (Descartes 1984: 12)

But why think that knowledge requires such incorrigibility? I examine two answers to this question – one rather dismissive, the other more subtle and illuminating – before presenting my own diagnosis.

Ordinary knowledge and 'scientific' knowledge

The first answer distinguishes ordinary knowledge from scientific or philosophical knowledge. On this reading, a philosopher like Descartes was interested in acquiring *scientia*, a body of systematic belief from which error had been definitively removed. The pursuit of *scientia* is a special epistemic project, far more rigorous than ordinary inquiry; and the sceptical doubt preparatory to this pursuit is simply irrelevant to common or garden belief. Science aims at an epistemic state different in kind from ordinary knowledge, and even those engaged in Descartes' project are under no compulsion to abandon their pre-scientific beliefs; nor could they without losing their sanity (Wolterstorff 1996: 189–93).

In fact, Descartes appears to be in two minds about whether the project of seeking *scientia* can be in this way insulated from the maintenance of ordinary belief.[1] Much of the time, he writes as if someone who undergoes his Therapy of Doubt must be prepared to overthrow *all* of his opinions (not just those purporting to be scientific) and reconstruct his epistemic position from the ground up: sceptical doubt, once absorbed, should undermine ordinary knowledge (Burnyeat 1997b: 118–20). But if scientific knowledge were (as Wolterstorff argues) simply a higher grade of belief, then this wouldn't follow: we could retain our ordinary, low-grade, beliefs during the search for *scientia*.

On balance, I think Descartes held that his sceptical doubt should undermine any corrigible belief, whether scientific or not. Reading him this way we can explain why Descartes lays down 'a provisional moral code' which would enable the doubter to live without belief until the work of reconstruction was finished (Descartes 1985: 122–6). This moral code is strikingly reminiscent of that which the Pyrrhonean sceptics thought would govern their 'life without belief', a life which was the final result of their sceptical dialectic. But unlike the Pyrrhonians, Descartes didn't exhort us to undertake the Therapy of Doubt in order to reach a state of tranquillity, free of epistemic worry. On the contrary, he urges us to forsake belief only so as to gain securer possession of it later on.

Nothing is more obvious than that we usually accept inconclusive evidence as adequate grounds for rational belief. So, if my reading of Descartes is correct, it looks as if he is setting up an artificial epistemic standard and then insisting that we abandon any beliefs which fail to live up to it. Locke thought that Cartesian scepticism amounted to precisely that: an inappropriate demand for demonstrative knowledge (Locke 1975: 634–6). If so, we have an explanation of why so many philosophers can't take the sceptic seriously. But why then do so many others find the sceptic disturbing? There must be something in common or garden belief, in the ordinary claim to know, which at least suggests a requirement of incorrigibility.

Pure inquiry

Ordinary belief aims at knowledge, but our pursuit of knowledge is hardly untrammelled. There are all sorts of pragmatic constraints which force us to base our beliefs on evidence of varying quality; we seriously guard against only a small proportion of the errors to which belief is subject. As a result, different people may believe rather different things on the basis of just the same evidence because of differences in their situation. I may feel obliged to rule out sources of error which leave you quite unworried, and *vice versa*. Bernard Williams reads Descartes as proposing that we eliminate these pragmatic constraints and embark on a *project of pure inquiry* whose only aim is truth (Williams 1978: Chapter 2).

The project of pure inquiry which Williams describes makes good sense in outline. Anyone entirely devoted to constructing an accurate picture of the world around them would arrive at a set of beliefs which was both different from and much more likely to be true than those I now find myself with. Wouldn't such beliefs have a certain authority for me? Wouldn't they be epistemically better, having a stronger claim to the title of knowledge than my own beliefs? To be sure, there are experts in every field, and we defer to their opinions. But ordinary experts do not aspire to incorrigible knowledge. Why should the pure inquirer?

The ordinary expert's inquiries are less constrained by lack of time and interest than our own but they are still so constrained. The expert needs to act and give advice, to close some matters in order to consider others. The pure inquirer operates under no such restrictions: limited resources are no longer an issue, we suppose. Given this unrestrictedness, wouldn't it be arbitrary to be satisfied by some level of evidence less than conclusive grounds, grounds which guarantee the incorrigibility of your claims to know? Once seduced by the ideal of pure inquiry, how can we avoid attempting to validate all sources of evidence and rule out all possibilities of error? Purity requires incorrigibility.

But such purity is a pious illusion rather than a product of our ordinary concept of knowledge. Any finite inquirer, however disinterested, will have to strike a balance between the comprehensiveness of his belief system and its veridicality. Does he want a lot more beliefs at the cost of a little more falsehood or fewer beliefs to ensure a greater likelihood of truth? Striking this balance is a matter of determining what level of inconclusive evidence suffices for belief. No inquirer can do this without considering matters beyond the strictly evidential. Only then has he the materials to deliver a non-arbitrary answer to the question: what level of inconclusive evidence is sufficient for rational belief? So inquiry can't be so pure after all; there is no hope of fixing our beliefs by reference to evidence alone.

Certainty and objectivity

Williams notes a further pressure to break free of the pragmatic constraints on inquiry, one he thinks implicit in the very idea of truth (Williams 1978: 64–8; see also Clark 1972: 759–62). Truth is an objective, perspective-independent, feature of belief, and belief surely aims at truth. Someone like the pure inquirer whose sole desire is to represent the world as it is must strip away those things that tend to make belief parochial and rise above their peculiar perspective on reality. In particular, the pure inquirer needs to escape from those pragmatic constraints which give each of us a partial and biased view of the world, and the value of such inquiry lies implicit in very idea that the search for knowledge is a search for objective truth.

But the demand for objectivity alone cannot motivate pure inquiry. States which register how the world is, independently of ourselves, need not be a product *solely* of how the world is. Williams admits that even the pure inquirer is not after omniscience – some truths are of more interest than others – and it is these interests that determine which bits of the world we wish to have represented to ourselves. I may form a view about p where someone else would draw back, without our representing the world in contradictory ways, because having a view about the truth of p is more important to me than it is to them. What objectivity requires is that people with the same evidence shouldn't be entitled to form contradictory beliefs, not that all people with the same evidence must form the same beliefs. The interest relativity of belief rationality on which I am insisting implies only that enquirers with similar evidence may differ in what matters they think their evidence sufficient to support a belief about.

Craig suggests a different, but related motivation for eliminating prag-matic considerations from the justification of belief (Craig 1990: sections X and XII). In Craig's view, to know that *p* is just to be a good source of information about *p*. He then observes that someone is a good source of information about *p for me* if he is as likely to be right about *p* as my concerns require. This introduces a certain relativity into the idea of a good informant and thus, one might think, into the concept of knowledge. But, according to Craig, there is a pressure to objectivise our judgements about who is a good informant. We each have an interest in collecting information while it is available, without knowing when, or why, or under what pressures it might be needed. We also have an interest in ensuring that other people collect information which is useful to us, whatever the variations in needs and situation between us. The role of our shared knowledge concept is pre-cisely to mark objectively good sources of information and the only way of ensuring objectivity in this respect is to eliminate variable pragmatic factors altogether from our judgements of who is a good informant. Thus, the concept of knowledge contains the seeds of a demand for certainty.

But, as Craig himself admits, this move to certainty is far too quick. Clearly, when we collect information, seek informants, or recommend infor-mants to others, we usually do so in ignorance of the purposes for which the information will be used, by whom, and under what conditions. It is also true that this will incline us to set a higher standard for being a good source of information than might arise from the particular circumstances we find our-selves in. But it doesn't follow from this that there is any pressure whatsoever to set the standard at an impossibly high level. What objectivisation requires is that the pragmatic constraints on belief formation embodied in the concept of knowledge be widespread and shared rather than local and peculiar. Indeed, Craig's own hypothesis about the function of the concept of knowledge predicts that the epistemic standard set will be one it is perfectly possible to meet: if 'know' exists to mark approved sources of information, it would be of no use whatsoever if every accessible source failed to satisfy it. So Craig's hypothesis does not motivate the demand for certainty.

Certainty and control

I said that Williams was on to something when he traced the sceptic's demand for certainty to his insistence that we transcend the pragmatic limitations on our epistemic processes, but we have yet to see why anyone should accede to this demand. I suggest that the answer lies in the need to ensure that we are accountable for our beliefs by demonstrating that we have control over them. And this reading of the debate helps to explain what we find in Descartes' *Fourth Meditation* (Owens 2000).

The message of the *Fourth Meditation* is not entirely plain, but two points come through well enough. First, if we are to be responsible for error, our beliefs must be under our control; second, to be under our control, belief must be subject to the will. Descartes is quite specific about how error occurs: I commit errors in cases where I form a belief even though 'I do not perceive the truth with sufficient clarity and distinctness' (Descartes 1984: 41). But why should 'sufficient clarity' be equated with 'certainty'?

At this point, Descartes appears to link certainty with the idea of *true* freedom. Speaking of an evident truth, he says:

> I could not but judge that something which I understood so clearly was true; but this was not because I was compelled so to judge by any external force, but because a great light in the intellect was followed by a great inclination in the will, and thus the spontaneity and freedom of my belief was all the greater in proportion to my lack of indifference.
> (Ibid.)

I feel indifferent about a proposition when there is evidence both for and against it, and though I may still (wrongly) decide to believe it and risk falling into error, 'the indifference I feel when there is no reason pushing me in one direction rather than another is the lowest grade of freedom' (ibid.: 40).

So I am accountable for error because I am misusing my free will when I affirm something on the basis of inconclusive evidence. A fully rational person just could not assent to a proposition for which there is inconclusive evidence: evidence is the only reason for belief, and inconclusive evidence will leave him indifferent. But why should inconclusive evidence leave him indifferent? And why should it deprive him of true freedom in forming a belief, if he can go ahead and form beliefs anyway? Indeed, if true freedom is not required for accountability, what role is it playing in Descartes' story?

We can connect the search for certainty with the idea of true freedom provided we replace Descartes' conception of freedom as subjection to the will with the notion of reflective control. It is fairly clear what is supposed to be troubling the believer confronted by inconclusive evidence for *p*: he could get himself to regard inconclusive evidence as sufficient for belief only by bringing to mind pragmatic considerations. But, as Chapter 2 established, reflection on pragmatic considerations cannot rationally motivate the formation of belief: rationality alone won't guarantee that you can get yourself to believe something simply by judging that the inconclusive evidence before you is sufficient, given the importance of the issue, etc. This is why, where the evidence for *p* is inconclusive, a rational believer will be indifferent between *p* and not-*p* and unable to exercise reflective control over whether he believes that *p*.

Of course, beliefs still get formed because non-evidential factors (desire, for instance) exercise a non-rational influence on them beneath the level of reflection, but how can we be responsible for such beliefs? Descartes thinks that we are still accountable for them because they are the product of an act of will, of a form of control which is not tied to reflection on evidence (Descartes 1984: 260). But, in Chapter 5, I'll suggest that Descartes is wrong: we cannot control our beliefs by means of the will. If responsibility requires control then we must be capable of governing belief by reflection on the reasons for it.

The only apparent cure for the impotence of reflection is to strip away the pragmatic constraints on belief and seek to ground our convictions in evidence alone. But, as I showed in Chapter 3, reflection on inconclusive evidence can never motivate a claim to knowledge; we need conclusive grounds to re-establish reflective control over belief. The sceptical demand for certainty arises out of the recognition that if we allow anything less than conclusive grounds to motivate the formation of belief then pragmatic considerations must be allowed to determine what level of inconclusive evidence is sufficient; and once they are permitted to intrude, reflective control over belief is lost. That, I suggest, is the root of the Cartesian idea that we are truly free in forming a belief only when we are certain.

Cartesian scepticism

I have been urging that Cartesian scepticism rests on the notion that both knowledge and rational belief require certainty. Most contemporary philosophers who discuss scepticism take themselves to be discussing Descartes' scepticism, but only a minority treat that scepticism as resting on a demand for certainty. For them, the demand for certainty is unmotivated and so no interesting form of scepticism can arise out of it. And, at least some of the time, they read Descartes as if he shared this assumption. Having appreciated how the drive for certainty can be motivated, we can see the *First Meditation* for what it is.

I have already quoted Descartes' opening demand for certainty.[2] Having made this demand, he begins his attempt to generate a comprehensive doubt by reminding us of perfectly ordinary sensory error. Commentators usually treat this as a mere softening-up exercise. They warn us not to attribute the following fallacious inference to Descartes: *each* of our experiences might be wrong, therefore they might *all* be wrong (Stroud 1983: 413–14; Williams 1983: 339–41). In their eyes, things get really serious only when the *sceptical hypotheses* are introduced: the idea that we might be permanently dreaming or else the victim of some evil demon who perpetrates a comprehensive deception. Only then is Descartes entitled to draw the sceptical conclusion that *all* our experience might be illusory.

I read the *First Meditation* rather differently (Owens 2000). What matters to Descartes is the simple fact that there is some reason to doubt every one of our experiences: in each case we can (with sufficient effort) think of a similar experience which misled us in the past. And this point, which can be established without any recourse to the sceptical hypotheses is, in Descartes' view, quite sufficient to undermine sensory knowledge all by itself. Reviewing the argument of the *First Meditation* in the *Sixth*, Descartes says that while trusting the senses 'I had many experiences which gradually undermined all the faith I had had in the senses' (Descartes 1984: 53), and then quotes examples of towers which looked round at a distance but square from close up, and so forth. It is clear that sensory knowledge has been thoroughly undermined long before Descartes mentions that 'to these reasons for doubting I recently added two very general ones' (ibid.), i.e. the dreaming and the evil demon argument.

So what, on my reading, is the point of the sceptical hypotheses? We can best answer this question by filling out the passage I quoted earlier:

> Reason now leads me to think that I should hold back my assent from opinions which are not completely certain and indubitable just as carefully as I do from those which are patently false. So, for the purpose of rejecting all my opinions, it will be enough if I find in each of them at least some reason for doubt. *And to do this I will not need to run through them all individually, which would be an endless task.*
>
> (Descartes 1984: 12 [emphasis added])

The sceptical hypotheses provide us with a doubt that will apply to all our experiences. By invoking them, we can succinctly make a point which could have been made much more long-windedly without them: our senses (and reasonings) are fallible.[3]

If my reading of Descartes is correct then much contemporary discussion of scepticism is simply irrelevant to the problem raised by Descartes. From the time of Kant onwards, philosophers have come forward with arguments intended to show that even if it must be admitted that each individual experience might be illusory, it is incoherent to suppose that all experience is illusory.[4] Suppose those arguments succeed in their purpose by providing us with an *a priori* guarantee that many or most of our experiences must be veridical. How would this frustrate the Cartesian sceptic? The Cartesian sceptic insists that we are not entitled to any of the beliefs we base on experience unless we have some way of telling which experiences are veridical and which are illusory. Unless the *a priori* guarantee provides us with a way of doing this, it can't reinstate perceptual knowledge. To use a well-worn analogy, we might know *a priori* that not every bank note can be a counterfeit without having any way of knowing of any individual note whether it is genuine or not.[5]

Nor did Descartes himself settle for such an unspecific reassurance. True, he argued that a benevolent God could not mislead us about the existence of the corporeal world whose fundamental (geometrical) nature we clearly and distinctly apprehend; we can rule out the sceptical hypotheses *a priori*. But God's guarantee extends well beyond such generalities:

What of the other aspects of corporeal things which are either particular (for example that the sun is of such and such a size or shape), or less clearly understood, such as light or sound or pain, and so on? Despite the high degree of doubt and uncertainty involved here, the very fact that God is not a deceiver, and the consequent impossibility of there being any falsity in my opinions which cannot be corrected by some other faculty supplied by God, offers me a sure hope that I can attain the truth even in these matters.

(Descartes 1984: 55–6)[6]

Descartes devotes the rest of the *Sixth Meditation* to the rather unpromising task of demonstrating that a responsible believer can avoid *all* errors of both outer and inner sense, that experience need *never* mislead us. Why would he have made this futile attempt to cure the senses of their fallibility if all he needed was a divine assurance that the corporeal world is approximately as we think it to be and that our senses are usually reliable? At the end of the Meditations, Descartes is forced to admit that 'in this human life we are often liable to make mistakes about particular things', but this is because 'the pressure of things to be done does not always allow us to stop and make such a meticulous check' (ibid.: 62). The problem, as ever, is that pragmatic considerations intrude upon the belief-forming process.

What if I am right and Cartesian scepticism is founded on the demand for certainty? So much the worse for Cartesian scepticism, many would say. Perhaps we should take from Descartes just what we need – namely the sceptical hypotheses – and carry on our own debate as usual, ignoring the presuppositions about knowledge which he brought to it and in their place substituting our own high-tech creation for the evil demon: the brain in the vat. Doesn't the brain in the vat hypothesis raise problems for us all, whether or not we are wedded to certainty? By scrutinising our reaction to it, we shall discover that the worries it raises are, at bottom, much the same as those presented by ordinary error. They stem from the very thing which makes certainty seem compulsory: the need for reflective control over belief.

Our scepticism

At first, let us think of the brain in the vat as a hypothetical creature whose cognitive processes we are evaluating, rather than as someone we might actually be. The brain is being electrically stimulated so as to produce experiences of an Oxford St. shopping trip and memories of an otherwise unremarkable London life but in fact it is sitting in a vat of nutrients on Mars and has never been anywhere near London. We may suppose that the brain has, as we would put it, no grounds for suspicion. Nothing in the brain's experience or memory should lead it to imagine that it is anywhere other than Oxford St. Prompted by an imaginary philosopher, it might acknowledge the possibility that things are not as they seem, but why should this thought worry it? All the philosopher has done is to provide a graphic illustration of human fallibility, and is the brain not entitled to fallible beliefs?

So long as this all remains hypothetical, complacency reigns. For sure, the brain's beliefs about itself and the world around it are largely erroneous – it knows very little – but, applying our usual epistemic norms, we find no fault with it. The brain in the vat is wrong but rational: it is entitled to claim the knowledge it claims. Assessing hypothetical beliefs like this, we seem to apply normative principles which are insensitive to the contingencies of the subject's environment. A subject who believes what his senses tell him and has no reason to doubt them (as we would say) has a right to his convictions, has good evidence for them, whether or not there is a shred of truth in his experience. His senses' reliability as sources of information, which is indeed a contingent matter, does not seem to come into it.

The advantage of keeping things hypothetical is that we can evaluate the brain in the vat's beliefs without having to form any (non-normative) beliefs of our own: we just apply our epistemic norms to an imaginary situation. Now let us leave the standpoint of the detached epistemic evaluator and take up that of the engaged epistemic deliberator. What should I believe? My senses and my memory all tell me I am walking down Oxford St. I know that it is possible that I am wrong about this and that time will show me that I am wrong. To put it another way, I know that the evidence I currently have on this point is never going to be all the evidence I could have, that I could always wait for more: subsequent experience might reveal that I am being somehow taken in. This reflection may disturb me, yet I don't wait for more evidence to come in; I form a view. Why?

I might try to vindicate my decisiveness by insisting on the phrase used above: there is *no* reason for doubt, therefore there is *no* reason to wait. But when I say there is no reason to doubt that I am in Oxford St., I can't mean that there is literally no evidence against this; rather that the evidence against it is insufficient to motivate a reasonable doubt. My belief that I am walking down Oxford St. could turn out to be false in many different ways. Some of these are more likely than others: it is more probable that I have misread the road name than that I am in bed asleep, dreaming vividly of a Christmas shopping trip. But both sorts of error have actually occurred in the past (as Descartes (1984: 13) reminds us), so I have some grounds for thinking they might occur again.

That I am a brain in a vat seems even less likely, but I know (by testimony) that experiences can be brought about by electrical stimulation of the brain, or *via* a virtual reality machine, and so there is some chance that such a thing might be happening to me now. When I say that there is *no* reason to believe this, what I mean is that I don't have sufficient grounds to take seriously the possibility that I am being deceived in that way; I am entitled to form a view without looking into it. Our question can now be restated: why is the evidence in favour of this sceptical hypothesis insufficient to motivate a doubt about my perceptual beliefs and all that is based upon them?

It is true of each of the sources of error just noted that there is some context in which it is reasonable to take it seriously. This is obviously so in the case of everyday perceptual illusions, etc. but it is true even of the possibility that I might be a brain in a vat. Suppose I notice some inexplicable discontinuities in my experience and at the same time learn that virtual reality technology is progressing fast. The difference between this and my earlier predicament is that I now have more evidence, or evidence more specific to my case, of the feasibility and likelihood of comprehensive deception. Might it not be reasonable for me to begin investigating the limitations of virtual reality technology, to see if that could explain the course of my experience? There must be *some* course of experience which would make it reasonable for me to wonder whether I am en-vatted.

On the other hand, suppose I read, on a slightly cranky web site, that virtual reality experiments are taking place near me. Here the grounds for doubt are more specific than the mere technical possibility of virtual life but quite insufficient to justify a serious doubt. So there is a spectrum of such cases running from those in which I have insufficient evidence to those in which I have sufficient evidence to take this hypothesis seriously, and the question remains: what determines whether my evidence is sufficient?

This question can be answered only by mentioning the constraints on my ability to investigate all possibilities of error, to assimilate whatever evidence these investigations might yield and to retain it in memory for future consultation. Inconclusive evidence alone could never justify my ceasing to look for more of it; pragmatic considerations determine when I have enough evidence to form a view. But here I encounter a familiar difficulty: reflection on such constraints cannot get me to make up my mind. I can happily say that the hypothetical brain in the vat is entitled to ignore the possibility that it is a brain in a vat because there is insufficient reason for it to look into this possibility, given obvious limitations on its time and cognitive resources. But I can't get myself to exclude this possibility just by telling myself the same story.

Our everyday epistemic norms allow us to ignore various conceivable sources of error, as they do not require conclusive grounds for belief. We are happy to employ these norms when *evaluating* hypothetical beliefs, when determining what it would be rational or irrational to believe. However, we can't *form* beliefs by telling ourselves that we have sufficient evidence for them, by reflecting that, given the pragmatic constraints on us, we are entitled to assume we are not making certain sorts of mistake. Limitations on our time and cognitive resources are not the sort of thing reflection on which can move us to belief. Therefore, fallibilist epistemic norms which mention such considerations can't constitute a method of forming rational beliefs, a way of exercising doxastic control. And since we can't govern our belief with these fallibilist epistemic norms, we can't really be held responsible to them. Or so the sceptic says.

That's my diagnosis of scepticism. It explains the charm of scepticism by linking it to the juridical theory of responsibility, to the plausible idea that we can be held to certain norms only in so far as we control whether we conform to them. It connects our scepticism with Descartes' scepticism, with a demand for certainty motivated by the desire for reflective control over belief. Finally, it explains our ambivalence towards scepticism: our uncertainty about whether to take the sceptic seriously. So long as we are using them to evaluate beliefs, our ordinary epistemic norms are perfectly fine and the sceptic appears untroubling: it is only when we try to regulate our beliefs by reflecting on whether they conform to these norms that sceptical worries begin to bite. Of course, beliefs get formed anyway but, the sceptic thinks, this failure of control puts them beyond the pale of rational assessment.

A target missed?

My diagnosis is unfamiliar, and many will complain that it simply misses the sceptic's point. I can't review all the different ways in which the sceptic's case might be restated but I shall address some of the more pressing concerns.

Sceptics usually present themselves as querying the rationality of the beliefs we already have; they don't ask which beliefs we could form if we tried. They are seeking a reflective endorsement of our beliefs, rather than insisting on a Reflective Motivation for them. For example, Descartes begins the *First Meditation* by devoting himself to the examination of his current opinions and thence to their demolition when they don't measure up. The exercise of epistemic control here seems to be more a matter of filtering out unfounded beliefs than commanding ourselves to adopt well-founded convictions. So how does this fit with my diagnosis of scepticism as the product of an inability to *motivate* belief by reflecting on the reasons for it?

Once we look into how the process of reflective endorsement is meant to work, this contrast between endorsement and motivation evaporates. Descartes attempts to get us to abandon our current beliefs by reminding us of certain sources of error, thereby forcing an acknowledgement that we ought not to hold these beliefs. So far as I can see, there is no important difference between this and the attempt to undermine belief by asking us: would you really feel entitled to form these beliefs in the face of this possible source of error? In either case, the answer is meant to be a 'no', and for exactly the same reason. Of course, as Descartes concedes, we are liable to persist with the beliefs we already have regardless of these negative reflections. But it is equally true that new beliefs will continue to be motivated by inconclusive evidence, our reflective veto notwithstanding.

A second worry about my diagnosis of scepticism centres on the notion of a sufficiency of inconclusive evidence. Is the legitimacy of this notion really what is at stake between the sceptic and his opponent? Shouldn't the sceptic simply deny that we have any evidence at all on the matter before us? The sceptic's point is not just that I could always collect more evidence and yet don't. For all I know, I might have *no* evidence; the future might show that I had precisely *no* reason to think I am walking along Oxford St. because the sensory experiences which are my grounds were completely unreliable. That is why the sceptic needs the sceptical hypotheses and can't rely on ordinary illusion to make his point.

But, as already noted, it is hard to see (from the outside) why the truth of a sceptical hypothesis would undermine the rationality of belief. When we evaluate the brain in a vat's beliefs, we seem to ignore contingent facts about the reliability of his sensory experience: the brain is wrong but rational. And if he is rational, his experience must be providing him with evidence for his belief, their illusory character notwithstanding. From the normative point of view, there is no difference between local and general illusion. What the sceptic needs is a way of criticising and undermining our epistemic evaluations in our own eyes, and to do this he must avoid making contentious assumptions about the rationality of belief.

The sceptic might try the following reasoning. The occurrence of the particular stream of experience I now enjoy is logically consistent both with my walking along Oxford St. and with my being en-vatted on Mars. The laws of logic and even the laws of nature (as we think them to be) are perfectly compatible with either scenario. So I have no more evidence in favour of p than of not-p, and surely in this situation I ought to remain agnostic. Even if pragmatic factors are allowed to motivate the formation of rational belief once the evidence has tipped in p's direction, they cannot rationalise belief in p when there is just as much (or as little) evidence in favour of not-p. *Pace* James (1956), I am not free to believe just because it is desirable that I should believe.

Here, it might look as if the sceptic is undermining our epistemic norms from *within* by invoking a principle I myself endorsed in Chapter 2, namely that one can't use non-evidential considerations to break evidential ties.[7] But, in fact, the sceptic is simply presupposing that a sensory experience as of p, in itself, gives us no reason to believe that p. Our reaction to the hypothesis of the brain in the vat (*qua* evaluator) contradicts this – the brain does have reason to think it is on Oxford St., and the mere possibility of en-vatment does not constitute 'adequate grounds for doubt'. It simply isn't true that the en-vatted brain has as much reason to believe p as not-p. The sceptic will not carry conviction if he blankly rejects this norm.

The sceptic's leverage

Any attempt to query our fundamental epistemic norms looks like a paradoxical endeavour. To show these norms are *wrong*, one needs an independent normative standpoint from which to operate. But one needs also
epistemic standards which have some appeal to us, we who now form beliefs
and claim knowledge with a clear conscience. For the sceptic to have any
hold over us, we must share some normative ground with him. And what
shared ground can there be if he regards almost all of our beliefs as irrational?

This question can't be evaded by basing sceptical argumentation on the
agreed fact that belief aims at the truth. The sceptic might invoke this
norm and then ask us how we know that following our (fallibilist) norms
of belief formation will lead to the formation of true beliefs. But suppose
we respond by taking advantage of those very norms (the ones which entitle
us to rely *ab initio* on perception and induction, etc.) to answer his question?[8]
Why do these norms need to be grounded in the norm of true-belief formation together with some other (uncontentious) factual premises before we
are entitled to rely on them? For example, why do we need to provide
non-perceptual reasons for thinking that our sensory experiences are in
fact a reliable guide to the truth before we are entitled to rely on them?
A stand-off ensues: we have got more (underived) epistemic norms than
the sceptic accepts, and the sceptic has no way of arguing us out of them.

What *does* give the sceptic the leverage he needs to undermine our epistemic norms, what accounts for his troubling aspect, is not a shared epistemic
norm at all but rather a purported requirement on norms as such, be they
ethical, prudential or epistemic. For the sceptic (and for many of his internalist opponents) genuine norms are rules we can use to regulate our mental
lives, rules which are a source of Reflective Motivation for us. This suggests
a test the sceptic can run on any epistemic norms we happen to hold, a test
that has no normative presuppositions. The test is this: see if you can get
yourself to believe something simply by reflecting that such a belief would
satisfy these norms. If you can't, the sceptic asserts, these norms are no
good to you. Rules which can't guide epistemic deliberation shouldn't
govern epistemic evaluation either. Our fallibilist epistemic norms fail this
test. Only infallibilist norms could satisfy him on this point. Hence the probative force of the sceptic's argumentation and the felt need for certainty
arise from the very same source.

For the sceptic, this loss of reflective self-discipline is fatal to epistemic
rationality: we should have no convictions at all rather than allow our
minds to be filled with beliefs over which we have no reflective control.
Yet, even those persuaded by the sceptic to judge that they ought not to
believe most of what they do believe, and ought not to form the beliefs
they otherwise would, find themselves retaining the one and acquiring the
other, much as before. Sceptical doubt lacks the impact of a real doubt: in

Hume's words, the sceptic's arguments 'admit of no answer and produce no conviction' (Hume 1975: 155). Our norms' failure to pass the sceptic's test does nothing to undermine their psychological efficacy, and this suggests that it does nothing to undermine their authority either.

The sceptic is trying to persuade us that our reasons rationalise our beliefs and support our claims to knowledge only if the judgement that we have those reasons could motivate conviction. He invites us to test our principles of belief assessment in the crucible of theoretical decision making, and finds them wanting. But since Reflective Motivation is false, such a test is inappropriate: if the possibility of reflective motivation is not required for rational belief formation, its absence neither shows belief to be irrational, nor compels the abandonment of belief. Belief arises when the uncertainty presupposed by deliberation gives way to the impression that we have a conclusive ground, and this transition is one that reflection on inconclusive evidence cannot accomplish.

Scepticism and total control

Several recent commentators on scepticism have sought to account for its appeal by postulating an ideal of presuppositionless thought, which we are meant to find attractive (Williams 1978: 64–7; Nagel 1986: Chapters 5 and 7; Stroud 1989). According to this diagnosis, the sceptic takes our fundamental epistemic norms, those which underwrite our reliance on perception, memory and induction, and asks us to provide them with a non-circular justification. The sceptic tempts us to embark on a search for some Archimedean point from which our belief-forming practices can be seen to be right and proper, a search which must inevitably fail. But, I insisted, this demand for a justification of our fundamental norms must be *motivated* before it poses a real threat. Nagel attempts to motivate it by restating it as a demand for epistemic control. I want to conclude this chapter by distinguishing Nagel's diagnosis of scepticism from my own.

Nagel's diagnosis

In belief, as in action, rational beings aspire to autonomy. They wish to form their beliefs on the basis of principles and methods of reasoning and confirmation that they themselves can judge to be correct, rather than on the basis of influences that they do not understand, of which they are unaware, or which they cannot assess. That is the aim of knowledge. But taken to its logical limit, the aim is incoherent. We cannot assess and revise or confirm our entire system of thought and judgement from the outside, for we would have nothing to do it with. We remain, as pursuers of knowledge, creatures inside the world who have not created

ourselves, and some of whose processes of thought have simply been
given to us.

(Nagel 1986: 118)

Nagel regards the metaphysical problem of free will and the epistemological
problem of scepticism as siblings: offspring of the desire to choose 'everything about ourselves, including all our principles of choice – creating ourselves from nothing, so to speak' (ibid.).[9]

It is not hard to see what Nagel has in mind. There is a notion of control,
total or *unconditional* control, according to which we control something only
if we also control all the factors which govern the exercise of that control. On
this view, the fact that my desires and beliefs control my actions does not give
me control over my actions unless I control my desires and beliefs as well.
Now it is quite obvious that if the exercise of control can be explained at
all, it will, in the end, be governed by factors over which we have no control.
For example, if control is exercised by means of reflection on reasons, there
must come a point at which we simply accept certain phenomena as good and
sufficient reasons and don't require that this judgement be motivated by
reflection on some further set of reasons. Therefore, the idea of total control
looks incoherent, just as Nagel says.

The demand for total control usually appears in the practical sphere but
Nagel argues that it has a theoretical analogue and this is what gives rise
to scepticism. To establish reflective control over belief, we need reasons
reflection on which will assure us of our epistemic good standing, and total
reflective control over belief requires that we never accept such a reason as
a reason unless we can motivate this acceptance by reflecting on some further
reasons. For example, one can treat a sensory experience as of *p* as a reason
to believe *p* only if one can find further reasons to think that one's sensory
experiences are reliable. And those further reasons (perhaps beliefs, perhaps
experiences) themselves stand in need of reflective validation. Clearly this
process must come to an end somewhere and when it does, total control is
lost.

Need the sceptic demand total control?

Nagel is right to say that the problem of scepticism arises because some of
us aspire to autonomy in both belief and action, but he is wrong about the
sort of autonomy to which we aspire. My diagnosis of scepticism leaves
total control on one side. What my sceptic uses to make trouble is the non-
pathological demand for reflective control implicit in Reflective Motivation.

For example, suppose an experience as of *p* provides a good reason to
believe that *p* (against a certain pragmatic background). Provided the judgement that this experience provides sufficient evidence for *p* can motivate us to
believe that *p*, Reflective Motivation grants us reflective control over our

acquisition of this belief. We don't have to provide grounds for that higher order judgement. We don't have to find further reasons, independent of the experience in question, reflection on which will convince us that this experience is sufficient evidence for belief. Of course, there may be such reasons – we may be able to appeal to some further experience, memory or piece of induction to underwrite our confidence in the probative force of this experience – but this is not required for us to control beliefs based on that experience. In *my* sceptic's view, there is nothing wrong with taking certain normative judgements as foundational provided they can motivate us.

Reflective Motivation articulates a limited, feasible notion of reflective control, one sufficient to make room for blame and justification. As Part 2 will show, we *do* have such reflective control over decision and action, a control which is direct without being total or unlimited. I can motivate a practical decision by reflecting on pragmatic constraints on the decision-making process, as well as on the reasons in favour of the various options. Having taken a desire to be a sufficient reason for action, I might be able to find an independent reason for thinking it sufficient, but equally I might not. Either way I can exercise reflective control over what I do by judging that the desire provides a good reason for action.

It is because we have reflective control in the practical sphere that the sceptic can plausibly tie responsibility for belief to reflective control over belief, insisting that justification and rationality are in play only where there is an analogue of practical freedom. Having established that even this prosaic form of freedom does not extend into the theoretical realm – that we can't motivate our beliefs by reflection on the reasons for them – the sceptic concludes that we can take no responsibility for our beliefs and therefore should not seek to form or maintain them. No yearning for presuppositionless thought is needed to tempt us down the sceptic's path – just the juridical theory of responsibility.

To shore up his opposed diagnosis of scepticism, Nagel must explain why the pull of the Archimedean point should be felt by us all. Why should we be impressed by the demand for a non-circular justification of each of our normative judgements? Why should we be any more impressed when this demand is based on a patently unrealistic notion of control? By contrast, all my sceptic needs is a coherent and realistic notion of control together with the juridical theory of responsibility. One can discover adherents of that theory among the most unreflective humans beings, and their adherence to the juridical theory of responsibility is independent of any desire for total control. To tie scepticism to such an incoherent demand is to underplay its power to seduce. We will neither understand it, nor free ourselves from it until we locate its charms in something more familiar and far more plausible.

Appendix to Part I

Renouncing belief?

In Part 2, I suggest that we break the link between rationality and reflective control, and insist that belief is subject to norms of reason even though we lack epistemic freedom. But perhaps we have arrived at the point where this seems the sole expedient only by ignoring an obvious way out. Why not simply deny that knowledge is the aim of belief?

I teetered on the brink of this in Chapter 2 when the evidentialist floated the idea of breaking the link between belief and the claim to know. On this view, belief in p would be a state of being disposed to act as if p were true, a state whose strength was proportional to the evidence in p's favour. There is here no problem about deciding when we know that p is true: we just give the possibility of p (and of not-p) the appropriate weight in our deliberations, and we can get on with life much as before. Wouldn't this give us all we want out of belief while avoiding those features of belief which make it doubtful that we can maintain reflective control over it? There is no need to specify what level of evidence is sufficient for belief (i.e. sufficient to justify a claim to knowledge), nor to bring in those pragmatic considerations which seem to abolish reflective control over belief. Each level of evidence in p's favour justifies its own degree of belief in p (and a reciprocal degree of belief in not-p); no level calls for that special cognitive commitment to p which generates sceptical worries.

There is a long-running debate about whether we can dispense with our knowledge-based notion of belief and live life without it (Jeffrey 1992; Foley 1993: Chapter 4; Burnyeat 1997a). To resolve this matter, we would need to consider all the reasons which have been given for renouncing knowledge claims, and not just the sceptical ones (I am thinking here of paradoxes like the lottery and the preface). We would also need to describe the place that knowledge claims have in human life: in science (do scientists claim to know their theories, or merely accept them?), in law ('guilt established beyond a reasonable doubt'), in our inter-personal relations (can I feel anything like anger or gratitude unless I lay claim to knowledge?), etc. Rather than embark on such a large project, I'll confine myself to querying one motivation for abandoning belief (as we know it): the idea that we can thereby outflank the sceptic and regain reflective control over our cognitive lives.

I start from the idea, floated in Chapter 1, that each person is authoritative about whether belief in p is reasonable for him or her. On this view, my judgements of my own rationality are not subject to brute error: a rational person might be persuaded that he ought no longer to believe p but not that it was unreasonable for him to have believed p in the first place. I'll grant this assumption. Now suppose we can factor reasons for belief in p into two components: a certain level of evidence for p and the non-evidential considerations which make that level of evidence sufficient to justify belief. If I am authoritative about when belief in p is rational, this must be because I am authoritative about the level of evidence I have for p: my claim to know the level of evidence I have for p is indefeasible.

Equipped with sceptic-proof knowledge of my evidence for p, I can now make judgements about what level of confidence I ought to have in p. Of course, these judgements won't determine whether I ought to claim to know that p unless I introduce pragmatic considerations into my reflections, and once that is done, reflective control over belief is lost. But it seems I can avoid this result by refusing to form a view as to whether p: I simply judge how much evidence I have in p's favour and acquire a suitable degree of belief in p, a degree of belief which is under my reflective control. By abjuring knowledge claims, I maintain control over and responsibility for my mental life, and thereby defeat the sceptic.

What I want to focus on here is the assumption that reasons for belief (i.e. for knowledge-linked belief) can be factored into two discrete components – evidential and non-evidential. It is only on this assumption that my authoritative judgement about whether or not I am reasonable can be taken to imply an authoritative knowledge of some purely evidential matter. And it is only given this that we can replace our ordinary beliefs with sceptic-proof levels of confidence. Now I am prepared to allow that epistemic norms are *a priori* truths and the evaluations they support are known to us simply by virtue of our rationality. And I have often spoken as if the considerations these norms invoke can be divided into an evidential and a non-evidential component. But should the latter really be assumed?

In Chapter 2, I tried and failed to distil a purely evidential component from the normative constraints on belief formation. I established that this can't be done by treating the non-evidential component as prudential. I then concluded that there must be pragmatic constraints on rational belief formation which are not prudential, in addition to whatever evidential factors are relevant. But why assume that there are *any* purely evidential constraints on rational belief formation, such that we can first specify the level of evidence in favour of a certain proposition and then, as a separate matter, determine whether that level is sufficient for reasonable belief? Why assume that the pragmatic constraints on belief formation can be factored out of our judgements about which beliefs are rational, leaving some evidential residue to act as a source of reflective motivation for (partial) belief (Williams 1996: 191–201)?

Of course, we do make judgements about how much evidence we have for various propositions, about how likely they are to be true, but such judgements employ an objective notion of evidence and are no more immune to brute error than are our beliefs about any ordinary matter of fact. For example, I may have a view on whether John's testimony is reliable, but this view can be mistaken without any failure of rationality on my part: I may simply be wrong. The claim that John's testimony is good evidence is defeasible: it is established by checking enough of the various ways in which this claim might be false. And what counts as 'enough' here is determined by the importance of the issue, etc. I can't judge the quality of my reasons for believing in John's reliability without bringing in pragmatic considerations. So I can't control my belief in John's reliability by reflecting on my reasons for it.

The same is true even when the evidential issue is an 'internal' one. For instance, my judgements as to whether a certain belief is consistent with the other things I believe can be wrong without any failure of rationality on my part. Not every inconsistency is one I ought to pick up on; not every contradiction is one a reasonable person could not miss. Here, again, there are issues about how much I should search for contradiction or guard against logical error, and any such judgement about this will have to take pragmatic factors into account. So even 'internal' constraints on belief cannot be enforced by means of reflection. And how are we going to distil, from our judgements about when an inconsistent belief set is reasonable and when it isn't, some more subjective but purely evidential constraint on beliefs which a rational subject can automatically know whether they satisfy and can enforce by means of reflection?

To sum up, there are many philosophers who think that we can be held to account for any deviation from epistemic norms and that such responsibility requires control over belief. Some might try to protect this view from the difficulties I have raised for it in Part 1 by insisting that the epistemic norms tell us not whether we can claim to know p on the basis of certain evidence but rather what degree of belief in p is justified by that evidence. But this manoeuvre is problematic. In taking control of belief, we must make judgements about the strength of our evidence. These judgements cannot concern the objective evidence for a proposition because a rational person can be wrong about that: such judgements could not be a source of reflective control. But nor can judgements about subjective evidence be a source of reflective control unless we think we can separate the evidential from the non-evidential elements in the evaluation of belief. So, even were it possible to live without claiming knowledge, we might still be unable, by renouncing knowledge, to re-establish control over belief.

Part 2

Freedom and responsibility

Chapter 5

Freedom and the will

The business of Part 2 is, first, to elaborate and defend a theory of freedom and control based on Reflective Motivation and, second, to investigate the connection between control and responsibility. I spent Part 1 laying out grounds for being sceptical of Reflective Motivation as applied to belief. Reflective motivation tells us that we can control our beliefs by reflecting on what we ought to believe, a hope which my consideration of how beliefs are actually motivated was meant to dispel. But throughout Part 1, I implied that Reflective Motivation did provide a sound basis for thinking about how we control action and a convincing account of our practical freedom. In Part 2, I set out this theory of practical freedom.

According to one view, subjection to the will is the key to freedom: after all, a paradigm case of something subject to the will is free action. Now, in Chapter 2, I suggested that what distinguishes actions from other psychological phenomena is that actions are governed by practical norms: an action is justified by reference to its desirability. Furthermore, I think that this fact about the rationality of agency is what makes agency subject to the will: an action is subject to the will because it is an event whose function is to promote the agent's ends (Pink 1996: 192–200). At the same time, I rejected the pragmatist idea that beliefs are governed by practical norms. Thus I implicitly argued that beliefs are not subject to the will, that they are not free in that sense. They escape the control of the will because their function is not to promote the agent's objectives (Pink 1996: 160).

If there is any such thing as freedom of belief, it is a judgement-based not a will-based form of freedom. I devote Chapters 6 and 7 to elucidating a judgement-based notion of freedom: reflective control. But before that, I focus briefly on the alternative, will-based, notion of freedom with two purposes in mind. First, I have more to say about what subjection to the will means, and thereby deepen the contrast with judgement-based notions of control. Second, I intend to establish that the will-based notion of control won't do, not only as an account of intellectual freedom but also as an account of practical freedom, its applicability to action notwithstanding. Even if, in the end, there is no freedom of belief and the juridical theory of responsibility must be abandoned, our efforts to elucidate reflective control will not have been wasted: the notion of reflective control is needed to make sense of our practical freedom.

Intellectualist versus voluntarist conceptions of control

It is often said that we have practical freedom if we are capable of doing what we decide to do, because we decide to do it. But this phrase could be used to express two quite different theories of practical freedom. 'Decision' might refer to a practical judgement – the judgement that I *should* raise my hand. On the other hand, 'decision' could refer to an executive event, the formation of an intention, a state which ensures that I *will* perform the act decided upon when the time comes. (A similar ambiguity affects the word 'choice'.) The former reading leads on to a judgement-based or intellectualist notion of practical freedom, the latter to a will-based or voluntarist notion.

If asked to explain the difference between intentions and practical judgements, many philosophers would say just this: practical judgements can be true or false while intentions can not. This statement is fine so far as it goes, but doesn't tell us enough. Beliefs are usually distinguished from desires in much the same way, and yet practical judgement is no more a form of belief than intention is a form of desire (or so I'll argue). We need some more discriminating characterisation of the difference.

What is the will?

While almost everyone admits that action originates in desire, not all writers see the need for acts of will over and above desire. For philosophers like Hobbes, Nietzsche and Ryle, the will is a myth with a purpose, the locus of an incoherent metaphysical freedom, a stick for moralists to beat us with, or one more excrescence of a bankrupt dualist psychology. Now I agree with these sceptics to *this* extent: I see no reason to think that every voluntary action is preceded by an act of will (distinct from the beliefs and desires which motivate it) – an action can be intentional without originating in an intention – but I do see an important role for an executive event, distinct from both judgement and desire, in the production of much of our rational agency.

The will enables us to co-ordinate our actions over time as neither desires nor practical judgements could. Suppose I am convinced that I must endure a painful operation for the sake of my health. To judge that I should undergo a painful operation is not to be in a state which will *ensure* that I am motivated to enter the hospital at (what I believe to be) the appointed hour. To desire to undergo that operation is not to be in such a state either. But to intend to enter the hospital at that time is to be in a state which, so long as I am in it, guarantees that I will (at least try to) go. Failure to (try to) ϕ when one intended to ϕ and now believes that the time for ϕ-ing has arrived means that one must have abandoned the intention to ϕ; at some point, one ceased to be set on ϕ-ing. Nothing similar is true of either practical judgement or desire: each provides some motivation for ϕ-ing but neither settles the motivational question.[1] The will commits the agent in a way that his desires and judgements do not: the will is an executive phenomenon.

Medieval philosophers were especially sensitive to this distinction between will and practical judgement. Free will was controversial throughout the High Middle Ages but, at least among orthodox Catholics, this controversy took the form of a clash between intellectualists and voluntarists, rather than between metaphysical libertarians and determinists (Kent 1996: Chapter 3). Both parties to this dispute were metaphysical libertarians – for both one had freedom of action only if the psychological sources of action were also free. All seemed to think that real freedom involved that total or unconditional control I set to one side in Chapter 4. But they disagreed over whether the source of free action lay in the will or in the judgement.

Voluntarists were inclined to argue that we do not have freedom of practical judgement and therefore they insisted that our freedom of action is ultimately a freedom of the will, that I act freely provided I act 'at will'. Intellectualists tended to think that once the will breaks free of practical judgement, it ceases to be a source of responsible agency and becomes a mere appetite. They maintained that we act freely only where our action conforms to a free practical judgement.[2] In contemporary thought, libertarian metaphysics is highly controversial, and most philosophers attempt to ground human freedom in a metaphysically modest and scientifically realistic notion of control. But the issue between intellectualists and voluntarists remains wide open.

For contemporary voluntarists, the fundamental way you exercise self-control is by taking a decision to do something at a future time and then executing that decision when the time arrives (Pink 1996: Chapters 1 and 3; see also Bratman 1999b). Plan adoption (the simple plan involved in walking across the room quite as much as the complex plan which governs a successful holiday) is the basic expression of practical freedom. This seems wrong to me. True, the ability to formulate and stick to a plan is a tool without which it would be virtually impossible to manage our complex lives, but is it really the essence of self-control? Isn't self-control about being able to do what you think you ought to do, whether or not this involves making a plan (however etiolated)? In the case of simple actions, planning and intention formation are unnecessary, yet one remains in control. And when you have made a plan which you no longer think to be a good one but find yourself following it nonetheless, against your better judgement, you are no longer exercising control over your actions; you remain responsible here only in so far as you *could* reassert judgemental control over your agency.

Is belief subject to the will?

I have suggested that an event is under the control of the agent's will when it is governed by practical norms. This might sound puzzling. Surely an event is under the control of my will when my will can influence that event in some fairly direct way. What has that to do with normative facts?[3] Take belief. Belief would be subject to the will if we could believe things at will. Now it may very well be that beliefs acquired at will – i.e. with a view to the desirability rather than the probability of the belief – are irrational. But why should this normative fact prevent the agent's interests motivating belief via an act of will?

In principle, the will could directly cause anything at all. But the mere fact that something is produced by my will, that my will motivates it, does not put me in control of it. I am in control of it only when my judgement as to whether it ought to be produced at will can determine whether it is produced at will. I am in control of the products of my will when the will itself is under my reflective control. We are interested in subjection to the will only in so far as subjection to the will is a form of control, is something which (on the juridical theory) might underwrite the agent's responsibility for his or her own agency. And the agent exercises control by means of higher order normative judgements about what ought to happen. These judgements are arrived at precisely by applying the relevant norms, so norms do constrain what can happen at will in the sense of that phrase which connotes control and therefore (on the juridical theory) responsibility.

We can see how normative facts constrain the exercise of control by returning to the case of belief. Suppose I want to be cleverer than my students, and this causes me to acquire the belief that I am cleverer than my students. The fact that I want to be cleverer than my students is not even a *prima facie* reason for thinking that I am. Therefore, I could not have arrived at this belief by judging that I ought to acquire it because of its desirability: I could not have exercised reflective control over my wilful acquisition of this belief. By contrast, the action of popping a pill with a view to inducing this belief is an action I could perform because I judged that such an action would have a desirable consequence: I could have exercised reflective control over my wilful performance of this action. Therefore the will is an instrument by which I can control my action but not an instrument by which I can control my beliefs.

I have established that something is subject to control *via* the will only if it is governed by practical norms. Action satisfies this condition, and so we have a possible explanation of why actions are free: actions are free because they are subject to control *via* the will. But this explanation is superficial because the voluntaristic notion of freedom which it invokes will not cover all that we take to be free. In particular, it does not apply to the will itself.

Is the will subject to the will?

Our wills as well as our actions are free. We think of ourselves as having direct control over what we intend to do quite as much as over what we actually do: we control the will itself. This belief in the freedom of the will is not, in my view, symptomatic of an adherence to libertarian metaphysics. Ordinary people do not think of themselves as free to choose their desires or their beliefs, even though every action originates in desire and belief. It is not a fear of our actions being determined by things over which we have no control which makes us insist on the freedom of the will; rather it is a feature specific to the will. On a voluntaristic conception of freedom, this feature must be that the will is itself subject to the will, that we can decide to do things at will. But, as I shall now argue, we can't take practical decisions at will, any more than we can form beliefs at will: 'we cannot will what we want to, just as we cannot judge what we want to' (Leibniz 1981: 182). So a voluntaristic conception of freedom has no obvious application to the will.

I have already established that beliefs are not subject to the will because a belief could not be justified simply by reference to the desirable consequences of having that belief. Something similar is true of practical decisions: what makes a decision rational is not the advantages of the decision itself but those of the action decided upon. Therefore, we can't rationally take a decision simply because making that decision would be beneficial. This point rarely makes itself felt because taking a certain decision is usually desirable just when and where the action decided upon is also desirable. Yet these two things can come apart.

Suppose you are offered a large prize for *deciding* to consume a mild toxin (Kavka 1983). It would be unpleasant, as well as unnecessary, to implement this decision: you receive the prize regardless of whether you actually consume the toxin. But to get the prize you really must take the decision and to take a decision is, of course, to commit yourself to implementing that decision. Can you reasonably decide to perform such an undesirable action simply because of the advantages of having taken this decision? Surely not. It can be reasonable for you to decide to drink the toxin only if drinking the toxin is a sensible thing to do and it isn't. On the other hand, the prize for taking this decision might rationally motivate an action which will *cause* you to decide to drink the toxin (take a pill, for instance). Since the prize for deciding to drink the toxin outweighs its unpleasant side-effects, the consequences of such a decision-causing action will, on the whole, be desirable. This is a case where it is rational for you to do something which will bring about an irrational decision.

We can now explain why our rationality does not give us the power to take a decision simply by reflecting on the desirability of that decision. Not every desirable end promoted by taking a decision is one which could be used to justify that decision – for example, a prize for taking the decision to consume a toxin will not justify that decision because it will not justify the action decided upon – so far as rationality goes, one can't get oneself to take this decision simply by reflecting on the advantages of having decided to drink the toxin. In this, intentions differ from actions, since there is no such restriction on the desirable ends that may be used to justify action (Pink 1996: 192–200).

We must conclude that the will is not subject to the will as actions are, and we are left without an account of how the will can be under our control.[4] In the next two chapters, I suggest that our control over both will and deed, over decisions and agency, should receive a common explanation in terms of their connection with *practical judgement*. If, as I think, reflection on what we should decide has much the same authority over the formation of intentions as it has over bodily movements, then deciding to ϕ is indeed something we control in this broader sense.

'Direct' versus 'indirect' control

I have argued that belief is not subject to control *via* the will. A voluntaristic theory of freedom offers us a very implausible conception of what it would be for us to control our beliefs and thereby deprives the debate about epistemic freedom and rationality of much of its interest. In the rather extensive literature on 'doxastic voluntarism', almost everyone adopts a will-based conception of freedom, either overlooking or ignoring the possibility that there may be other and more palatable ways of articulating the claim to control our beliefs. By adopting a voluntaristic conception of control one effectively abandons the idea that we can exercise control over belief.

Is this entirely fair? The doxastic voluntarist might concede that we cannot exercise direct control over belief by means of the will. But what of *indirect* control? The literature on doxastic voluntarism is replete with discussions of the possibilities of controlling belief by means of our action (Alston 1988). And action surely is subject to the will. Why isn't this enough to give us the sort of control over belief which could underwrite our responsibility to epistemic norms?

The problem with controlling our beliefs by means of our actions is that such exercises of control are not subject to epistemic norms at all. If we induce belief by means of a deed, the norms of practical reason determine the rationality of that deed. Action is governed by practical considerations: the theoretical rationality of a belief has, at best, an indirect bearing on whether we should take steps to induce that belief. Now, I take it we are interested in control over belief because we hold ourselves accountable to epistemic norms, and many of us are inclined to think that such responsibility requires control. If so, what we need is a form of control governed by epistemic norms, one which can underwrite a direct responsibility for implementing those norms. No action-based control of belief can give us that.

There are self-help manuals which assure us that by rehearsing positive thoughts in our auditory imagination we can banish negative attitudes and unhelpful beliefs about ourselves. Suppose that were true. Then we could act to get rid of these undesirable mental states solely on the grounds that it was bad for us to have them (regardless of whether they were evidentially well founded or not), and such actions might be perfectly reasonable: it would be rational to induce beliefs which were themselves irrational. The exercise of this sort of belief control is governed by practical and not by epistemic norms, and therefore the fact that we have control of this sort over belief can do nothing to explain why our beliefs are responsible to epistemic norms. But the whole point of trying to construct a notion of control which will cover belief is precisely to explain how beliefs can be subject to *epistemic* norms in a way consonant with the juridical theory of responsibility.

Would it help if we restricted our attention to actions designed to make our beliefs more rather than less truthful? Say I judge that I ought to believe that my students are more talented than I now think and I set about trying to convince myself of this. I may suspect that I am inclined to underestimate the students' abilities, and so I scrutinise their essays more carefully (or talk with my less misanthropic colleagues). Suppose I thereby succeed in getting myself to believe what I think I ought to believe: does this show that I have the right sort of control over belief?

No. Action, however motivated, is not an instrument of control which can underwrite a direct responsibility to epistemic norms. Actional control of belief underwrites only a *conditional* responsibility to conform our beliefs to epistemic norms when it is prudent (or morally obligatory) so to do. Actional control ensures that we are accountable for irrational belief only where there is something that can or should be done about it: this sort of doxastic responsibility is entirely derived from responsibility for action. Where there is no action which it is sensible to undertake with a view to regulating belief – perhaps no action available to us would be at all efficacious, or perhaps those actions which would ensure our beliefs' conformity to epistemic norms are imprudent (or immoral) – we have no responsibility to obey epistemic norms.

Some adherents of the juridical theory of responsibility might settle for this result. On their view, if our agency is the only thing we control then our responsibility cannot extend beyond our actions and the (foreseeable) consequences of our actions: we are responsible for our beliefs only in so far as we could, and should, influence them by means of our agency. But (as I argue in Chapter 8) we cannot shrug off our epistemic responsibilities simply by highlighting the difficulty of controlling our beliefs by means of our actions. We believers are held to epistemic norms even when there is no action which we should perform with a view to implementing them. Irrational belief is not excused just because there is nothing the agent can *do* about it. Belief's responsibility to epistemic norms is unconditional, not derived from our responsibility to norms of practical reason.

The beauty of reflective control is that it is a *ubiquitous* and *generic* form of control. Unlike actional control of belief, it is always available to any rational creature, and it is a way of implementing any rational norm. The instrument of reflective control over belief is higher order judgements about what epistemic norms dictate, and if reflection on such considerations alone could rationally motivate belief we would have a form of control over belief which is governed directly by epistemic norms. Such reflective control would indeed underwrite a direct responsibility to epistemic norms.

Doxastic voluntarism

In all of the examples of actional control over belief so far discussed one gets oneself to believe that *p* by doing something else: inducing the belief that *p* involved taking a pill, associating with the right people, or even rehearsing an improving thought. In the language of the doxastic voluntarism debate, I have considered only 'indirect control' over belief. But what if we could convince ourselves of *p* by means of a *basic* action, an act of trying to form the belief that *p* which didn't involve doing anything other than trying to form that belief (Adams 1985: 8–10). Would such causally direct actional control over belief underwrite a direct responsibility to epistemic norms?

I think not. The problem with actional control over belief is simply that it is control by means of an action: whether the action is basic or not is beside the present point. Suppose that we could sometimes form beliefs without doing anything else. Still this basic action of belief formation would, like all other actions, be governed by the norms of practical reason. For example, if the basic action were a *trying* to form the belief, that attempt would be rational if and only if the formation of the belief was a desirable result. This normative fact alone suffices to ensure that our capacity to perform this basic action cannot give us a type of control over belief whose exercise is governed by epistemic norms and therefore cannot (on the juridical theory) underwrite a direct responsibility to those norms.

In Chapter 2, I considered the pragmatist idea that the norms which govern the formation of belief are practical norms, with an evidential constraint added. Had this version of pragmatism stood up to scrutiny, we could have made good sense of the idea that epistemic norms can be implemented by means of an action, that actional control of belief could underwrite a direct responsibility to epistemic norms. But pragmatism failed: beliefs are not subject to the will precisely because belief formation is not governed by practical norms. So actional control, however direct, cannot ground our responsibility to epistemic norms.

Nothing I have said is meant to resolve the issue which I take to be central to the current debate about doxastic voluntarism: can we ever form beliefs simply by trying to form them? Can belief ever be induced directly, by means of a basic action? On the answer to this query hangs the extent of our *practical* responsibility for belief. Suppose my beliefs were like bits of bodily agency in that I usually could bring them about without doing anything else first. That would widen the scope of our practical responsibility for belief considerably. But my concern is exclusively with our responsibility to conform our beliefs to (unconditional) epistemic norms and no amount of actional control over belief could underwrite that responsibility. So far as I can see, the truth or falsity of the claim that we can induce beliefs by means of basic acts has no significance for epistemology, internalist or otherwise.[5]

Epistemic activity and the justification of belief

We have seen that belief is not subject to the will. But recently several writers have conceded this point while still maintaining that our responsibility for belief derives from our responsibility for certain activities which help to fix what we believe. In their view whether the resulting beliefs are justified is determined entirely by whether these epistemic actions are justified. Since these activities are subject to my will, the normative quality of my beliefs (if not the creation of the belief itself) is placed back under the control of my will (Kornblith 1983: 39; Montmarquet 1993: Chapters 2–3; Hookway 1994: 225; Zagzebski 1996: 219–31).

To render this plausible, we must restrict our attention to a special class of belief-causing actions – those motivated by a desire to get at the truth by means of evidence – otherwise a belief reasonably induced by means of a drug, say, would thereby be reasonable. The formation of a belief is often preceded by a certain amount of investigation, consideration and evaluation of evidence (what, in Chapter 1, I called first-order inquiry), processes which certainly look like intentional activities. The thought under examination is that once we have assessed these epistemic actions, once we have decided whether the inquiry was reasonable, no further question remains as to the normative status of the beliefs which result from it.

Inquiry involves evaluating evidence, taking certain possibilities seriously (or not, as the case may be), engaging in statistical or deductive reasoning, etc. These all sound like activities – certainly the verbs involved are *grammatically* active – but are they activities in any more substantial sense? I have argued that activities are events subject to the will, events whose justification lies in how desirable their occurrence would be. Applying this notion of activity to the elements of an inquiry, we find genuine activities intimately entwined with events which are certainly not actions, though they are often referred to by means of exactly the same form of words. This ambiguity encourages the idea that in assessing the actions which form part of the process of inquiry, we are also assessing the beliefs which result from that inquiry.

For example, a phrase like 'evaluating evidence' can be taken at least two ways. If I am a judge, I can decide to spend an evening reading the trial papers and I may do this after weighing the importance of getting the verdict right against the loss of time and mental energy involved. Here 'evaluating evidence' is an action fully subject to the will. What is not an action in any sense is the formation of a belief about guilt or innocence (and of the other beliefs which lead to it), something which may occur as the result of reading the papers: a belief in guilt cannot be justified by reference to the desirable consequences of having that belief (and so cannot be rationally motivated by reflection on such considerations). So if 'evaluating evidence' includes forming a view of whether the evidence is sufficient to establish guilt, it is no longer pure activity but at best a hybrid process. Nor does our control over the activity which produces this belief give us any direct control over (or responsibility for) the belief itself.[6]

How about 'taking seriously the possibility that my friend is lying'? Is this an activity? Say I believe that p on the basis of his testimony, and then come to doubt it. Abandoning the belief in p is no more something I do (no more subject to my will) than the acquisition of that belief was. True 'taking the possibility seriously' may involve not just the loss of a belief but also some consequent activity. Perhaps I determine that it is now rather important to resolve the matter and find out whether my friend is a liar, and so I set out to collect some evidence. Here it is the other way around to how it was with the judge: an event which is not an epistemic activity motivates an event which is. The collection of evidence (and its assimilation and consideration) surely are subject to the will: they are things we do in the expectation of certain desirable consequences, such as the formation of an accurate belief on the matter. But the loss of trust in my friend which preceded these activities was not itself an action. To theorise effectively about the process of belief formation, we must keep these disparate elements apart.

Verbs like 'calculation' are a fertile source of confusion here. 'Calculation' could refer either to an activity intended to arrive at a belief or else to a process which includes the formation of that belief. If calculation includes belief, a calculation can be reasonable only if the belief formed (as well as the activity which precedes it) is reasonable. But if calculation does not include belief, an activity of calculation which it was perfectly reasonable to engage in might lead to a quite unreasonable belief. True, it may be reasonable for me to engage in the activity of calculating my tax bill only if it is reasonable for me to believe that this activity will result in a reasonable belief about my tax bill. But the fact that I reasonably believe that calculating will deliver a reasonable belief does not imply that calculating actually will deliver a reasonable belief. So the normative status of the activity of calculating cannot determine the normative status of the resulting belief unless it is taken to include the formation of that belief, and thus ceases to be something I can do at will.

A further source of potential confusion is the idea that believing actually involves taking certain practical decisions. For example, Harman (1980) says that to accept p is to decide not to inquire further into whether p.[7] Since we do have control over our decisions, it might look as if this gives us control over belief as well. Now Harman is certainly right that if a rational person forms the belief that p he will normally cease to inquire into whether p. Such a person usually has no further reason to inquire into whether p: so long as she believes p, she takes herself to know that p and therefore to know that evidence against p must be misleading.[8] But a believer in p might have an extraneous reason to inquire into whether p – that is, a reason to collect evidence on whether p and consider how it supports p. For example, she may wish to convince someone else of p and needs to construct a plausible case for it. So there is no *necessary* connection between belief in p and practical decisions about epistemic actions and therefore no cause to identify the adoption of the belief with the taking of such a decision. Rather the belief usually rationalises and motivates this decision.

Once these points have been fully appreciated, it is no longer plausible to suppose that the normative status of the actional components of a process of inquiry alone determine whether the beliefs that result from inquiry are justified. Surely someone can collect just the right amount of evidence to resolve a matter and spend just the right amount of time and effort considering the evidence, and yet form a belief about it which is unjustified (or fail to form a belief which would have been justified). He might do this because he forms an inaccurate view of the balance of evidence, or he might be insufficiently impressed by the need to make up his mind, etc. This failure will amount to a careless or unreasonable *action* on his part only if one thinks that believing is itself an action.

In fact, most of the writers I am now considering agree that believing is not subject to the will, which is precisely why they seek to derive the normative status of beliefs from that of the actions which cause it.[9] But our control over these actions yields only an *indirect* control over belief and, as already argued, such indirect control cannot underwrite the *direct* responsibility of belief to epistemic norms. There are only two possible ways forward. One involves detaching control from the will and arguing that it is a reflective control over belief which makes us responsible to epistemic norms. I explore this line of thought in the next two chapters. The other way out is to abandon the whole idea that responsibility requires control, a move I recommend in Chapter 8.

Chapter 6

Locke on freedom

There is no shortage of off-hand references to 'intellectual autonomy', 'the spontaneous application of concepts', 'freedom of judgement' in our philosophical tradition. These idioms gesture towards a notion of freedom and control which, it is hoped, applies beyond the practical realm, bringing our cognitive lives within the scope of our responsibility, even if our cognitive life is not subject to the will. In far shorter supply are serious attempts to develop this notion of control. One person who did write extensively about these issues was John Locke, and I spend this chapter expounding and criticising a line of thought to be found in his work. I do not endorse his conclusions but they are a useful foil for those of Chapter 7. I offer what follows as one possible reading of Locke: anyone who looks at the text will discover a rich and stimulating discussion rather than a single, consistently maintained, view.[1]

Epistemic control

Locke states unequivocally that 'to believe this or that to be true does not depend upon our will' (Locke 1965: 133) and yet he is equally clear that we have duties and obligations in the epistemic realm, as much as in the practical. Nor does he think epistemic duties could be imposed on us were it beyond our control whether we fulfil them or not: Locke is a firm adherent of the juridical theory of responsibility. For him, there must be an element of freedom in thought, otherwise 'ignorance, error, or infidelity could not in any case be a fault' (Locke 1975: 717). At first, Locke appears to equate freedom with subjection to the will and implicitly denies that our control extends further than our agency (Locke 1975: II, XXI, 5–30). But he goes on to develop a broader notion of control, one intended to apply both to the will and to belief.

I begin with the problems raised by belief, then look to what Locke says about the will and finally turn back to apply what he says about freedom of the will to belief.

Locke looks for epistemic control in several places, not all of them equally promising. One element in the picture is the investigations and deliberations which lead up to the acquisition of a belief. Clearly these are voluntary actions, and they exercise a formative influence over our beliefs. Locke compares knowledge to perception in that it is '*neither wholly necessary nor wholly voluntary*'. We can choose whether or not to look at something and how closely to scrutinise it, but we can't choose how we'll see it once we attend to it:

> [A]ll that is *voluntary* in our knowledge is the *employing* or withholding of any of *our faculties* from this or that sort of objects, and a more or less accurate survey of them: but they being employed, *our will hath no power to determine the knowledge of the mind* one way or the other; that is done only by the objects themselves, as far as they are clearly discovered.
>
> (Locke 1975: 650–1)

This is a neat and simple account, but it can't be the whole story. We have a *direct* responsibility for our beliefs, and for Locke, such a responsibility presupposes direct control over belief. On the above model, our influence over our beliefs is no more direct than that we have over the character of our perceptual experience: such experiences are neither reasonable nor unreasonable, precisely because they are not under our direct control.[2] Of course, we can exercise an indirect control over our experiences (e.g. by re-orienting our sensory organs), but here our responsibility is for the actions which influence our experience and not for the experience itself. Yet we are held to account for our beliefs as we are not for our sensory experiences. Is there any more direct form of epistemic control which might underwrite this responsibility?

Knowledge and opinion

Locke draws a big distinction, familiar from pre-modern philosophy, between knowledge on the one hand and belief or opinion on the other.[3] To have knowledge is to perceive the agreement or disagreement of ideas, to enjoy an intellectual intuition of the truth of a proposition. To have a belief or an opinion is to register that a proposition is more or less probable given certain evidence and then to give your assent to that proposition (or not) on that basis.[4] Judgement in accordance with reason, rather than (intellectual) perception, is what is needed to bring this off. Once belief is in play, a question arises – how much evidence is required for us to be entitled to assent to a certain proposition? And according to some pre-modern thinkers, in resolving this question we have an opportunity to exercise direct control over belief.

For example, Aquinas tells us that

> things are apprehended, which do not convince the intellect, and hence allow the intellect to assent or not assent – or at least to suspend assenting or not assenting for some reason – and in such matters to assent or not assent is within our power and subject to our command.
>
> (Aquinas 1983: 154)[5]

So not only can we decide whether to attend to a certain issue and how much time to devote to it, but we can decide when we have sufficient evidence to enable us to assent to a proposition, when we have done enough to resolve the matter. In Aquinas' view, there is scope for decision in the realm of belief which doesn't exist in the realm of knowledge.

Does Locke agree? Here is what he says:

> In propositions where though the proofs in view are of most moment, yet there are sufficient grounds, to suspect that there is either a fallacy in words, or certain proofs, as considerable, to be produced on the contrary side, there assent, suspense, or dissent, are often voluntary actions: but where the proofs are such as to make it highly probable and there is not sufficient ground to suspect, that there is either fallacy of words . . . nor equally valid proofs yet undiscovered latent on the other side . . . there, I think, a man who has weighed them, can scarcely refuse his assent to the side, on which the greater probability appears.
>
> (Locke 1975: 716)

Locke seems to agree that where the proofs are inconclusive we have liberty of indifference: the will is free to determine which way our assent should go.

But this is not a happy reading of Locke. First, it flatly contradicts the claim he started out with, that belief does not fall within the scope of the will. Second, it sits very uneasily with Locke's oft-repeated rejection of the whole notion of liberty of indifference, of the idea that we are truly free only when reason leaves it undetermined what we should do or think (Locke 1975: 283–4). Third, it simply isn't true that where the evidence is inconclusive we can believe whatever we like. If the evidence for and against a Republican victory in the next Presidential election is evenly balanced, I can't get myself to believe that they will lose by reflecting that I would thereby sleep more easily in my bed. Of course, wishful thinking might lead me to this conclusion, but such wishful thinking is not an exercise of cognitive self-mastery.[6]

A careful reading of Locke's words inspires second thoughts. First, we notice a requirement that there be *grounds* for assent, dissent, suspense: the suspicion of a mistake or the expectation of new evidence. The epistemic judgement is based on evidence, not on the desirability of the belief. Second, if we are to render Locke's position both consistent and plausible, I think we must treat his use of the phrase 'voluntary *action*' here as a slip. Substituting for 'voluntariness' the more general notion of 'freedom', we can get away from the idea that we are dealing with an action. Indeed, Locke is quite clear that something can be free without being subject to the will, without being an action in that sense: our wills are free but he thinks it nonsensical to suppose that the will is ever subject to the will. To understand Locke's view, we must first explicate Locke's notion of free will and then return to apply it to belief.

Locke on freedom of the will

Locke begins the chapter of his *Essay* entitled 'Of Power' by dismissing the notion of free will altogether. One's actions are determined by one's will, and one's will is determined by one's desires: there is no room for any further control over the will. He takes the Hobbesian line (Hobbes 1839a) that a man's actions are free in so far as he can do whatever he wants to do and simply denies that any similar notion of freedom is applicable to the will (Locke 1975: II, XXI, 14–29). But later in the same chapter Locke begins to speak of liberty of the will.[7] What Locke really objects to is not free will as such but rather a certain conception of what it would be for the will to be free, one which models freedom of the will too closely on freedom of action. An action is free if it is subject to the will, but it is nonsense to suppose that the will is itself subject to the will.

So what can 'freedom of will' mean if not subjection to the will? Locke locates practical freedom in a certain deliberative capacity: ultimately a free person must decide and act in accordance with her desires but she is also able to postpone action and reflect on the options. For Locke, the mind is able 'to suspend the execution and satisfaction of any of its desires, and so all, one after another . . . to consider the objects of them; examine them on all sides, and weigh them with others. In this lies the liberty that man has' (1975: 263).[8] Once this examination is concluded, the agent must take that option which appears to offer the greatest prospect of happiness; but this necessity to pursue what appears to be the greater good (upon reflection) is no restriction on our freedom (ibid.: 264–5).[9] A free will is a will which accords with our (considered) practical judgement.

Note that there is no role for liberty of indifference even when the question is whether we should suspend the implementation of our desires or not. The occasions of suspension and the amount of examination will, in a rational person, be 'proportionable to the weightiness of the matter, and the concernment it is to us not to mistake' (ibid.: 278). Suspension is no *deus ex machina*, no random intervention in the causal process leading to action; rather the capacity for practical deliberation is something which a free being possesses and can use when the occasion demands. Once deliberation should be brought to a close, the rational agent can reflect that this is so, cease evaluating the options and act in accordance with his considered view of what is best.

Here Locke can be seen as answering the question 'What makes our will free?' by offering us a certain reading of Reflective Motivation. Recall that, according to Reflective Motivation, if a mental state is reasonable that state could have been motivated by reflection on the quality of the reasons for it. For Locke a free and reasonable decision is one that could have been arrived at by suspending the satisfaction of importunate desire, reflecting on what was good for us and then implementing that judgement in action. On this interpretation, Reflective Motivation does not require that we be able to circumvent desire altogether and act on the basis of practical judgement alone. What it does presuppose is the capacity to restrain desire until such time as we judge our desires have come into line with our real needs and interests, a capacity which a man being stretched on the rack, for instance, may lack. Reflection exercises a kind of veto over rational behaviour – we can postpone action until our will conforms to our practical judgement – and this power of scrutiny and of veto is reason's way of controlling the will.

Locke and Hume

It is illuminating to confront Locke's picture of the rational control of action with Hume's scepticism about the whole idea of practical reason. Hume asserts '*first* that reason alone can never be a motive to any action of the will; and *secondly* that it can never oppose passion in the direction of the will' (Hume 1978: 413).[10] Locke would heartily endorse the first of these propositions: he never tires of insisting that it is the uneasiness of desire, and not our judgement of what is best for us, which moves the will. When desires conflict, it is the most pressing which wins out. Hume himself could have written the following words: 'good, though appearing, and allowed never so great, yet till it has raised desires in our minds and thereby made us uneasie in its want, it reaches not our wills' (Locke 1975: 262). So where lies the difference between them?

Hume thinks that if 'reason alone can never be a motive to any action of the will', it follows immediately that 'it can never oppose passion in the direction of the will' because ''tis impossible reason could have the latter effect of preventing volition, but by giving an impulse in a contrary direction to our passion; and that impulse had it operated alone would have been able to produce volition' (Hume 1978: 415). Here Hume is overlooking the possibility that reason has the power to suspend the operation of a desire and make room for practical reflection without having the power to motivate an action altogether contrary to desire. This is exactly the possibility on which Locke insists. Reason can veto action and enforce deliberation so long as our practical judgement is out of line with our desire. Until desire comes into line, practical judgement cannot be implemented and the rational agent cannot act.

This suspension gives desire time to reform itself and gives us time to do things which might influence it (e.g. paint the unattractive features of the rejected option in more vivid colours). Our control over the content of desire is indirect but, in this, desire is no different from belief. As we have seen, I can exercise an indirect control over my beliefs by collecting and assimilating evidence; and, as we'll see, for Locke, our freedom of thought consists in an ability to directly suspend the formation of belief and thereby allow time for the exercise of such an indirect control.

But, a Humean might respond, these suspensions and vetoes must be motivated by desire in some way; reason alone cannot move us to postpone action and deliberate any more than it can motivate us to act. True (the Lockean will reply), it is such things as our 'concernment' in the question, the felt importance of getting it right, which will motivate the suspension; but this is not a motive for acting one way or the other. Rather it is a motive for acting in accordance with a well-founded judgement; it is a motivation for allowing reason to govern action. Provided there are incentives to deliberate which are not simply motives for deciding one way or the other, reason can control what we do and thereby make us free in both our decision making and our action.

I have portrayed Locke as rejecting the will-subjection theory of control and as instead locating our freedom in the connection between the will and practical judgement. But couldn't we read Locke as putting forward a special form of the will-subjection theory of control, one which hypothesises that our judgement as to whether we ought now to take a practical decision influences our will *via* a further act of will? This thought might be reconciled with Locke's insistence that the will itself is not subject to the will by interpreting that claim as a rejection only of the more extreme idea that we can will to will a specific action (as opposed to being able to determine at will whether to take any decision at all).

But Locke never qualifies his assertion that the will is not subject to the will in this way, and he nowhere speaks of the will as the faculty which suspends the action of the will.[11] Indeed, he clearly needs to maintain that our practical judgement (or understanding) has a direct influence over *whether* we will (as opposed to *what* we will), an insistence which makes philosophical sense. If judgement has no direct influence at this point, how would it ever come into contact with the will? Clearly a regress threatens, and the only non-arbitrary way of terminating it is to allow practical judgement unmediated access to the will. For Locke, our freedom lies right there.

Locke on freedom of understanding

Now we have Locke's theory of freedom before us, how are we to construe 'freedom of understanding'?[12] A good way into Locke's views on this is to look at his discussion of wrongful assent. Locke begins with a question: 'if assent be grounded on likelihood . . . it will be demanded how men come to give their assents contrary to probability' (Locke 1975: 707). One case is where a man's powers of reasoning are simply inadequate to the task of absorbing the evidence before him (ibid.: 709). Locke seems uninterested in this sort of example because, I suspect, it isn't a case where the irrational belief is reprehensible. A man who cannot reason is, in that respect, like a beast. What really interests Locke are instances in which a failure to conform your beliefs to the evidence renders you liable to blame. Where there is responsibility, there is sure to be some element of freedom also.

We can divide cases of culpable epistemic irrationality into two classes. First there are those where we fail to have what Locke elsewhere calls 'a perfect indifferency for all opinions' (1996: 211). Now 'indifferency' doesn't mean that one cares not which topics one has views about so long as they are all (likely to be) true. On the contrary, Locke is constantly emphasising that we have far greater 'concernment' in some subjects than in others. Rather 'indifferency' fails when one allows one's needs and interests to determine not just on which subjects one seeks to form an opinion but what opinion one forms. The trouble with the learned man who has been shown to be wrong but won't concede the point, or the lover who can't credit reports of his mistress' infidelity, or the man who declines to open his mail because he fears his finances are not in good order, is that each is biased in favour of a particular view. Therefore, either they refuse to attend to evidence which would undermine their current belief or else they decline to give such evidence its proper weight.

Locke's other examples feature people who don't care enough about the issue under consideration: they needn't be biased on the matter, they just don't put enough effort into finding out the truth about it. Locke is no rigourist about belief: he happily concedes that 'where the assent one way or the other is of no importance to the interest of anyone . . . there 'tis not strange that the mind should give itself up to the common opinion, or render itself to the first comer' (Locke 1975: 717). What irks him is that in matters of great concernment, in particular where the truths of religion and morality are at stake, the average person puts so little effort into forming a tenable view. Either he does not consider carefully enough the evidence he already has or else he can't be bothered to collect sufficient evidence. There are several explanations for this epistemic laxity. One is sheer laziness, more or less excusable depending on the pressure of the burdens which everyday life places on us. Another is haste or 'precipitancy'. Yet another is fear of authority and of the weight of tradition. People without any preconceived opinion might accept the received view simply through fear of challenging it.

Locke's account of the rationality of belief chimes well with that I sketched in Chapter 2. Non-evidential factors have a crucial role in determining not just how much trouble we ought to take over certain issues but how much evidence we require before we can form a reasonable view. Where our concernment is great, a higher level of evidence is required than when it isn't. What's more, this feature applies as much to practical judgement as to any other:

> it is a very wrong and irrational way of proceeding, to venture a greater good for a less, upon uncertain guesses and before a due examination be made, proportionable to the weightiness of the matter, and the concernment it is to us not to mistake.
>
> (Locke 1975: 278)

So how does 'freedom of understanding' come into the picture? As we have already seen, where there are grounds to suspect that the evidence before us is faulty or that important new evidence will soon appear, we have the power to suspend judgement, provided the matter is of sufficient concernment. Culpable error occurs when we misuse this power of suspension, either by not suspending judgement when we ought to or by suspending judgement when we ought not. True, Locke says, it is in

> the nature of the understanding constantly to close with the more probable side, but yet a man hath a power to suspend and restrain its enquiries, and not permit a full and satisfactory examination, as far as the matter in question is capable, and will bear it to be made.
>
> (Locke 1975: 715)

We are now in a position to see why Locke thinks that epistemic irrationality can be culpable. Of course, what we believe is, in the end, fixed by the apparent weight of evidence, just as what we do is determined, in the last analysis, by the strength of various desires. And we have no direct control over either the strength of our desires or the apparent weight of the evidence. But where there are grounds for thinking that we have not collected evidence sufficient to settle the question, we can suspend judgement until we have had an opportunity to collect new evidence and to reconsider the probative force of that which is already before us. The problem with all the characters just described is that they misuse this power of suspension, reflection and reconsideration. Some of them stick to their guns when they ought to suspend judgement in order to protect a belief which is close to their heart; others don't suspend judgement when they ought, to spare themselves the effort required to deal with the matter properly.

I have extracted from Locke's text an elegant theory of freedom and responsibility which can be applied to belief and to the will, while subjecting neither belief nor the will to the will. Locke's theory makes no use of liberty of indifference: both he and Descartes think we have freedom of judgement in cases where, since the evidence is overwhelming, we couldn't believe otherwise. But while Descartes also takes the traditional line that belief is an appropriate object of blame only because on occasion (where the evidence is indecisive) we have an epistemic liberty of indifference and can assent to an error, Locke denies that belief is ever subject to the will.[13] For Locke, our epistemic responsibility derives exclusively from the fact that belief can be suspended until deliberation compels conviction (or lack of it): that is what makes our judgement free, and no more is required to make sense of the idea of governing one's beliefs by reference to the norms of reason.

Beyond Locke

Locke is trying to defend the Enlightenment doctrine that each individual has a special responsibility for his or her own beliefs: the buck stops with each of us, not just for our actions but for our convictions. And he wants to ground this individual responsibility in the reflective control which each person exercises both over what he or she thinks and over what he or she does. But I doubt Locke has told us what 'reflective control' means, even for the case of action, and it is only because of this omission that his account has any application to belief.

An adequate theory of reflective control must address the following question: how can reflection on what I have reason to believe (or do) exercise a *direct* influence on what I believe (or do)? To put it another way: how could my judgement about what *I* should believe (or do) have any more immediate motivational impact on me than my judgement about what *you* should believe (or do) has on you? For the advocate of reflective control, we each have a special capacity to apply reason to our own beliefs by means of higher order normative judgements: I can determine what I believe by reason alone. Any failure to apply reason to my own beliefs is a culpable breach of epistemic norms. It is also true that I may be able to influence your beliefs by forming a view about what you ought to believe; but I have no special capacity to apply reason to your beliefs by means of such judgements. If your beliefs fall into irrationality, the responsibility is yours, not mine.

In Chapter 1, I observed that it was unclear how higher order normative judgements could have any motivational impact except via the first-order reasons they were judgements about. Surely, the only truly direct influences on what I believe (or do) are reasons for belief (or action) – evidence and desire – themselves. My higher order judgements can perhaps exercise an indirect influence by moulding the content of my first-order reasons, by getting me to attend to new things and ensuring that I register their significance;

but it is the first-order reasons that, in the end, determine what I believe (or do). And such indirect influence hardly constitutes a form of direct control: after all, my judgement about what you ought to believe (or do) can help to determine what *you* believe (or do) by refocusing your attention without giving me direct control over (or responsibility for) *your* beliefs and actions.[14]

A Lockean might reply that while only reasons for ϕ-ing can get me to ϕ, the desire to deliberate about whether to ϕ can prevent me from ϕ-ing. Equally, a strong desire to be right about whether p can ensure that I continue to worry about whether p and fail to form the belief that p, even if only evidence for p can convince me of p. Now these desires directly motivate the person whose desires they are. My desire to be right in what I think or do will have a direct motivational impact on my mental life, while my desire that you be right in what you think or do could have only an indirect influence on yours. My desires motivate deliberation by me straight off, but they motivate deliberation by you only indirectly, only *via* your desires (and other reasons). So don't we now have a form of direct control that applies to both belief and agency?

But we have quite lost the idea that one can exercise an influence on one's own mental life simply by means of higher order judgement, by forming a view of the normative standing of one's beliefs and desires. I have direct control over my belief if my judgement about whether I ought to believe that p helps to determine whether I acquire that conviction. But there is nothing in what Locke says to indicate why these higher order judgements should have any direct influence over what happens. On Locke's model what determines whether I form a belief or not is whether I *desire* to deliberate further, not whether I *judge* that I ought to. On Locke's model, if I have an aversion to further deliberation, my higher order judgement that I should consider the matter further lacks the motivational resources to stop me. Yet it is clear that someone who judges that he ought not to form a view, and yet can't prevent his aversion to further deliberation ensuring that a view is formed, has lost control over his beliefs. And the same is true of action.

Should Locke restore reflective control by postulating a desire to believe and act in accordance with these higher order judgements?[15] Such a desire seems strange: why should I desire to believe what I think I ought to believe (rather than what the evidence supports). Why should I desire to do what I think I ought to (rather than to act in accordance with my first-order desires)? And even if such desires do exist in some people, why should we suppose that they are present in any rational creature, in any creature with reflective control over its mental life, and that these desires are always strong enough to overcome any countervailing desire? I'll argue that our practical judgement has an intrinsic authority over our actions which our theoretical judgement does not have over belief. That is why our practical judgement is a source of rational motivation independent of desire.[16] But no such thing is true in the theoretical realm.

The authority of reflection

Higher order normative judgement is the instrument of reflective control and we have reflective control when such judgements have an intrinsic authority over what we think and/or do. What is it for a judgement to have intrinsic authority? Chapter 7 is devoted to this question, but I shall introduce the general idea now by means of a political analogy which Aquinas borrows from Aristotle.

Aquinas contrasts the control we have over our passions with that we exercise over our bodily members. He assimilates our relationship to our bodily members to that between a master and his slaves. The slaves are deemed to have no will of their own, but are simply instruments of the master's will: they cannot rebel against their master, though they might fail to execute his commands. As a result, if anyone is responsible for what a slave does, it is his master. Similarly, our bodily members have no will of their own: they might malfunction, but they can't rebel; and so if anyone is responsible for what they do (as opposed to what happens to them) it is their owner. On the other hand, Aquinas likens a man's relationship to his passions to that between a king and his subjects. The king rules over his subjects, but the subjects have wills of their own and may oppose the king. So can the king be responsible for his subject's behaviour?[17]

This political analogy might suggest that managing your passions is like reasoning with a fellow citizen about how he should act. Perhaps the king can influence his subjects – but only by persuading them that the course of action he recommends is wise, independently of the fact that he recommends it. On this picture, the king has the right to advise and warn, but the responsibility for what they do rests with his subjects. I doubt this was what Aquinas had in mind. We usually think of a king as having *authority* over his subjects: he has the right to command them. What the subjects have reason to do is not independent of what the king commands. The king has a direct responsibility for the actions of his subjects, a responsibility he does not have for those subject to another king, precisely because he is in authority over the former. If we rule over our own passions, then we can determine what we ought to feel simply by judging which passions are appropriate – these judgements are a source of rational motivation for us – and so we are responsible for the feelings that result.

Let us apply all this to belief. If we each ruled over our own convictions with a political authority, there would be a clear sense in which we controlled our convictions. Not that our convictions would be like slaves. It is quite possible for us to believe things that we think we ought not to believe and for these recalcitrant beliefs to have some rational motivation. But had we a political authority over our convictions, our judgements about what we ought to believe would themselves be a source of rational motivation for belief. What we ought to believe would be determined (at least in part) by what we thought we ought to believe, giving us an authority over our own beliefs which we do not have over the convictions of others. Each of us would possess a direct reflective control over our own convictions, a control which many philosophers think epistemic responsibility requires.

But Aquinas' model suggests another possibility: one could model my relation to my own beliefs on the political relationship between myself and other citizens. I have no authority over my fellow citizens. I can reason with and attempt to persuade them: we can share in the process of deliberation. But the fact that I think they ought to do such and such in itself gives them no reason to do that thing. My advice is only as good as the quality of the reasons behind it; my opinion stands or falls on its merits. In Chapter 7 I argue that this is a better model of how we stand to our own convictions. My opinion about what I ought to believe has no more authority over my beliefs than the next man's opinion; what it would be reasonable for me to believe is determined entirely by the evidence available to me (etc.) and not at all by what I think I ought to believe. Of course, I can deliberate with a view to influencing my convictions, just as I attempt to reason with someone else about what they should believe. But I no more rule my own beliefs than I do those of another.

On the other hand, political rule *is* the right model of how we stand to our own will: we have authority over what we decide to do, as well as what we do. Which intention it is reasonable for me to form is not independent of what I think I ought to do: so my practical judgements are a source of rational motivation. True, our intentions can perfectly well deviate from our practical judgement, and deviate for a reason: an errant will is not like a broken arm. But such *akrasia* of the will is intrinsically irrational because it flouts the authority of our practical judgement, as a broken arm can not. What I doubt is that this model can be extended to belief (or to the passions): in my view, we stand to our own beliefs not as the king stands to his subjects but as one citizen stands to another.

Chapter 7

A theory of freedom

In Chapter 1 I posed the following question: how can reflection bear any weight in an account of freedom? Self-consciousness, that awareness which we have of our own mental states, of our purposes and activities, does seem central to our personhood, in part because without it we cannot have that form of self-control which makes us free. Yet self-consciousness can't be the whole story: freedom is about control, and control is a power to move things; but how can our self-consciousness, our ability to reflect on our motives, itself be a source of motivation? Unless reflection on our reasons can move us, like the reasons themselves, it can hardly be the mark which distinguishes autonomous agents from mere playthings of impulse.

Can reflection move us?

Imagine a creature whose beliefs and actions are determined by the same sorts of reasons as are our own. It can wonder whether a certain proposition is true and amass evidence for and against; it can ponder what action to perform and contemplate the desirability of the various options. Our creature engages in first-order theoretical and practical deliberation, and what it thinks and does is influenced by this reasoning in the normal way. Moreover, our imagined creature rarely believes or acts contrary to reason. In fact it rarely asks itself whether the items it treats as pieces of evidence are good reasons for belief or whether the characteristics it treats as desirable generate good reasons for action; it rarely forms a view about the rationality of its convictions or the prudence of its actions.

Not that it is incapable of such second-order deliberation. The creature *can* turn inward. It can reflect (with satisfaction) on how well-motivated its thoughts and actions are, on the near perfect fit between reason and outcome. Yet these thoughts have no motivational impact. While its gaze is fixed on the world, it discovers all sorts of reasons for thought and action, reasons which move it appropriately. But when its attention turns inward, when it executes a normative ascent, its deliberations become motivationally inert. Even if our creature thought ill of its own beliefs and actions and the reasoning behind them, this would have no direct impact. All the creature can do from the reflective standpoint is to contemplate the normative quality of its mental life. To engage with this life, the creature must give up thinking about how well-evidenced are its beliefs, how rational its actions, and attend to first-order questions. Let us christen our creature (somewhat tendentiously) the *reflective automaton*.[1]

Are we human beings reflective automata? Many writers insist that we can govern what we think and do by reflecting on our reasons. If so we must have a capacity which the automaton lacks and which looks as if it might be crucial to our freedom. Perhaps the motivational inertness of its higher order judgements deprives the reflective automaton of rational freedom, the absence of unreason from its life notwithstanding. Yet there is something strange about the idea that we can exercise control over our mental life simply by asking ourselves how reasonable it is.

Take practical judgements. No one should deny that our judgements as to what we ought to do can have a causal influence on what we actually do: in principle, anything can cause anything. The somewhat strange idea is that we have, in our practical judgements, a further source of rational motivation over and above that provided by the practical reasons on which we reflect when making those judgements. How could reflection be an independent source of rational motivation; how could the *judgement* that I have reason R to ϕ, as opposed to the *fact* that I have reason R to ϕ (a fact of which I am *non-reflectively* aware) move me to ϕ? The answer must be that *Reflective Rationalisation* is true, my judgement that I have reason R to ϕ (whether right or wrong) gives me a reason to ϕ over and above that yielded by my awareness of R itself. *Rational Motivation* then yields the result that, if I am rational, this judgement must provide a motive to ϕ.[2] But how can this be?

True, a capacity for reflection makes a big difference to our motivational psychology, even if we are reflective automata. For a start, a being capable of reflection will likely, *ipso facto*, have needs and interests different from those of an unreflective creature: it might enjoy exercising its capacity for reflection, for example. Furthermore, it will be able to form desires with a second-order content: its own beliefs, desires and emotions, its own psychological makeup, may become an object of practical reasoning. But for a reflective automaton, at least, it remains the case that all motivation is unreflective. If an automaton wants to cultivate the desire to play the piano, that want has a second-order content but it is the want itself, and not the automaton's judgement of its value as a reason, which moves it to action.

In general, the thought that it has a reason R to ϕ gives the automaton no more or no different a reason to ϕ than R itself. Should the automaton's judgement of what it ought to do (or think) diverge from the actions it would perform (or the beliefs it would have), and should it want to implement its judgements, the automaton can adopt various self-manipulative stratagems – take drugs, have itself bound to the mast, or simply fix its attention firmly on the relevant considerations in the hope of raising desire 'in a due proportion to the value of that good' (Locke 1975: 262) – but here the motivational impact of the judgement derives entirely from the desire to have the judgement implemented and the actions which that desire generates. So the automaton has the sort of reflective control over its life which Locke grants us over ours, but its reflective judgements are not themselves a source of reasons and thus have no direct influence on its thought and behaviour. The automaton has no direct control over its own beliefs and actions.

How might it be otherwise? How can the reflection that we have reason R to ϕ give us, we non-automata, any more of, or different, a reason to ϕ than R itself? We should not suppose that reflection reveals, or even creates, reasons whose content is simply unavailable to an unreflective being;[3] it is considerations of which we can have a purely non-reflective awareness which constitute the subject matter of reflection. So how can reflection be an independent source of motivation? To see how, let me revert briefly to the political analogy I introduced in Chapter 6.

Should the state go to war? The citizens may each have an opinion on this question, a reasonable and perhaps correct opinion, based on a concern for the public good. But their opinions are not authoritative. The king's opinion is law. His authority rests not on the fact that he has knowledge of, or is moved by, a set of considerations unavailable to the citizenry but simply on his position. Indeed, the king's view of whether the state should go to war ought to be based on the very reasons which move his more public-spirited citizens. But because he is the sovereign, his opinion has an intrinsic authority. Similarly, our practical judgements might have an intrinsic authority over our own actions, not because they are motivated by a special sort of reason, independent of mere unreflective inclination, but simply because they are reflective, simply because they represent our own verdict on what we have reason to do.

Our practical judgements are themselves a source of practical reasons and thus of rational motivation. As I indicated in Chapter 2, there is a very big difference between thinking and doing in this respect. Our reflective judgements about what we ought to do have an authority over our actions (and over the formation of intentions) which our judgements about what we should believe do not have over our beliefs: that is why we control our actions (and intentions) as we do not control our beliefs.

When contemplating what action to take, the reflection that time has run out, that we ought now to decide, does seem capable of moving us. Practical judgement involves more than a passive registration of how sensible it would be to take a decision – it can ensure that we take that decision. The same is not true of belief. Here we are like the reflective automaton: we can register how sensible it would be to form a belief at this particular stage, but this judgement does nothing to motivate that belief. We have a facility for self-command in the practical sphere which the reflective automaton lacks. Its reasons control its actions, but *it* does not. That is why it is not free. And that is why our freedom is confined to the practical sphere. But can we really credit the idea that our thinking we ought to do something can, in itself, get us to do it? Is this not to run up against the plausible Humean claim, which Locke carefully accommodates, that judgement alone can never move us to action?

The authority of reflection: agency

Let us see how the authority of reflection manifests itself in the practical sphere. Our subject begins by asking himself what he should desire. Then the subject forms a view about what it would be best for him to do, all things considered. Finally, one of two things may happen: if the time for action is now, action is the result; if the time for action has yet to come, a decision is made to act at the appropriate moment. Things can go wrong at all three points. First, the subject might get his interests wrong. Second, he might engage in faulty deliberation about what he should do in the light of them. But the most important possibility for our purposes is the third: his decisions and action might fail to conform to his judgement about what he should do. This is *akrasia*, a form of practical irrationality.

It is crucial to appreciate that this element of irrationality is quite independent of any which might afflict the first two stages of practical deliberation. Suppose I am under some illusion about what I want, or else that I deliberate badly and judge wrongly what I should do to get it. There is an element of irrationality in all this. But if I then fail to do that which I have wrongly determined it would be best for me to do, I am guilty of an *extra* bit of irrationality: I lack the self-control to which every rational agent should aspire. My views about what I ought to do have a right to control my actions which is independent of the cogency of those views: my practical judgements have an *intrinsic authority* over what I do, not merely an authority which derives from the beliefs and desires which should motivate such action. Of course, the practical judgement must make *some* sense in terms of the agent's perceived needs and interests, otherwise it would be hard to see it as a judgement of the agent at all. But the judgement's authority, its ability to determine the rationality of both intention and action, is not a product of its cogency.

Several writers have suggested that *akrasia* is not always irrational (e.g. McIntyre 1990: 392–4; see also Audi 1990). Suppose I fail to act on my practical judgement because of certain relevant considerations of which I am tacitly aware but I overlooked when making the judgement; they sap my motivation and prevent the erroneous action. Huckleberry Finn judges that he ought to return his slave friend Jim to Jim's owners but finds himself incapable of doing so. Here what Huck actually does (arguably) reflects what he has reason to do better than does his practical judgement. And since rationality is a matter of responsiveness to reasons, doesn't Huck act rationally, the fact that he contravenes his practical judgement notwithstanding? No. It is certainly true that Huck may be doing what he ought to do and doing it for the right reasons, but it does not follow that Huck's behaviour is an example of rational agency. Part of what constitutes practical rationality is a self-control which the person exercises by means of her practical judgement, and here this self-control is absent.

The problem with *akrasia* is not that one does what one has good reason not to do; rather it is the failure of practical judgement to dictate decision and action as it should. In this my relation to myself is quite different from my relation to other people. I may investigate their interests and, after sympathetic deliberation, form a view about what they ought to do. Do they have any reason to act on my judgement? Only if it accurately reflects those considerations which ought to move them. My judgement has no intrinsic authority over them. That is why I am responsible for my own actions as I am not for theirs.[4]

The will's authority

Some philosophers might wonder whether I have mislocated the locus of authority in practical deliberation. Perhaps the thing I have special reason to conform my action to is not my practical judgement but rather an executive phenomenon: my intention. I govern my activities by framing plans and deciding to implement them; weakness of will occurs when my actions diverge from my intentions rather than from my practical judgements.[5]

But, as we saw in Chapter 5, such a will-based account of the notion of control is unable to explain why we think we control our intentions as well as our deeds. Furthermore, we can't locate that self-control which is constitutive of a rational agent in his capacity to form (and adhere to) intentions, because it isn't true that failing to carry out one's plans is, in itself, a symptom of irrationality. I can be *akratic* in forming an intention I think I ought not to form as much as in performing the wrong action; when this happens, not doing what I intend to do may be perfectly rational.

Suppose I decide to do something that I think I ought not to do, and then fail to carry out my intention. Here my intention is clearly irrational. Is my failure to implement it also irrational? Were my failure to carry it through due to the influence of my opposing practical judgement, this would surely be a sign of resurgent rationality rather than renewed irrationality. An intention has no authority of its own to determine which action is rational: its function is simply to perpetuate the motivational force of practical judgement over time. It is reasonable for me to maintain and carry out my intention to ϕ only so long as it is reasonable to stick by the practical judgement that I ought to ϕ. Not doing what you intend to do is irrational only when your intentions reflect your view of what ought to be done.

But what if I don't follow through on my unreasonable intention because of a failure of nerve, say, one that would have occurred whatever my practical judgement? Here I lack a certain sort of self-control, a self-control which is often essential to rational agency over time but not one constitutive of rational agency as such. The rational agent is someone who implements her practical judgement in action; whether she does this by forming a prior intention to act is a secondary matter.

Intrinsic authority

An important point of clarification: I am not saying that my judgement that I ought to ϕ in itself provides me with a positive reason to ϕ in just the way my first-order beliefs and desires provide me with reasons to ϕ. When asked to justify my ϕ-ing, I will omit mention of the fact that I judged I ought to ϕ. If this judgement *did* provide a reason for ϕ-ing, it would be sensible to ask whether this was an overriding reason to ϕ, or whether it might be outweighed by my first-order reasons for not ϕ-ing, in which case it might (on balance) be rational for me not to ϕ, even though I judge that I ought to ϕ. But this question is bizarre: we have obviously misconstrued the intrinsic authority of practical judgement.

Instead, we must treat my practical judgement as having a *power of veto* over my actions. My action cannot be rational unless it conforms to my practical judgement, no matter how strong the considerations in the action's favour. Conformity to my practical judgement is not in itself a reason to perform some action (on this point Hume is right); rather it is a precondition for my reasons to issue in a rational action. The fact that a proposed action does not conform to my practical judgement is, in itself and in so far as I am rational, sufficient to motivate forbearance. But the mere fact that I judge that something ought to be done does not suffice to make the deed rational and so is insufficient to motivate compliance. What fully rational action requires is congruence between the first-order reasons (of which I am non-reflectively aware) and my higher order practical judgement (where such a judgement is made).[6]

The authority of practical reflection over action rests on a certain asymmetry. My practical judgement remains perfectly rational even if, incontinently, I fail to carry it through into action. But my action cannot be rational so long as it fails to conform to the verdict of practical reason, however unfounded that verdict may be, and however understandable the rebellion against it. This asymmetry of reason generates a certain motivational asymmetry: if, *akratically*, I begin to act when I think I ought to refrain, this will not, in so far as I am rational, move me to change my mind about what I ought to do. But my judgement that I ought to refrain will stop me, in so far as I am rational. It is the judgement that should be controlling the action, not *vice versa*.[7]

The function of reflective control

I have now located the source of that direct control which we have over our actions: we can command the deed because of the intrinsic authority of our practical judgement. But my account of this authority makes it look rather negative: our reflective control resides in a power of veto over our actions, not in the power to give ourselves new reasons for action. Is countermanding really the same as controlling?

Locke maintains that we have direct control over both belief and action, and he traces this control to our ability to suspend a decision on a theoretical or a practical matter until such time as we think we have sufficient reason to take the decision, given the importance of the issue, and so forth. In Chapter 6, I complained that this power of suspension was insufficient to give us reflective control over whether we act or not. The reflective automaton is also, on occasion, moved to deliberate about both theoretical and practical matters. It, too, will be sensitive to the importance of the issue and the limitations on its cognitive resources; it, too, will have a stronger desire to be right about some things than about others and will have beliefs about how to get this desire satisfied by means of (first-order) deliberation. These beliefs and desires will usually suffice to motivate the required amount of thought. What the reflective automaton lacks is the ability to get itself to open (or close) its mind on a practical question simply by *judging* that it has good reason so to do.

This is precisely the ability we ourselves possess, at least in the practical sphere. We have a judgemental veto which we can use to prolong (first-order) practical deliberation (or to begin it where we can't form a sensible view without deliberation). Thus we do have direct control over whether we hesitate or act, deliberate or decide, and this form of direct control has a positive role to play in determining what we do. As Locke observed, it enables us to wait until the strength of our desire for a good is proportional to our judgement of its worth before acting.

My account of practical freedom is Lockean in a number of crucial respects. It locates practical freedom in a special power we have to veto action and permit further scrutiny of the options until our desires and our practical judgement concur. Furthermore, the subject matter of this deliberation will be the desirability of the various options and the conclusion of the deliberation can be implemented only in so far as it reflects what we actually desire. Neither Locke nor I suppose that our judgements as to what is good can move us to act, regardless of our desires. But I deny that the veto-power of reflection derives from some desire that the results of reflection be implemented, from a need (which may be more or less strong) to act in accordance with our considered view of what we ought to do. Hume is wrong to think that all motivation has its source in desire. Only by dropping this assumption can we bring out the intrinsic authority of practical judgement and with it the nature of the freedom which we enjoy in deciding what we shall do.

The impotence of reflection: belief

Does my judgement about what I should believe have an intrinsic authority over belief? Again, there are three stages in higher order theoretical deliberation: I form a view about what the evidence and the constraints on my cognitive resources are; I deliberate, wondering whether I ought to believe that p in the light of all the relevant evidential and pragmatic factors; and then I form a view about what I ought to believe. Once again, failures might occur at all three stages but at this point theoretical deliberation diverges from practical. If I arrive at a faulty judgement about what I ought to believe, there is no rational requirement on me to conform my first-order belief to this higher order judgement. If my first-order belief is well grounded in various evidential and non-evidential considerations, that belief continues to be rational, my higher order disapproval of it notwithstanding. I have no veto over the rationality of my own beliefs, my higher order judgements are not a source of rational motivation for belief, and thus I have no reflective control over which beliefs I adopt.

On my way to a meeting, I see a clock which tells me that I am running late. I believe the clock is correct and consequently feel rushed. Let us suppose that this belief is a perfectly rational one – I have no reason to doubt the clock – but wishful thinking leads me to form the opinion that I ought not to believe the clock. In this situation there is a clash between my first-order belief and my judgement about what I ought to believe but, this clash notwithstanding, my first-order belief remains perfectly rational. By contrast, if wishful thinking leads me to form the practical judgement that I ought not to rush in any case because the meeting is not so important and yet I find myself rushing regardless, then my behaviour is irrational, the whimsicality of my practical judgement notwithstanding. My behaviour displays a lack of that self-control to which every rational agent should aspire.

My judgements about what I ought to believe lack the intrinsic authority over my beliefs which my practical judgements enjoy over my actions. The thought that I should not believe p gives me a reason not to believe p only in so far as that thought is well motivated. If it isn't well motivated, my beliefs can be rational whether or not they conform to it. It follows from this that when it comes to motivating belief, I stand in the same relation to myself as I do to others. I may form a view about what someone else ought to believe in the light of all the relevant considerations, but my view gives him a reason not to believe that p only in so far as it reflects considerations which should move him; it has no authority of its own. Exactly the same is true of my views about what I myself ought to believe. So I lack the reflective control over my own beliefs which I have over my deeds.

Theoretical akrasia

Few would deny that my actions may defy my practical judgement, but can my first-order beliefs really diverge from my judgements about what I ought to believe? One relatively unproblematic way in which this can happen is where I have a belief which I think I ought not to have because there is insufficient evidence to support it. I may find myself with an invincible conviction of someone's guilt, even if, on reflection (or perhaps after the discovery of new evidence), I think the matter requires more thought and so the outrage which it generates is unreasonable. Here I might say something of the form 'I believe *p* but I ought not to', a perfectly unparadoxical belief to have about oneself, though it registers a regrettable cognitive lapse. My second-order judgement no more destroys my first-order belief than my negative assessment of my own anger prevents me from being angry.[8]

If my opinion about what someone else should believe diverges from what they actually believe, at least one of us is in error, but there need be no irrationality on either part: I might just have got their reasons wrong.[9] According to the doctrine of authoritative self-knowledge floated in Chapter 1, to discover such a clash within yourself is to discover not just that you must be wrong in some respect but that you are actually being irrational, that you are holding a combination of beliefs that you couldn't possibly have good reason to hold. Either your first-order belief is not well motivated (i.e. is irrational) or else your judgement about what you ought to believe is erroneous, and since a rational person necessarily knows what his or her own reasons are, making an error about what you ought to believe is also symptomatic of irrationality. Much the same is true when your practical judgements diverge from your actions. This can't be a case of brute error: some irrationality is going on, something you have no good reason to think or to do.

But this parallel should not obscure a profound difference. In the practical case, we discovered an asymmetry with motivational implications: your practical judgement can render the action it concerns irrational, but that action can't render your practical judgement irrational (though the good reasons for that action may). By contrast, your theoretical judgement can no more render the belief it concerns irrational than that belief can render your judgement that you ought not to hold it irrational. Of course, when you realise that there is a clash here, you also realise that you have reason to remove that clash, but there are two ways of resolving this clash, and, in the theoretical case, the mere fact of a clash gives you no reason for going one way rather than the other. By contrast, when your actions diverge from your practical judgement, your practical judgement is making your actions irrational, not *vice versa,* so (unless you have *independent* grounds for suspecting that your practical judgement should be revised) you should resolve the clash by making your action conform to your practical judgement.

If what we do fails to correspond to our judgement about what we ought to do, there is reason to conform our action to the judgement of conscience, a reason which is not just a requirement of coherence between the two. But the claims of conscience do not extend to belief.

Theoretical versus practical reason

We have a reflective control over action which has no epistemic counterpart: action is free as belief could never be. I have just put this down to the intrinsic authority which practical judgement has over action, an authority which has no parallel in the theoretical sphere. Is it possible to say anything more about the origins of this practical authority, anything which might explain why it has no theoretical analogue?

Inconclusive reasons and the authority of reflection

The special authority of practical judgement is rooted in certain facts about practical reason, facts which explain both our sense of freedom in deciding how to act and the absence of such freedom and control in the theoretical realm. Chapter 3 established that to feel entitled to believe that p I must think of myself as possessing a conclusive ground for p; by contrast, I can be in a position to decide to ϕ without imagining that I possess a conclusive reason for ϕ-ing. The reasons I have for ϕ-ing are reasons I know I could still possess even if ϕ-ing were not the best thing for me to do – they are defeasible – but I can't believe p unless I think I have grounds which I couldn't have unless p were true.

For example, I might decide to buy a house on the grounds that I don't want to pay rent and need security of tenure, but when I actually move in it may turn out that I am more oppressed by the trouble of maintaining the house than I expected. Here the considerations reflection on which led me to buy the house still provide good reason to buy, but it just turns out that there were better reasons not to buy. Contrast this with the case where I believe that house prices won't rise next year because I take myself to have learnt this fact from the testimony of various pundits. Here, I could hardly have learnt this fact if it weren't true that house prices won't rise: the ground I take myself to have for believing in a flat housing market would not exist if the market were going to inflate.

To feel entitled to believe that p is to think yourself possessed of a conclusive ground for p in the face of which you could do nothing other than believe that p. To have doubts about whether you ought to believe that p is to have doubts about whether you have such a conclusive ground. This fact accounts for a further difference between theoretical and practical reasoning. Even if ϕ-ing is the best thing for me to do, the reasons in favour of doing the opposite don't lose their probative force in my eyes just because I have decided to ϕ: they may, for example, provide grounds for rational regret. There is no analogue of this in the case of belief and evidence: if I believe that p, I must think of the evidence for not-p as misleading and therefore worthless.[10] If contrary evidence motivates doubt about p, it thereby undermines my belief in p (Williams 1973b: 172).

Given all this, how could my judgement that I should believe p move me to believe it? There is no question of my deciding whether to believe that p by making a judgement about when I have sufficient inconclusive evidence for p. There is no question of my invoking the limitations on my cognitive resources to persuade myself that I do have sufficient evidence to make up my mind about whether p. Without a conclusive ground to think p true, no judgement about how I ought to make up my mind on the evidence before me can move me. On the other hand, if there is a conclusive ground to think p true, my opinion as to whether I ought now to believe that p can play no role in determining whether it is rational for me to believe that p: the truth of p has been established and, for that reason alone, I ought now to believe it.

By contrast, since the reasons in favour of ϕ-ing (rather than not) can present themselves as inconclusive, there is room for further input into whether I ought to ϕ, there is room for a judgement about whether the (defeasible) reasons in favour of ϕ-ing are sufficient to make ϕ-ing a reasonable thing to do. Reflection on the importance of the issue and on the need to take a decision can persuade me that the present considerations are sufficient to resolve the matter. Not that this further input is required for agency: action can be rationalised by inconclusive reasons without practical judgement. But there is room for the agent to make ϕ-ing the only reasonable option simply by judging that they ought to ϕ; once I have decided on ϕ, this judgement ensures that I can't be rational unless I ϕ.

Freedom of practical judgement

Aquinas traces our practical freedom to a prior freedom of practical judgement: we are free in our actions because we are free in our judgements. As I noted in Chapter 6, he maintains that where evidence is inconclusive, it is up to us what we believe. Since practical reasons are always inconclusive, Aquinas concludes that practical judgement is always free. Our action is free, as the behaviour of animals is not, because we can control our action by means of 'the free judgement of reason' (1983: 70–1, 102–4, and 126–7). I have denied that belief is free, but I think Aquinas is right about practical judgement. Practical judgement is under our reflective control and our freedom of will derives from this freedom of practical judgement.

Practical judgement is free in much the same sense that intention formation is free:[11] neither is subject to the will, but both are based on inconclusive reasons and both are, as a result, subject to the authority of practical judgement. For example, I can make a judgement about whether this is the right time to make a practical judgement and this higher order judgement will, like the practical judgement itself, be based on a sufficiency of inconclusive reasons. But, once made, this higher order judgement helps to determine the rationality of practical judgement. A practical judgement can't be rational if I think I ought not to make it, any more than the formation of a given intention can be rational if I think I ought not to form it.

Given all this, can I ever *know* that I ought to ϕ? If I make my practical judgements on the basis of inconclusive reasons and, as Chapter 3 claimed, knowledge requires conclusive grounds, how can I ever know what I ought to do? And if we are in a position to believe something only when we feel entitled to claim to know it, can I even believe that I ought to ϕ? We must indeed distinguish practical judgements from beliefs. To judge that one ought to ϕ is to *decide* that one ought to ϕ rather than to *believe* that one ought to ϕ. But we must also keep a hold of the distinction I insisted on in Chapter 5 between decisions as judgemental and as executive phenomena: practical judgements are not intentions. By using the language of decision here, I am not implying that practical judgements are without truth value, I am not denying that their correctness is a function of the way the world is; I am saying just that they cannot be items of knowledge.

Intentional explanation

One final point of clarification. Nagel has described (and criticised) a view according to which the fact that my reasons for ϕ-ing are always inconclusive by itself guarantees that I am always able not to ϕ, that I am always able to act on the weaker reason and so free to do as I please, whatever my reasons (Nagel 1986: 115–17). As Nagel remarks, if this line of thought were cogent it would make it very hard to understand how the fact that my reasons favour ϕ-ing rather than not ϕ-ing could ever *explain* why I do one rather than the other. Yet it seems to be essential to the whole idea of rational autonomy that my actions should be explained by my reasons.

Whether or not this is a just criticism of the view Nagel is attacking, it has no application to my position. I am not looking to the inconclusiveness of practical reasons to open up some sort of explanatory gap, present in the lead-up to an action but absent in the generation of belief, in which to locate our practical freedom. In fact, inconclusive reasons play a key role in generating both belief and action: the inconclusive evidence of my senses generates belief by getting me to think I am perceiving, while the inconclusive reasons for holidaying in South Africa rather than in France ensure I go to South Africa by getting me to think I ought to holiday in South Africa. There is no more randomness, arbitrariness or chance in one causal chain than in the other. We can explain either what I think or what I do by pointing out that I had sufficiently strong reason to think or do that thing.

The difference between belief and action lies not in the mere presence of inconclusive reasons in the causal chain leading to action but in how they mesh with the subject's reflective judgement. Such inconclusive reasons can play a role in practical reflection, a role without theoretical parallel. I can decide to do something by asking myself whether I have sufficient inconclusive reason for doing it and such reflection helps to determine whether my action is rational or not. I can equally form a view about what I ought to believe in the light of the balance of inconclusive evidence (etc.) but I can't motivate a belief by reflecting on whether I have sufficient inconclusive evidence for it. So reflection on inconclusive reasons can move me to action as it can't move me to belief. There is no explanatory gap, just an explanatory difference.

Conclusion

In Chapter 1, I introduced the notion of reflective control by elaborating some views to be found in recent philosophical literature. In the rest of Part 1, I suggested that this notion of reflective control applied to action and intention but not to belief. Now we have a full theory of reflective control before us, we can see exactly why practical reason diverges from theoretical reason in this regard. What we have yet to discover are the implications of this result for epistemic responsibility. Clearly, theoretical reason does not presuppose intellectual freedom and so we appear to have intellectual responsibility without intellectual freedom. But unless we control our beliefs, how can we be held to epistemic norms? To answer this question, I must turn to another topic broached in Chapter 1: the juridical theory of responsibility.

Chapter 8

The scope of responsibility

What is responsibility? What exactly is the juridical theory of responsibility a theory of? To be responsible is to be (potentially) an object of disapprobation, both to yourself and to others. But disapprobation can take many forms: shame, disgust, blame, indignation, resentment, condemnation, guilt, contempt, derision. Which reaction's range of application delineates the scope of responsibility? Clearly not all of them are tied to responsibility: I am ashamed of the unsightly wart on my nose, though I am not responsible for it. In order to assess the juridical theory, I must attempt to characterise responsibility – and the reactions definitive of responsibility – without reference to control and then see whether responsibility, so understood, applies only to what is under our control.

To get the debate going, I need to make some assumptions about the extent of our control. Now I have argued at some length that while action is both subject to the will and under our reflective control, belief is neither. But in this chapter I aim to convince even those who don't accept this rather controversial conclusion about belief that the juridical theory of responsibility is wrong, so I do not take belief as my sole example; I focus just as much on desire and emotion. Many writers, including some of the juridical theory's firmest supporters, agree that neither desire nor emotion is subject to the will; nor are they inclined to think that a rational person can mould his affective life simply by making higher order judgements about it.[1] So here we have a less controversial example of something which escapes our direct control. Of course, many of these same writers will doubt whether our desires and emotions are governed by reason at all, since this implies responsibility; and, they think, responsibility presupposes control. That is the very point at issue in this chapter, but before grappling with it, let me attempt to characterise responsibility.

Blame and responsibility

Among the sentiments which constitute (or give expression to) a negative assessment of the character and attributes of other people, we can discern two broad classes. In the first we find shame, humiliation, embarrassment (directed towards oneself) and disgust, contempt, disdain, derision and scorn (directed towards another). In the second class, the self-directed emotions are guilt and remorse, while the other-directed emotions are indignation, resentment, reproach, condemnation and, above all, blame. It is not hard to see that these two kinds of feeling are appropriate under rather different conditions. Responses of the first type fit both my warts and my agency; but, on the face of it, I could not reasonably feel guilty about my own wart or indignant at and resentful of yours. These reactions would be uncalled for unless we were thought to be *responsible* for our warts. No such story is required to make sense of wart-shame. This suggests the following hypothesis: responsibility is just that feature of persons which makes the second class of reactions (call them the *blame reactions*) appropriate.

This hypothesis is independent of the juridical theory of responsibility, but juridical theorists tend to endorse it. For them, the reason guilt, blame and indignation, etc., are deemed appropriate to our agency but not to our warts is that only the former is under our control.[2] I, too, find the hypothesis plausible, but it doesn't seem to support the juridical theory: on the face of it, blame reactions are not tied to control in the way that the juridical theory suggests. Say I become convinced, on inadequate evidence, that my brother has stolen money from me and then I discover my error. Here I should feel guilty about having thought ill of him (even if I did nothing about it) and others would blame me for my unjustified suspicions. What goes for belief goes also for desires and feelings: if I wish that my grandmother were dead or feel jealous of her wealth, guilt would hardly be out of place whether or not I have done anything to hasten her end. Yet neither my beliefs nor my wishes are under my direct control.

The juridical theorist who acknowledges that beliefs, desires and feelings are beyond our direct control yet seem to be objects of blame can respond to this fact in one of three ways. First, he might try to distinguish two forms of blame reaction – the 'moral' and the 'non-moral', perhaps – and insist that emotions like guilt are moral emotions, and therefore indicative of responsibility, only when they are applied to the voluntary.[3] But once this move is made, we can no longer get a grip on the notion of responsibility by reference to these sentiments alone; rather we need the notion of responsibility in order to discern the truly moral sentiments. How then are we to assess the juridical theory of responsibility? The danger here is that the juridical theory will cease to explain anything and become part of a stipulative definition both of responsibility and of a certain class of 'moral' emotions.

Rather than discerning different forms of blame, the juridical theorist might prefer to distinguish appropriate from inappropriate blame and say that our responsibility extends only to those things which render this feeling reasonable or appropriate. I can experience severe guilt for an action no reasonable person would blame me for – e.g. the death of a child who ran blindly out into the road before I could stop – and perhaps the guilt I feel at wicked desires or malicious thoughts is no more sensible. But those not already convinced by the juridical theory will wonder why they should agree. On the face of it, it seems perfectly appropriate to blame someone who yearns for his grandmother's demise, or thinks ill of his brother on inadequate evidence, in a way that it isn't at all appropriate to blame me for running over the child.

Sidgwick opens up a third escape route for the juridical theorist when he distinguishes two senses of the word 'ought':

> [I]n the narrowest ethical sense what we judge 'ought to be' done, is always thought capable of being brought about by the volition of any individual to whom the judgement applies. . . . In a wider sense, however – which cannot conveniently be discarded – I sometimes judge that I ought to know what a wiser man would know, or feel as a better man would feel, in my place though I may know that I could not directly produce in myself such knowledge or feeling by any effort of will. In this case, the word merely implies an ideal or pattern which I ought – in the stricter sense – to seek to imitate as far as possible.
>
> (Sidgwick 1981: 33)

There are indeed ideals of thought and feeling (and of conduct too) which are supererogatory, which we try to live up to without blaming ourselves should we fall short of them. But Sidgwick's point can rescue the juridical theorist only if *all* the norms governing thought and feeling are of this type. But, as already observed, we do blame ourselves when our beliefs and desires fall so far short of our ideals as to lapse into vice. In this respect conduct, thought and feeling seem to be very much on a par. But the last sentence of the Sidgwick passage suggests a more promising strategy for the juridical theorist. Perhaps he should defend the idea that responsibility requires control by arguing that, despite appearances, we don't really blame either beliefs, desires or feelings: rather blame reactions are directed towards the voluntary causes and effects of such psychological states. I'll now scrutinise this popular line of thought.

Responsibility without control

Take anger and the associated vice of intemperance. Anger often finds expression in abusive or even harmful behaviour. Suppose the anger is unjustified. Then the behaviour which expresses it will be unreasonable, as when, annoyed by an elderly pedestrian blocking my path, I curse him as I pass. The juridical theorist can observe that though we may have no direct control over our anger, we do have direct control over whether and how it is expressed. So, perhaps when I am blamed for my road rage, say, what I am really being blamed for is honking my horn at a driver who is simply observing the speed limit, rather than for anything I may feel about that driver. But this can't be right. As I have already noted, I can blame myself for unreasonable emotions which never get expressed at all. Furthermore, even when they are expressed, their expression may not be under my control (Adams 1985: 4–6).

Suppose I am furious with you. There are manifestations of my annoyance of which I remain unaware (perhaps because of the anger itself) or am unable to control, such as gestures, tone of voice, etc., behaviour which poisons my relations with you. I might try to avoid you, but that itself could well cause serious damage (were you a lover or a colleague). If such involuntary behaviour had a purely physiological explanation, I could not be held to account for it; but, where it expresses a psychological state itself subject to rational assessment (like anger), I am culpable. I am responsible for the harmful effects of my anger even though neither my intemperance nor its manifestations are under my direct control.

At this point, a defender of the juridical orthodoxy could switch tack and observe that I do have an indirect control over, and thus a responsibility for, both my intemperate character and the involuntary behaviour which manifests it. Aristotle famously claimed that we become virtuous by habituation, by doing virtuous things; vice has a similar origin (Aristotle 1925: 28–9). Kant, too, observes that we acquire generous feelings by performing generous deeds, and he lays it down that we have a duty to cultivate feelings which ease the work of duty (Kant 1996: 161–2 and 204–5). I can cultivate temperance by persistent self-restraint, attending anger-management classes and so forth. My irascibility won't instantly disappear but, on this view, I am not to blame for that; my responsibility is to *try* to cultivate a cool temper. If I am to blame for anything, it is for omitting to try.[4]

Suppose two of us suffer from road rage. We each assiduously attend anger-management classes and do our relaxation exercises in the car simulator with the same level of commitment, but the therapy works for you and not for me: I still feel inclined to drive people off the road at the least provocation. Perhaps I can now restrain myself, but my suppressed rage makes me a less skilful and attentive driver (in ways I might not even notice, being beside myself with annoyance) and puts my fellow road users in some danger. Nor can I avoid driving altogether if I am to discharge important practical obligations. Here one's reproaches would be tempered by a knowledge of my efforts at self-improvement, but one should hardly cease to blame me, as one would cease to blame you: continued guilt on my part would be not at all inappropriate. Yet I tried just as hard to conquer my anger as you did yours. So my guilt and others' blame cannot be directed at my failure to try.

Suppose I put more effort than you into anger management and eventually achieve the same result. Am I not more to be admired than you, precisely because it was so much harder for me to become temperate? Perhaps. But what I am trying to do, and what is so hard for me, is precisely to become as temperate, as good a person in that respect, as you are. After such a struggle, I may end up a better person than you overall because I am better in respect of courage and endurance, but that does nothing to diminish my responsibility for my feelings.

Virtues and talents

The Kantian line of thought under discussion makes the responsibility we have for our own ethical character too indirect; it makes it look too much like our responsibility for cultivating skills and talents. No one is to blame simply for speaking French badly or for being a poor pianist. Nevertheless, one can acquire an obligation to develop these talents, by taking on a job as a teacher for example. Of course, one's efforts may not be wholly successful but one should make a serious and continuing effort to acquire the skill one ought to have. Failure to try makes blame appropriate, and we are liable for the consequences of such culpable incompetence. On the Kantian view this is precisely how responsibility for anger is to be understood. Temperance can be considered a skill I must acquire if I am to be able to discharge my duties and avoid being helpless in the face of my own fury.

But this fails to take the measure of the difference between virtues on the one hand and skills, talents and abilities on the other: I have a direct responsibility for virtue and vice but only an indirect responsibility for talents, etc. As far as talents go, my responsibility is focused on the actions I might take to cultivate them rather than on the presence or absence of the talents themselves. For example, I might have an obligation to learn the piano, but this obligation can be overridden by the need to devote time to my French so I can teach it well. Here, I will end up a bad pianist but I will not be to blame for this since I was not, all things considered, obliged to learn the piano properly. On the other hand, suppose I am intemperate and should attend group therapy sessions, but family obligations override this requirement. Am I no longer to blame for my intemperance because I can't spare the effort required to cure it? Can I free myself of any guilt on the matter simply by reflecting on these practical constraints? Surely not.

The point here is that the possession of the virtue (and the absence of a vice) has an ethical significance which is quite independent of the (ethical) feasibility of the actions required to cultivate it. So even if virtue can be the product of voluntary action, it doesn't follow that our responsibility for our moral character is a mere by-product of our responsibility for our actions. Similar points apply to the retention of virtue. I might simply forget how to play the piano if I don't practise sufficiently, and 'I have for-gotten' may be sufficient excuse for error (provided I had no time to practise). But I can *never* excuse intemperate behaviour on the ground that I have forgotten how to be temperate (because I couldn't keep up my relaxation exercises) (see Aristotle 1925: 143).

Perhaps the juridical theorist can account for the difference between virtues and talents as follows: while skills and talents are often required for the discharge of moral obligations, there is no necessity about this. By contrast, it is a necessary truth that such traits of character as temperance, courage and sensitivity ease the work of virtue, both by making us aware of what virtue demands in a given situation – ensuring we notice the needs and reactions of others – and by counteracting temptations and other moti-vational obstacles to virtue: that is what makes it look as if these traits of character have an intrinsic ethical value, even though our responsibility for them is no more direct than is our responsibility for skills and talents. The problem with this line of thought is that certain physical capabilities seem no less essential to the moral life than the character traits we call virtues. How could someone without a minimally functioning body (including accurate sensory organs as well as limbs under proper control) hope to dis-charge his moral obligations? Yet no one would hold him directly responsible for his poor eyesight or weak left arm; no one would put these physical defects on a level with cowardice or intemperance.

I don't want to deny that when assessing someone's culpability for vice, we do take into account unusual features of his personal history. The rage of someone terribly abused as a child is less resented than that of a person with a normal upbringing, and temperance in such a person is the more admired. But this should not be taken to indicate that his culpability some-how depends on the degree of control, direct or indirect, which he is thought to exercise over his anger. Rather, what gives us pause are doubts about whether this person's emotions are responsive to reasons at all, given his un-usual upbringing. As I have argued all along, it is one thing for a state to be subject to reason and quite another for it to be under our reflective control.

In this section, I have argued that virtues are unlike talents in that one can't reduce our responsibility for virtue and vice to our responsibility for performing actions which tend to cultivate the virtues and eliminate the vices. And since we have no other means of exercising control over these character traits, the idea that direct responsibility requires direct control must itself be called into question.

The good person

Responsibility implies the propriety of blame but this can hardly be a suffi-cient condition for accountability: I blame my kettle for leaking all over floor and my dog for waking the neighbours, without holding them responsible in anything other than a purely causal sense. Similarly, it is a vice in a kettle that it leaks and a virtue that it doesn't. We could save the hypothesis that blame delimits the scope of responsibility by distinguishing different senses of 'blame' and 'virtue', but this would be to follow the juridical theorist down the path of stipulation. Instead I'll argue that responsibility is what is registered when blame is applied to persons *as such*.

In the last section, I argued that people are held to account for the extent of their virtue as they are not for their skills and talents. In making this point, I concentrated on what I took to be a moral virtue – temperance – but, I shall argue, there are non-moral virtues (distinct from talents, etc.), and the point applies equally to them. A person of virtuous character is a good person, someone who is good, not *qua* pianist or *qua* conversationalist but *qua* person. Obviously, one's moral virtues contribute to this assessment of one's merit as a person; so do certain non-moral qualities. But not all of one's qualities are relevant to whether one is a good person, any more than all the qualities of a kettle are relevant to whether it is a good kettle. My hypothesis about responsibility is that one is held to account for one's merit as a person; one gets blamed for those things (both moral and non-moral) which are thought to make one a bad person.

Juridical theorists have linked virtue, responsibility and personal worth in this way, though they insist that all three notions apply only to what is under our control. If a person's true self is that for which he is directly responsible, then the juridical theorist's true self does not extend beyond those aspects of his character which are under his direct control. For example, in Descartes' eyes there is 'only one thing in us which could give us good reason for esteeming ourselves, namely the exercise of our free will and the control we have over our volitions. For we can reasonably be praised or blamed only for actions that depend upon this free will' (Descartes 1985: 384). Considering someone with a generous character, Descartes remarks that 'nothing truly belongs to him but this freedom to dispose his volitions, and he ought to be praised or blamed for no other reason than his using this freedom well or badly' (ibid.).[5] This etiolated notion of the self is both an inevitable and an implausible consequence of the juridical theory of responsibility.

Hume on responsibility

Hume roundly rejected the juridical theory of responsibility: 'sentiments are everyday experienced of praise and blame, which have objects beyond the dominion of the will or choice' (Hume 1975: 322). But Hume also held that the distinction between virtues and talents on which I am insisting was merely 'grammatical' (ibid.: 312–13). According to Hume, we approve of traits and features in others which give us pleasure, such as cheerfulness, wit and beauty; and, by empathy, we approve of what gives pleasure to those who have it: riches and good fortune, various skills and talents, etc.

My attempt to draw a distinction between two forms of approval or dis-approval – that tied to responsibility and that not – is, in Hume's eyes, futile (ibid.: Appendix IV and 1978: Book III, Sections IV–V).

Before looking at Hume's arguments for this sceptical conclusion, let us get his target – the virtue–talent distinction – into clearer focus. We say that someone is a good pianist but a poor linguist, a good conversationalist but a poor public speaker. These are forms of personal assessment but they do not claim to assess the person as such: they do not tell us whether this person is estimable as a whole, merely whether she is estimable in a certain respect. Now one might try to arrive at a *tout court* assessment of someone's character simply by assessing them piecemeal *qua* linguist, *qua* conversationalist, *qua* entrepreneur, etc., and then somehow weighing the negative and positive aspects of her character to produce an overall result. But this is not how we do it. Rather we think of certain desirable character traits, like generosity, as relevant to one's worth as a person and certain other character traits (perhaps equally desirable), like linguistic aptitude, as simply irrelevant. That is why we blame people for vice but not for lack of talent. My personal merit is my responsibility in a way that nothing else is, precisely because it involves an assessment of *me* in a way that nothing else does. This (and not some notion of control) is what grounds the idea that I am responsible for my virtues in a way that I am not responsible for my abilities and talents.

What does Hume have to say against all this? Hume notes that we admire Hannibal for traits of character which would normally be classified as psychological talents and physical abilities: his military skill, imperviousness to the cold, great energy and charisma. According to Hume, such admiration can outweigh Hannibal's obvious vices – his perfidiousness and inhuman cruelty – thus delivering a favourable verdict on his general character. Even where the scales tip the other way, as in the case of Pope Alexander VI, it is a matter of balancing talents such as judgement, prudence and powers of persuasion against vices like avarice, overweening ambition, to reach a verdict on the man as a whole. No decisive weight is attached to what Hume calls 'the social virtues' (e.g. generosity, justice) in these *tout court* assessments; if Hannibal and Alexander VI have a responsibility to avoid incurring guilt and blame, they have an equally grave responsibility to avoid occasioning shame and contempt.

But Hume has subtly misposed the question which seeks an overall assessment of someone's character. If you are asked 'Do you admire Hannibal?', you may very well answer 'yes'. But if you are asked 'Do you think Hannibal was a good man?', you will probably say 'No'. There is no contradiction here because the first question is not really seeking a *tout court* assessment of Hannibal at all; rather it elicits your opinion of those traits of character for which Hannibal is famous (i.e. which led to his military successes). If there was no context to this question, it would be hard to know how to address it ('Admire him *for what*?'). It is an important fact that the second question, 'Was Hannibal a good man?', makes perfect sense without any specification (however implicit) of the purposes for which the assessment is being made or the aspect from which he is being regarded. You know exactly what information would be relevant, namely information about his virtues and not about his talents.

We now have a viable alternative to the juridical theory of responsibility. On my view blame marks the scope of responsibility, and we are blamed for our vices, for those traits of character, manifested in thought, feeling and action, which make us bad people. Both of my opponents tend to erase the distinction between virtues and talents: Kant tries to assimilate our responsibility for virtuous character to our responsibility for skills and talents, with a view to preserving the idea that responsibility requires control; while Hume thinks that once the juridical theory has been abandoned, the virtue–talent distinction also will disappear. Both are wrong: we can build a theory of responsibility on this very distinction. And now that the concept of virtue has been brought into play, we can ask whether there are non-moral virtues and vices, whether we can be held responsible for defects of character which are not the special province of ethics.

Doxastic responsibility

Vice corrupts belief (Wallace 1978: 63–76; Adams 1985: 17–21): fear leads the coward to overestimate the danger; ingratitude causes me to forget the good you have done me; pride prevents me from abandoning a theory which you have just shown to be unsound. A courageous, grateful or modest person avoids these traps and forms beliefs in a reasonable fashion, and if a person is courageous, grateful or modest they are, to that extent, a good person. So part of being a good person is not allowing your beliefs to be perverted by vice. But we are still some way short of the idea that there are *epistemic* virtues, that having reasonable beliefs is part of what it is to be a good person, that one might be blamed for doxastic irrationality as such.

Epistemic vice

Take rules of etiquette. If I place my top hat on the floor rather than on my knees when paying a call, I have violated a norm of etiquette; but guilt and blame would be appropriate only if this behaviour were a manifestation of a vice such as lack of consideration. Those who don't know where to put a top hat may lack a useful social skill but they are not thereby bad people. Now, were epistemic norms like rules of etiquette, someone could be quite irrational and yet still be a good person, provided that irrationality was not symptomatic of some non-epistemic vice. On this hypothesis, epistemic rationality is a skill that one should acquire, but the lack of it does not, in itself, make one a bad person. Of course, I should still feel guilty for having believed, on inadequate evidence, my brother to be dishonest, but, on this hypothesis, what makes me feel bad is not the irrationality itself but rather the malevolence, or the absence of trust, it manifests. Maybe imprudence, too, involves the lack of a desirable skill rather than the presence of a deplorable vice. True, imprudence can be the occasion for blame, but perhaps this is so only when we see such imprudence as symptomatic of some vice, for example a cynical dilatoriness in someone entrusted with the financial affairs of a minor.

In fact, there are specifically epistemic vices, gullibility being one. If I believe, on the say so of the *National Enquirer* alone, that in 2028 a comet will collide with the Earth and destroy us all, I will be ridiculed by others and feel ashamed of myself when the comet fails to appear. Am I also blameworthy? Yes. I won't actually be blamed for crediting the *National Enquirer* unless some harm is done (or a risk of harm is created), but my gullibility would count against my claim to be a good person, even if no harm were done. Exactly the same is true of action. People are not held to account for bad actions that create no risk of harm: if I try to harm someone by casting a spell over them, I would be blameworthy, I would be a bad person, even though no one would blame me.

In order to be blamed for gullibility, the gullible person need not manifest a non-epistemic vice: this epistemic vice is quite sufficient. For example, if I neglect family responsibilities to prepare for the collision with the comet, I shall be blamed for this neglect and the stupidity it shows even though I am otherwise a good family man. The neglect need not involve voluntary action; perhaps my anxious anticipation of the collision distorts my emotional life in ways I cannot control. But even before anything bad happens, my gullibility means that I can't be an esteemed human being because I can't be trusted to think and feel as I ought.

There is a clear parallel with action. If I irrationally spend all my cash on a nice holiday and have to forgo all my pleasures for several months thereafter, I shall incur the contempt of others for imprudence and scold myself for my foolishness. But something else is also true. Imprudence threatens both one's own interests and the interests of others in one's care. The fool cannot be relied on to behave as he ought because there is a whole set of practical reasons to which he might remain unresponsive. We blame imprudence when it harms (or risks harming) significant interests, but even before this happens we think a man's imprudence makes him a bad man precisely because we can't rely on him to behave as he ought in the light of his reasons.

Dogmatism is another distinctively epistemic vice. Unlike the gullible man, the dogmatist need not rush to judgement; but once convinced of something he sticks to his opinion come what may, in the teeth of evidence which ought to undermine his certitude. By contrast, the weak-minded man hesitates and vacillates, finds it hard to form a view on any issue and abandons his convictions at the drop of a hat. These vices are a matter of having too much or too little confidence in one's own opinion. They are distinctively epistemic vices, not by-products of other character traits with their own ethical significance. Of course, I may have too little confidence in my opinion that the danger is slight, say, because I am a coward, or too much because I want to impress. But there is also such a thing as having the wrong level of epistemic self-confidence *tout court*.

Epistemic virtues and talents

As well as epistemic vices there are epistemic virtues. The wise man knows to whom credit is due, at what point to form a view, when to open his mind and when to close it. Wisdom is a virtue: it makes someone a good person. But one should not confuse epistemic virtues, like wisdom, with epistemic talents. It is a commonplace that cleverness and wisdom are two quite different things. The wise man forms opinions whose firmness properly reflects the strength of the reasons behind them. Epistemic talents, by contrast, are skills which give one the ability to form and retain beliefs. I might be highly epistemically virtuous and avoid all unreasonably strong or weak convictions without having the intellectual wherewithal to absorb and preserve much of our collective knowledge. Epistemic talents include theoretical imagination, a good memory, the ability to grasp complex hypotheses or the patience to sift through piles of tedious data until the truth becomes clear, and so on. Wisdom is perfectly consistent with intellectual mediocrity.

Epistemic talent is about identifying (i.e. becoming aware of) and retaining reasons for belief; epistemic virtue is about being suitably responsive to those reasons. Blame is in order where we fail to be the way (we are aware) we have reason to be. I may be unable to think up a certain hypothesis, or grasp a complex argument, or recall something I was told yesterday, without irrationality; in these cases the relevant reason is beyond me. But I can't without irrationality commit a simple logical blunder, or miss the relevance of the statement that p to my belief that not-p. It is not always easy to draw a line here – if it requires a moderately complex argument to establish a contradiction in my beliefs, is my inability to appreciate that argument a failure to respond to a reason of which I am aware, or is this a case in which I am unaware of the reason? – but that is the line we must draw in deciding whether someone is epistemically culpable.

We can see the need for an epistemic virtue-talent distinction by asking what sort of cognitive failings suffice to make one a bad man. If we hear it said of someone that they are slow on the uptake, or unretentive, we have not yet heard anything directly relevant to whether he is a good person. Someone may blame my poor memory for allowing us to miss the last showing of a film we wanted to see together, but they won't expect me to feel guilty at this lapse unless they think of it as displaying some further vice (e.g. a lack of proper concern on my part). On the other hand, to be told that someone is gullible, or bloody-minded or easily swayed, is to be well on one's way to forming a view of their worth as a person; it is demerits of this sort for which persons are accountable, if they are accountable for anything at all.

Hume rightly insists that a virtuous person must have a moderate degree of prudence and understanding (Hume 1975: 316). One's personal merit is not independent of these non-ethical virtues. Furthermore, some level of epistemic talent is required for any level of epistemic virtue: one can't be a wise man, a man of good judgement, without a certain level of intelligence and a functioning memory. But that is because no rational person can be devoid of these attributes, and only those subject to reason qualify as virtuous or vicious: virtue is about how you handle your reasons. The fact that virtue presupposes some cognitive abilities does not erase the virtue–talent distinction, even in the epistemic realm.

Exactly when is one obliged to cultivate epistemic virtue or epistemic talent? This is a practical question, a question about what deeds one should perform. Epistemology is not going to yield an answer here. The epistemologist's business is to describe the norms which govern the rational formation of belief, a process which is the domain of theoretical and not of practical reason. Confronted with theoretical irrationality, or the simple inability to form and retain beliefs, it is up to the ethics of action and the norms of prudence to determine what, if anything, should be done. But our responsibility for our beliefs extends beyond whatever responsibility we have to cultivate our epistemic virtues and talents. Some norms are not there to guide action, to govern the exercise of control: their function is to assess what we are.

To sum up, we can now see that the key concept for any theory of responsibility should be responsiveness to reasons, not agency or control. As well as actions, I am accountable for those states of mine (beliefs, desires and emotions) that are governed by reason, at least where I am capable of responding to those reasons. Neither the scope of the will, nor the power of reflection determines the boundaries of responsibility. Virtue and vice are matters of my responsiveness to different sorts of reason – ethical virtues concern ethical reasons, epistemic virtues concern epistemic reasons – and I am praised or blamed accordingly.

Responsibility and punishment

We rightly blame people for things over which they have no control, but it does not follow that we are entitled to punish people for things over which they have no control (Adams 1985: 21–2). Indeed most legal theorists hold that punishment presupposes control, that liability requires an action. No one is punished for thought alone: the object of punishment is action and not bad character.[6] To account for this fact, I would have to propound a theory of punishment which I do not have. Instead, I ask whether the two main theories in the field – the deterrent theory and the retributive theory – give us the resources to explain why we are punished solely for action even though our responsibility for our belief, desires, emotions is of the same sort as our responsibility for agency.

The deterrence theory

The deterrent theory insists that punishment is focused on acts. For example, Hobbes suggests that 'to punish those who do voluntarily hurt, and none else, frameth and maketh men's wills, such as men would have them' (Hobbes 1839b: 153). On this account, punishment is meant to provide us with a reason to conform to the law, but the desire to avoid punishment can provide us with a reason to conform only if conformity is the kind of thing which can be rationally motivated by the desire to avoid punishment. Now where that which constitutes conformity is subject to our will, the conformity can indeed be justified and motivated by its desirable consequences – the avoidance of punishment. So it is clear why Hobbes claims that punishment is appropriate for deeds alone. Beliefs (and emotions) are not subject to the will – one can't adopt a belief or an emotion simply to avoid punishment – and that is why, on the deterrent theory, we have no laws impinging on them directly.[7] The law could, and does, command actions which are designed to induce certain beliefs and emotions in its subjects (think of laws about school attendance and the penalties attached to truancy), but it does not command those beliefs (or emotions) themselves.

How does blame relate to punishment on the deterrent theory? One possibility is that blame is a form of punishment: such disapproval is just one more device for inducing pain in malefactors.[8] If we take a Hobbesian line on punishment, we might then argue that blame, too, can be imposed only where the will has control. But there is something wrong with the assimilation of blame to deterrent punishment. Williams argues that we cannot

> base the justification of blame just on its efficacy. No such account can be adequate, because it collides with one of the most obvious facts about blame, that in many cases it is effective only if the recipient thinks that it is justified. Blame that is perceived as unjust often fails to have the desired results, and merely generates resentment.
>
> (Williams 1995: 15)

Here Williams has put his finger on an important difference between blame and deterrent punishment. On the deterrence theory, legal penalties are intended to effect conformity to the law simply by playing on people's desire not to be punished. If someone conforms to a law he believes to be unjust or frivolous simply through fear of punishment, the legal sanction has served its purpose. By contrast, blame is intended to effect conformity to certain norms by getting people to recognise that they have violated norms which they had reason to obey.[9] Of course, blame may also induce conformity simply because those subjected to it find disapproval unpleasant, but blame's aim is frustrated if it serves only as a sanction. Successful blame prevents (not deters) future violations by getting its object to acknowledge that blame is justified,[10] and it is (potentially) appropriate wherever notions of justification are in play. The scope of blame is the whole space of reasons. Since blame is not pain inflicted in order to deter a repetition, one need not restrict it to what is subject to the will: we can be blamed for our character as well as our deeds.

On the deterrent theory, the deterrent effects of punishment may be insufficient to justify punishment – blameworthiness may also be required – but they are at least necessary. The deterrence theory can thus account for the fact that it is always action (and not character) which is the proper object of punishment without maintaining that we have a graver responsibility for our evil acts than for other wicked psychological states: that we are more blameworthy for the one than for the other. Punishment focuses on acts rather than wicked character simply because it can exercise a certain kind of rational influence over the former which it cannot over the latter.

The retributivist theory

Many feel that the deterrent theory overlooks the core function of punishment. When we act wrongly and so harm another, we incur a debt to that person (and to society?) which punishment repays. The repayment of that debt is an intrinsically good and necessary thing, regardless of its role in deterring evil deeds (or in reforming a bad character).[11] Suppose we accept the retributivist theory. The question then becomes: does one run up such a debt by means of bad thoughts and feelings as well as by means of wicked actions? The fact that only actions are punished may be taken as a sign that one does not, in which case we do have a responsibility for our actions (and other events under our control) which we don't have for our thoughts and feelings. In the eyes of many retributivists, punishment repays a debt which doesn't arise at all except where freedom exists.[12]

This talk of a moral debt redeemed by punishment strikes a chord in many people, but we should not imagine that it is confined to matters of agency. Take the notion of forgiveness and its counterparts: apology and reparation. One apologises for a wrong and forgives a debt which has been run up. This nexus of apology and forgiveness extends well beyond legal sanctions. Having entertained unfounded suspicions of your good character, I may confess this to you at a later stage and seek your forgiveness. I may also feel obliged to do something to make it up to you. And, if I am a scrupulous character, I might do all this even though my suspicions never came out and so did you no actual harm. Here I think of myself as having run up a debt which needs to be discharged.

The fact that legal sanctions are actually imposed only for bits of agency can be explained, consistently with retributivism, by reference to two factors. First, the burden of debt that needs to be discharged is likely to be greater if you allow your evil thoughts, etc., to express themselves in action. These actions may well have harmful consequences, for which you will be responsible; even if they don't, your lack of self-restraint is itself culpable. Legal sanctions are generally more serious than those involved in a private reconciliation, because of both their public nature and their severity, and it is only when you act that the extent of your indebtedness becomes sufficient to justify statutory punishment.

The other consideration which makes us look for agency before we punish is evidential. Since legal sanctions are quite severe, we need a higher standard of evidence than is required when we decide whether to ask for an apology. In announcing that Eskimos ought to be slaughtered, I am probably expressing a wicked and potentially harmful state of mind. But my words might be just bravado: usually one can't tell how serious I am until one sees what I do, or at least try to do. The evidential situation is much the same with intentions, and this may be why people are not punished simply because they confess to having a certain intention, even though (as I argued in Chapter 7) intentions, unlike beliefs, are freely formed.

To sum up, neither the deterrent theory nor the retributive theory tells against the idea that our responsibility extends beyond the sphere of our control. Rather, there are features special to punishment which explain why we punish only agency and not thought, desire and feeling. The relatively narrow scope of punishment should be no comfort to the juridical theorist.

Part 3

Memory and testimony

Chapter 9

Knowledge and its preservation

By the end of Part 2 we had reached a certain accommodation with the internalist view of epistemic justification. In the eyes of an internalist I am entitled to a belief only when I am aware of reasons which would justify that belief. One strand of internalist thinking goes further and insists that my awareness of reasons must motivate belief in a way which gives me control over belief, for only then can I be truly responsible for my convictions. But the internalist need not insist on this; he may accept that belief is a fit object for praise and blame provided it is responsive to reasons of which the subject is (non-reflectively) aware. It is not required that such responsiveness to reasons should amount to reflective control over belief.

Unfortunately, this compromise will not do. So long as we focus on belief formation it works well enough, but trouble begins the minute we turn our attention to how beliefs are preserved and transmitted. A realistic view of the workings of memory and testimony must acknowledge that a belief is retained in memory and disseminated through testimony without the retention and dissemination of the reasons which originally motivated the formation of that belief. If *justified* belief can be preserved and transmitted *via* memory and testimony then it looks as if we must break the connection between justification and awareness of reasons, allowing the probative force of a reason for a person to transcend that person's current awareness of it. But how can such a concession be reconciled with internalism?

Let me reiterate why I wanted to stick by internalism in the first place. Externalism about justification threatens to sever the link between justification and responsibility. If epistemic justification is simply a matter of whether our belief-forming processes are reliable and has little to do with anyone's awareness, or ability to become aware, of their reliability, then how can failures of epistemic rationality be imputed to us? In that case, unreasonable beliefs are no more down to us than a malfunctioning digestive system would be. But we can restore the link between justification and responsibility without going so far as to endorse the idea that S's beliefs must be justified by something of which S is now aware. Epistemic internalism, properly construed, is just the view that beliefs need to be justified and that what justifies beliefs are reasons, states of awareness. A given subject need not be aware of the reasons which justify his belief, provided he is entitled to presume that there are such reasons. In lumbering themselves with the idea that a reason must coincide in time and person with the belief it justifies, internalists do not define their position, they undermine it.

A framework

Radical internalists hold that a subject is justified in holding a certain belief only when that subject is aware of a reason for it.[1] Radical internalists have sought to underwrite our reliance on testimony by means of perception and induction alone, thereby freeing us from any dependence on reasons of which we are not aware. In their eyes, my experience of Paul's utterance 'It has snowed', combined with induction on past experience of Paul's testimony (or that of human beings in general), will enable me to conclude that what Paul says is true, in much the same way that the sight of ice on the sidewalk combined with induction on past instances, can justify the belief that it has snowed. Paul's assertion that it has snowed is just another piece of inductive evidence, like the ice on the sidewalk. In both cases, I am fully aware of the premises needed for the inference which supports the belief: no reference need be made to reasons of which I am not apprised (e.g. Paul's reasons).

Many radical internalists give memory a similar treatment. On their view, having forgotten my reasons for believing that it snowed yesterday, I can still know that it has snowed provided I can make an inductive inference from the fact that I appear to recall snow to facts about yesterday's weather.

I shall call such treatments of memory and testimony *reductionist*. As I show in the course of Part 3, the prospects for this reductive project are bleak. The outlook for memory is especially grim. How could we determine whether our memories are a reliable source of knowledge without at some point implicitly relying on memory? Any inductive investigation makes constant recourse to memory; why should this one be any different? The prospects for a reductive treatment of testimony are little better. How could a normal human being, in a natural life span, hope to ground all the knowledge she has acquired from testimony on induction from her own personal experience? No one feels obliged to embark on such an undertaking; and, if they did, the picture of the world thus produced would be exceedingly impoverished.

In Chapters 10 and 11 I'll argue that the role of both memory and testimony is to preserve knowledge which we (collectively) already possess, not to be a source of inductive evidence. We acquire empirical knowledge through perception and inductive inferences based thereon, but this is not the means by which we preserve knowledge. Human cognitive life would be impossible unless we had further (and irreducible) capacities to retain what we have learnt and to transmit it to others. In this chapter I lay out the general theoretical framework which my model of memory and testimony requires before going into details. But I'll begin with a brief discussion of perception, both because it is the source of all empirical knowledge and because it provides a useful comparison with memory and testimony.

Perception

A great deal has been written about perception and its role in the justification of belief. Some internalist philosophers (coherentists) hold that sensory experiences cannot themselves justify beliefs, rather it is our beliefs about them that do the justificatory work, in particular our belief that certain sensory experiences are a good guide to how the world is (BonJour 1985: Chapter 6; Harman 1973: Chapter 11). Clearly any attempt to justify a belief in the reliability of experience must lead straight back to experience. Coherentists are happy with such a justificatory circle, but their internalist rivals – foundationalists – are not. Foundationalists insist that we allow sensory experience to justify belief straight off without the mediation of a reliability belief, thereby avoiding a circle of justification (Pollock 1986: 81–3 and 175–9).

On this point, my sympathies are with the foundationalists, and I adopt their view of perception in what follows; but the issue about memory and testimony remains wide open. Foundationalists, quite as much as coherentists, have been tempted to treat reliance on testimony and/or memory as based on a tacit form of inductive inference. These two parties may disagree over whether an empirically justified belief in the reliability of sensory experience is required to ensure the evidential value of such experience, but they frequently concur in thinking that such a belief in reliability is required to underwrite dependence on either memory or testimony. In fact, I think that what the foundationalist says about perceptual knowledge is closer to (though not the same as) what all of us should say about memory and testimony.

Foundationalists grant sensory experience *prima facie* authority over belief:

If I have an experience as of *p* and have no adequate reason to doubt that I am perceiving that *p*, then I am entitled to believe that *p*.

Of course, sensory experience may deceive us and, what's more, experience itself when combined with a bit of induction may disclose that we are, or are likely to be, being misled. If things look one size from a great height but look (and feel) quite a different size at ground level, I will learn my lesson and cease to judge size from a great height. But what is undermining our faith in our senses here is precisely *further* sensory information with a bit of help from induction. And how could it be otherwise? There is no way of deciding whether your senses are misleading you other than by relying on some aspect of your sensory experience.

I endorse the foundationalist's sentiments here, but his principle must be read carefully. According to the principle, all that is required to justify a belief in *p* in the way of positive evidence for *p* is an experience as of *p*, provided there are insufficient grounds for doubt. The principle does not say that experience alone can justify belief. As I established in Chapter 2, evidence alone, experiential or otherwise, can never tell us when a belief is justified. The sceptic can always concoct some spurious worries about the reliability of our senses, and what renders his doubts spurious are the pragmatic constraints on our deliberations. These pragmatic factors determine what does and does not constitute sufficient grounds for doubt. The foundationalist need not deny this; what he rejects is the idea that the probative force of experiential evidence derives exclusively from our beliefs about its reliability.

Memory and testimony

To generalise the foundationalist's treatment of perception to cover memory and testimony, we need two new principles:

> If I seem to remember that *p* and have no adequate reason to doubt that I am remembering that *p*, I am entitled to believe that *p*.

and

> If *p* seems to me to be asserted and I have no adequate reason to doubt that I can learn that *p* from this assertion, I am entitled to believe that *p*.

If induction indicates that our memory or this testimony is not very reliable, we are obliged to have doubts and to refrain from going along with what we recall or hear. Yet being free to lean on memory and testimony at the outset, prior to any inductive evidence of their reliability, we can arrive at our current epistemic position without travelling in a circle.

But the reductionist has grounds for complaint here. 'What is so special about memory and testimony?' she will ask. If I see some ice on the sidewalk and infer that it has snowed, this experience gives me evidence of snow only given some prior inductive backing: why should it be any different when our evidence is the (apparent) statements of others on the subject, or an awareness of the contents of our own memory? For a foundationalist, perception is special in that when I have a direct experience of snow, what the experience purports to present me with is snow itself. By contrast, what memory of *p* and testimony that *p* purport to present me with is, at best, an indicator or symptom of *p* – my own memory and someone else's utterance, respectively. In allowing that a perception as of *p* itself gives one non-inductive evidence that p one hardly lets in the idea that a perception of a mere indicator of p gives one a similar sort of evidence (Burge 1997: 32–5; Christensen and Kornblith 1997: 5–11).

There is the pressure of necessity here: unless we give memory and testimony this *prima facie* authority, we shall be unable to reconstruct our epistemic position. But (the reductionist will say) if we are allowed to go in for these *ad hoc* manoeuvres in order to preserve our epistemic pretensions, why wouldn't some rather different moves do just as well? Why not suppose that my perceptual experience of a cloud gives me *prima facie* sufficient evidence of future rainfall, or the ice on the ground of past snow fall? Why not stipulate that my experience provides non-inductive evidence for all sorts of things which do not enter into the content of that experience but are well-correlated with whatever does?[2] We could then free ourselves from dependence on memory and testimony by relying on other forms of non-inductive evidence. But this line of thought is persuasive only because we are thinking of the *prima facie* authority of memory and testimony as a matter of their providing us with non-inductive evidence. This is to overlook the significance of the fact that both a memory as of p and testimony as to p present us with a *representation* of p: they are attempts by a rational being to represent how things are.

My contention is that memory and testimony enable us to tap the probative force of reasons of which we remain unaware. When I learn that it has snowed by hearing this from Paul, the evidence which justifies my belief is Paul's own evidence (his experience perhaps) and *not* some non-inductive evidence yielded by my perception of his utterance. Similarly, when I remember that it has snowed, the evidence which renders my current belief rational is the evidence which I then had for this proposition, whether or not I still possess it, *not* the fact of my recollecting the proposition now. It is precisely because memory and testimony involve awareness of a representation that they allow reasons which are not currently available to us (namely, the reasons which lay behind the production of that representation) to justify the beliefs which we currently have. Memory and testimony replenish your epistemic system with the probative force of old reasons, reasons already used to justify belief; they are not a source of new evidence, whether inductive or non-inductive.

We can now see the precise extent to which the foundationalist model of perceptual knowledge fits the case of memory and testimony. The parallel is clear: sensory experience, apparent memory and testimony all provide *prima facie* sufficient reasons for belief – we don't need an inductively justified belief in the reliability of any of these mechanisms to underwrite our reliance on them. But the difference is no less stark (Burge 1993: 476–81). Sensory experience is a source of (non-inductive) evidence, but all memory and testimony do is to *preserve* evidence: they don't *provide* any. When I am asked why I believe that p and I reply that I remember it or that I learnt it, I am not myself giving evidence for p. Rather I am indicating where to look for the evidence: I am deferring to someone else (or to myself at another time) for my reasons.

Two dimensions of rationality

It is clear that there are going to be two quite different questions we can ask about any belief acquired *via* memory or testimony. First, we can ask whether someone is entitled to rely on memory/testimony at all. The principles stating that, provided there are no grounds for doubt, you are entitled to accept something remembered or testified to are relevant at this point. Grounds for doubt include evidence of the unreliability of memory and testimony, or else the intrinsic unlikelihood of what they tell us. Second, we can ask whether, given that the person was entitled to rely on memory/ testimony, he ended up with a rational belief or not. Here what is relevant are the reasons possessed by the source of the belief (and how well their probative force has been registered and preserved). A person who passes the first test may still end up with an irrational belief, if the belief he inherited was itself irrational; and he may find himself in this position without having had any cause for doubt. We must distinguish the rationality of our believing (or not querying) a certain proposition from the rationality of the belief thereby acquired (or sustained).[3]

But one might wonder how anyone could rationally acquire or retain an irrational belief. Won't the fact that I am justified in accepting a belief by itself ensure that the belief accepted is a rational one? Take memory. Suppose I have a well-grounded confidence in what I appear to recall. Won't that suffice to ensure that the belief retained in memory is itself justified? I might be unable to produce good reasons for what I claim to remember, but if there are no grounds for doubting that I previously had such reasons, isn't this absence itself a piece of evidence which justifies the belief retained, as well as my retention of it? True, my original conviction may have been irrational, but if what now sustains that conviction is a well-grounded faith in the contents of my own memory, surely my current belief is justified, its sordid history not withstanding? Here, the objector moves from the premiss that I am entitled to believe p because I apparently remember it (in certain conditions) to the conclusion that my apparent memory of p (in those conditions) must give me sufficient evidence for the truth of p. This inference is unsound.

First, the absence of grounds for doubt sufficient to undermine my right to rely on my memory of p cannot be converted into the form of *inductive* evidence which (when combined with the piece of memory/testimony itself) justifies the belief that p. No such conversion can take place until we know what factors are likely to render memory unreliable – something we can learn only by using our memory. Only then can we be sure that there is no inductive evidence for memory's unreliability. The principles enunciated a few paragraphs back entitle us to accept what memory tells us prior to *any* empirical investigation of memory's reliability. We need them because the process of forming and justifying beliefs about the reliability of memory cannot even get going unless we are entitled to use memory *ab initio*. That is why these principles are substantive normative claims which many philosophers would dispute, not just banalities to the effect that we can rely on memory or testimony provided we have a right to rely on them.

Still, couldn't the fact that I seem to recall that *p* provide me with adequate non-inductive evidence for *p*'s truth? I investigate this suggestion further in Chapter 10, but we can note one *prima facie* objection here and now. Upon discovering that my original belief in *p* was irrational, wouldn't I admit that my recalled belief in *p* is also irrational? Wouldn't it be perfectly natural for me to describe my recalled belief in those terms? If so, that belief can hardly be justified simply by observing that I had no grounds to doubt my memory of *p*.

Sensory illusion

I have distinguished the rationality of a belief inherited *via* testimony or memory from the rationality of my acceptance of it: can a parallel distinction be drawn in the case of perception? Suppose I suffer from olfactory hallucinations but, having no reason to suspect this, I begin searching for the source of this foul odour. Here my belief seems to be supported by evidence (the illusory smell) and appears to be justified. But perhaps I think this only because I have overlooked the distinction between *belief* justification and *believer* justification. Should I rather say that, though it may be reasonable for me to rely on smell, in fact the hallucination provides me with no reason for this belief: I am justified though my belief is not?[4]

No. There is a default entitlement to believe our senses, but this entitlement depends on the fact that our sensory experiences provide us with (non-inductive) evidence for the beliefs which they engender, evidence which is, *ceteris paribus*, sufficient to justify belief. So a belief based on such an olfactory hallucination can be perfectly rational.[5] And it is absolutely essential that the hallucination should justify my belief. In basing this belief on an experience, I assume the responsibility of justifying that belief myself. I am not exercising any entitlement to shift that burden to someone else (or on to my earlier self). Should my sensory experience fail to provide sufficient grounds for the belief I base upon it, there is nowhere else for the blame to go: the buck stops with me. If this belief is unjustified, so am I.

The treatment of sensory illusion I have just rejected might be motivated by a desire to accommodate both internalist and externalist intuitions about justification. According to the internalist, justification requires awareness of a reason; according to the externalist, the mechanism by which a justified belief is produced must be a reliable one. Why not say that the olfactory experience here is necessary but not sufficient to justify my belief in the odour – that it justifies this belief provided my sense of smell is working properly, delivering generally reliable information about the world around me? Since the mechanism involves something of which the subject is aware – the experience – this should satisfy the internalist; and since this experience counts as a reason only if one is not subject to olfactory hallucinations, the externalist should also be content.

But to embrace this compromise, we must allow that the hallucinator's belief is unjustified without our being entitled to hold anyone (including the hallucinator himself) responsible for its lack of justification. No internalist should concede this, for it completely breaks the connection between justification and responsibility. The entitlements to rely on memory and testimony allow a subject to transfer epistemic responsibility and thus make room for a distinction between believer justification and belief justification. But, in the case of the hallucination the person responsible can only be the hallucinator himself. And since the hallucinator is perfectly sober, capable of responding to reasons appropriately, he surely bears the responsibility for justifying his beliefs. So, if he is justified in believing in the smell, his belief must also be justified.

Failures of reason

Even the most radical internalist must concede that justification is linked to responsibility only when there is someone who is capable of taking on that responsibility, someone who can be held to account for an unjustified belief. For example, it may seem to me that I am reasoning cogently when I run through a valid mathematical proof while under the influence of speed, but it is very unlikely that such mentation could justify a belief in the theorem proved – the proof is valid and it appears valid to me, but since my ability to discriminate good reasons from bad ones is much impaired by the drug my conviction is unfounded (BonJour 1998: 128).

Here I have an unjustified belief in the theorem, but unless I have grounds for suspecting my own sobriety I am not to blame for this belief (perhaps someone slipped speed into my tea just a few moments ago without my noticing). It would be mad to insist that before I can accept any mathematical proof, I must first assure myself that my brain is working normally. Rather, that is something I am entitled to presume in the absence of significant evidence to the contrary – otherwise all mathematical reasoning would require empirical support (Burge 1993: 463 and 1997: 28–9). So I have a right to this unjustified mathematical belief, provided I have no grounds for suspecting that I am incapable of carrying out the reasoning on which it is apparently based.

Now the radical internalist complains that if memory or testimony fails without giving the subject any grounds for suspicion he may end up having an unjustified belief, though he was in no way at fault. But this puts him in no worse a position than the subject convinced of the truth of a mathematical theorem while quite unaware of the influence on his brain of the drug he has just consumed. The latter has no grounds for doubting the cogency of his reasoning but its unreliability undermines any justification he may think he has. What exposes the subject to this element of epistemic luck is not some reliance on reasons of which he knows he is not aware. Rather it is a more general phenomenon: a subject may be entitled to think that a belief can be justified when, in fact, it cannot.

Still, isn't there an important disanalogy here? The drug surely impairs the rationality of the mathematical reasoner, but if I am misled by a plausible liar, or rely on a bad memory, I am not necessarily being irrational. In fact, I think the three cases are analogous. All involve a failure in the processes which enable reasoning to take place, but in none of the cases does this amount to irrationality. If I reason carelessly, or in a biased way, I remain capable of responding correctly to reasons of which I am aware: I just fail so to do. This is irrational, and is blameworthy. What is not blameworthy is being *unable* to respond to reasons properly, and that is the predicament of the drug-impaired subject. It is also the predicament of those who are entitled to rely on plausible but misleading memory and testimony: such failures cripple reasoning. The only difference is that the reasons the latter cannot respond to properly are reasons of which they know they are not aware.

In all three cases, the subject has an unjustified belief, but it does not follow that she is unjustified in having those beliefs. To be justified in having a belief, you must be entitled to hold someone responsible for justifying that belief. That person may be yourself *now*, yourself *then*, or some third party. But you can be entitled to hold someone responsible for justifying that belief even if that someone is not in fact responsible because he is incapable of discharging that responsibility (provided, of course, you have no reason to suspect this). And this is so even when the person in question is yourself. That is why a mathematician on speed is justified in having unjustified beliefs.

It should now be clear where moderate internalists like myself part company with externalists. Externalists maintain that the following situation can arise: a belief is unjustified; the person with the unjustified belief is perfectly capable of taking responsibility for it; he has not even attempted to transfer that responsibility to anybody else and yet he is not to blame for the belief's lack of justification. For example, externalists claim that an unwitting victim of olfactory hallucinations is entitled to the unjustified belief that there is a foul smell in the room. But the victim of olfactory hallucinations is perfectly capable of taking responsibility for this belief and so he must have a justification for it, otherwise he is at fault. To restore the link between justification and responsibility without being unfair to the hallucinator, we should insist – as internalists do – that his hallucination justifies his belief provided he has no reason to doubt it: both he himself and his belief are justified.

Belief and internalism

I have denied that we can justify our reliance on memory and testimony from the evidential resources which perception and induction make available to us. We must be prepared to accept things on authority both from our earlier selves and from others; only then can the process of querying memory and testimony get going. Once we are willing to depend on evidence we don't have, we can acquire reasons for rejecting such dependence in specific cases, but we can't set out with a neutral attitude to the blandishments of memory and testimony. How is the subject himself meant to feel about this intellectual dependence on other people and on his early self? Can he regard himself as anything other than slave to received opinion and un-examined prejudice (Descartes 1985: 218–20)? In dealing with this issue, I must return to a topic discussed in Chapter 3: the nature of belief and knowledge.

Belief as a block to deliberation

In Chapter 3 I argued that knowledge requires conclusive reasons. Several writers have endorsed the related claim that if one thinks one knows that p then one can't acknowledge that there is any evidence against p, that there is any reason to believe not-p (Dretske 1971: 216–17; Harman 1980: 168–70). In their view knowledge cannot admit of grounds for doubt. To know p is to know that p is true, and if p is true then anything which appears to be evidence against p is misleading: p has been established and all other phenomena are to be explained on the assumption that p.

This claim might seem rather strong but it stands up to closer scrutiny. Not only have many past philosophers endorsed it, but reflection on the everyday use of the word 'know' suggests it also. The statement 'I know that p but I'm not certain that p' sounds strange to most ears, at least where the second clause is taken to express a real doubt. We can explain this by supposing that a knowledge claim implies certainty and that certainty excludes doubt (Unger 1975: 98–103). Note this is perfectly consistent with the thought that if such and such a piece of evidence were to materialise I would change my mind. 'I know that p though I'm not *absolutely* certain that p' sounds better because it does not express a present doubt about p; rather it simply acknowledges the possibility that I might change my mind.

In Chapter 3, I argued also that one can't feel entitled to believe something unless one feels entitled to claim to know it. Given this, if knowledge requires certainty (i.e. the absence of doubt), so must belief. And indeed it does. As James remarks: 'The true opposites of belief are doubt and inquiry, not disbelief' (James 1950: 284). Belief in p is a state of mind which is an obstacle to first-order deliberation about whether p, tending to prevent the weighing of evidence for and against p.

Belief states, so construed, have an obvious utility. Rational belief in p cannot require the continued assessment of evidence for and against p, otherwise not only would we have to keep an eye out for such evidence, we would also have to store the evidence we already possess on the matter so that the significance of new evidence could be assessed in the light of it. But this is quite impractical given the number of issues on which we need to have a view. Once a question is decided, we close the books on it and throw away the evidence; deliberately retaining evidence for future consultation is a sign of doubt – an attitude perhaps appropriate to the scientist who is interested in the likelihood of various things and has a professional obligation to suspend judgement, but quite unsuited to the everyday believer (Harman 1986: 38–42, 46–9).

In Chapter 7 I argued that while reflection on our reasons cannot rationally motivate the formation of belief, it can motivate practical decisions. This was my attempt to elucidate the idea that we have a control over our decisions which we don't have over our beliefs. The point I am now making is different. It concerns not the formation of belief but rather what is involved in having a belief. It is a point which applies equally to decisions and intentions: we can be moved to take a practical decision by reflecting on the weight of reasons in its favour – to that extent decisions are under our control – but once the decision has been taken serious practical deliberation is over.

For example, a decision to holiday in South Africa signals the end of serious deliberation about where to holiday. Obvious constraints on our time and mental capacity compel us to take such decisions in advance of action: we can't get away with leaving every choice until the last minute (Pink 1996: 70–5). Once this decision is made, I feel entitled to forget precisely why I preferred South Africa to France, and lay all my other plans on the assumption that I shall holiday in South Africa. To open my mind on the question once more – to ask whether France might not have been a better choice – would be to abandon this intention.

Similarly, a rational believer in p does not wonder whether p is true: belief tends to prevent the sort of first-order deliberation about whether p which often does rationally motivate the formation of belief. This isn't a point about our lack of reflective control over the formation of belief; nor is it a point about the inefficacy of higher order theoretical deliberation; rather it is a point about a rational belief's lack of responsiveness to new evidence, once it is in place.

Some qualifications

My claim about belief requires a couple of qualifications. First, what is definitely excluded by belief is *serious* first-order deliberation, by which I mean the kind of deliberation which indicates an open mind about whether p. I may try to think of reasons for p in order to convince someone else, or for form's sake, but unless my own belief in p is seriously in question this is not deliberation in the relevant sense. Higher order doubts about my first-order beliefs may also motivate a search for (or consideration of) evidence.[6] This might happen because such doubts cause me to open my mind on the question, but it need not be like that: I may suspect that my first-order belief is unjustified and set out to investigate the grounds for it without thereby abandoning that belief. But such higher order deliberation is not serious in the relevant sense (however sincere) unless the belief's retention comes to depend on the outcome of the deliberation; once that happens, the belief has already been abandoned.

A second qualification: belief comes in degrees. Some beliefs are stronger than others and, in a rational person, the strength of the belief reflects the strength of the reasons for it. By this I do not mean that we can think p more or less likely: that would be a point about the *content* of the belief, not about its *strength*. A stronger belief is more tenacious than a weaker belief: we are more reluctant to abandon it, to re-open the books on the question or even change our minds altogether. This tenacity is a psychic force, a cognitive inertia which keeps the belief in place beyond the point at which awareness of evidence ceases to operate on it directly. In this sense a belief with a probabilistic content can be much stronger than a belief which is not probabilistically qualified.[7]

I must also firmly distinguish my notion of epistemic strength from the Bayesian notion of degree of belief. For a Bayesian, belief-strength is a quantity which obeys the axioms of the probability calculus and simply registers the amount of evidence in favour of a given proposition. So if I believe proposition p with a strength of 0.7, it follows that I believe proposition not-p with a strength of 0.3. In contrast, belief as I conceive it is an all or nothing state with a certain tenacity. The rational believer in p disbelieves not-p: he claims to know that p is true and that not-p is false. The strength of his belief is a measure of how difficult it is to get him out of that state, of how weighty are the evidential and pragmatic factors needed to shift him.[8]

Belief change

But if belief in p is a block to any consideration of the evidence against p, how can countervailing evidence ever get us to abandon this belief? The answer is that evidence can influence whether or not you hold a belief without it being weighted in a process of (first-order) theoretical deliberation. If I stumble across sufficiently impressive evidence against p, that evidence can overcome the cognitive inertia implicit in my belief and sow a doubt in my mind. And though this doubt is not engendered by reasoning, its production is a rational process, not a mere struggle between two psychic forces. Third parties can assess the rationality of doubt by asking how strong the new evidence is relative to that which motivated the original belief. Of course, this old evidence need not be available to the subject himself, but if he is rational it will be reflected in the cognitive inertia of his current belief. The earlier evidence can help to justify later belief and rationalise resistance to doubt, even though he is no longer aware of it.

Suppose I have a firm belief in the honesty of my accountant. To have such a belief is not just to think that the evidence currently favours his honesty: that would be consistent with having an open mind on the question, with carefully collecting and assimilating further data and being thoroughly on one's guard. If I trust my accountant, I simply don't consider whether a certain anomaly in the company's books should undermine my faith in him: I ignore it or explain it away on the assumption that he is honest. Nevertheless, my belief is not invincible. Certain events might arouse my suspicions, might sow doubts. They won't do this *via* a process of deliberation – I can't (seriously) consider whether these events should undermine my trust without already having ceased to trust; rather it is by undermining the belief that they make such deliberation possible. From the outside, the rest of us can see that my refusal to consider whether my accountant is dishonest is perfectly reasonable, even in the face of what is becoming a significant amount of evidence. But as the evidence mounts up, there will come a point when my conviction should be undermined by the evidence before me and inquiry must recommence.

I now have the materials at hand to answer that internalist worry about reliance on groundless prejudice. The internalist is right to require that belief be based on the awareness of evidence. Nevertheless it doesn't follow that a continuing awareness of this evidence is required to maintain that belief in a rational person. On the contrary, no genuine belief could persist in that way: beliefs, once formed, have a life of their own. If the internalist requires any more, he is in effect suggesting that we give up on belief altogether.

Chapter 10

The authority of memory

Nothing is more common than for us to continue to believe without rehearsing the reasons which led us to believe in the first place. It is hard to see how it could be otherwise. Were we obliged constantly to re-trace our cognitive steps, to reassure ourselves that we are entitled to our convictions, how could we ever move forward? We have probably forgotten why we adopted many of our current beliefs, and even if we could dredge the evidence for them up from memory, we couldn't do this for more than a tiny subset of our beliefs at any one time. Since inquiry involves a reliance on many different beliefs, progress is possible only if we can use established results in future deliberation without re-fighting the battles of the past.

But this plausible thought appears to conflict with another, that we should believe only where we have adequate evidence: rational belief must be based on evidence for the proposition believed. Now, one might quibble over what exactly 'have evidence' means. Is it required that whenever the belief comes to mind, so too does the evidence on which the belief is based? Or is it sufficient that one be capable of rehearsing this evidence? Either way, human beings are very often unable to satisfy this demand in respect of beliefs on which they happily rely. If this is illicit, inquiry must be reined in, constrained by our memory's inability to retain more than a fraction of the evidence relevant to the beliefs we formed at various points in the past.

Epistemologists have responded to this tension in several ways. Externalists simply drop the demand that belief be based on reasons. Radical internalists try to find evidence on which rational memory belief might be based. There are two internalist strategies here. One claims that certain empirical arguments underwrite the memory beliefs of the rational person, arguments which one can rehearse even if one can't recall the specific grounds on which one formed the belief in the first place. The other strategy simply asserts that memory beliefs have a *prima facie* authority, that one is entitled to rely on them without any justification, provided one has no grounds for doubting them.

I agree that we must have reasons for our convictions: to believe something is to believe it to be true, and if you don't have any grounds for thinking it true you shouldn't believe it. For example, information installed in our brains as part of our genetic endowment may exercise a beneficial influence on our behaviour, but such evolutionary 'memory' is not a repository of knowledge: to make it such we must have grounds for relying on it. Nevertheless, we must also get away from the radical internalist idea that having a reason to believe is a matter of being able to produce evidence. One's belief may be well grounded in past deliberation even if one is quite incapable of recapitulating that deliberation. And there is no need to invent some alternative support for the belief which one can now bring to mind. We are not creatures of the moment, unable to carry our cognitive achievements forward from one instant to the next.

Justifying memory?

Suppose I remember that Hitler committed suicide. I don't remember how I learnt this, nor can I lay my hands on anything that might count as (direct) evidence in favour of it. This is the situation we find ourselves in with the bulk of our factual beliefs: how do you know the boiling point of water or the dates of the First World War? It seems that either such knowledge is completely groundless or else it is based on the simple fact that you remember these things. But how can this memory be self-justifying? How can a belief be evidence for its own truth?

As already noted, some philosophers have sought to argue that memory beliefs are self-justifying. Either they think a memory belief is intrinsically self-justifying, so that if one appears to remember that p, one already has a good reason to believe that p. Or else they appeal to background knowledge about how one is likely to have acquired the belief in question: I know that I learnt most of my history from a number of reliable sources (teachers, reputable books, etc.) and therefore can claim that I am likely to have got the belief that Hitler killed himself from a reliable source. Either way, the very fact that I have this belief can serve as evidence for its truth.

In this section, I discuss the latter view on which memory is a source of inductive evidence (without intrinsic authority) whose probative force rests on the grounds we have for thinking our memory to be a reliable guide to the truth (Foster 1985: 106–16). Here we are supposed to start out with a neutral attitude to our own memory beliefs, to pretend that *a priori* we are as likely to be wrong as to be right in what we recall. But can we really regard our memory beliefs as we would the clicks of a Geiger counter? Our memory is not one more informational device which we can use or not as we please: it is fundamental to all cognitive transactions, including any that would be involved in establishing the reliability of memory itself.

Any investigation into the reliability of memory will make use of beliefs about the past (Meinong 1973). I may simply *recall* having learnt my history from trustworthy authorities. Or if I have little idea about the origins of my historical beliefs (or about the reliability of my sources), induction from past instances of memory success and failure may still assure me that my memory is to be trusted on historical matters. But I could hardly conduct such an investigation without using my memory to compare what I claimed to remember with what I later discover to be the truth. So in any such inquiry, some memories must be taken at face value, at least to start off with. An agnostic about memory could not even begin to determine which of his memories he should accept and which he should suspect.

My opponent might reply that I have ignored the possibility of an abductive investigation into the reliability of memory (Harman 1973: Chapter 12; Peacocke 1986: 164). Here, one takes all one's apparent memories and asks: what is the best explanation for the fact that I have all these memories? The answer might well be that I have the memories I do because the world was at least approximately the way I remember it as being.

The details of such an argument need to be spelt out, and until this is done it is hard to judge whether a sound abductive inference could underwrite our memory knowledge. But, however the inference goes, one can be sure it will be quite complicated: we must consider a wide range of memories and a reasonable selection of possible explanations for them and assess each by our chosen standards of abductive inference before we can arrive at the conclusion that our preferred explanation is the best. Memory will be involved at every stage in this process: not memory of the past successes and failures of memory but memory of what has already been established in reasoning – that such and such a subset of our apparent memories are well explained by a given hypothesis, that such and such is not as good an explanation of the whole set of apparent memories as the one we are now considering, and so forth. I could hardly hold in mind all the stages in such a complex argument. If it is written down perhaps I could get my head around any given stage of the argument at will, but my present sense that I could do this successfully if I tried must ultimately be based on my *memory* of what happens when I do try (Descartes 1985: 15; Pollock 1986: 46–58; Plantinga 1993b: 62–3; Locke 1996: 194). So an abductive investigation of memory's reliability is as dependent on memory as is an inductive investigation.

There undoubtedly are cases in which one learns things by utilising background knowledge about memory. Dennett asks how we would go about answering two questions: (1) Have you ever danced with a movie star? (2) Have you ever driven for more than seven miles behind a blue Chevrolet? Most of us, he says, would deliver a firm 'No' to the first question but would reply 'Don't know' to the second. Yet in neither case can we remember anything directly relevant to the proposition. So why treat them differently? The reason, Dennett suggests, is that we think that had we danced with a movie star we would now remember the fact, while we don't think this in the case of driving behind a blue Chevy. So our memories provide evidence for the proposition that we have never danced with a movie star but not for the proposition that we have never driven behind a blue Chevy for some distance (Dennett 1991: 146–7).

But is it always like this? Suppose I do remember having danced with a movie star. Must I have satisfied myself of the accuracy of my memory before accepting this proposition? Certainly, I might learn things which lead me not to accept the proposition: I might suspect that I was inclined to deceive myself on such matters. But in the absence of any beliefs about how accurate my memory was in this regard, what would my epistemic position be? Would I feel entitled to accept the verdict of my memory that I had danced with a movie star? Surely yes. But then I am not neutral: my default reaction to memory is acceptance.

Memory as *prima facie* evidence

In the face of such considerations, several philosophers have argued that memory's epistemic authority must be intrinsic. If I remember that Hitler committed suicide then I am simply entitled to continue to hold that belief unless and until countervailing evidence is presented to me (Chisholm 1977: Chapter 2; Pollock 1986: 83–7; Dummett 1992; and Burge 1993: 157–65). To put it another way, my recollections have *prima facie* authority: I can trust my memory without the supporting argument sketched above. Something like this must be right, but it remains to elucidate '*prima facie* authority'.

On one reading of this phrase what is being said is that memory gives us a form of evidence for *p*, '*prima facie* evidence', sufficient to establish the truth of *p* in the absence of countervailing evidence. This would be to model the epistemic role of memory on perception. In perception we have two separate states: the belief and the experience which furnishes *prima facie* evidence for the belief. But memory is an awkward fit for this model. When I remember that Hitler committed suicide, are there really two elements here: the belief that Hitler killed himself and the memory impression on which that belief is based? All I seem to find when I ask myself what I remember of Hitler's death is a series of beliefs. If my memory of Hitler's suicide were experiential (had I actually been present at the suicide and could visualise what happened) then I could have discerned two elements – the memory experience and the belief based upon it – but my topic is factual and not experiential memory (Owens 1996). Factual memory is a mechanism for preserving beliefs already acquired: it is not a source of quasi-experiential evidence.

Memory without belief?

Pollock wishes to restore the parallel between factual memory and sensory experience and with it the idea that memory provides evidence for belief. The belief-independence of sensory experience is established by considering cases in which we enjoy an experience as of *p* but don't trust our senses and therefore don't form the corresponding belief. In much the same way, Pollock (1974: 188–96) thinks, we can have a memory without trusting it.[1]

Say I seem to remember that I was born on New Year's Day: 1 January is the date which comes to mind whenever I ask myself when I was born. Such a memory may persist long after I become convinced that my memory for such facts is unreliable: New Year's Day still pops into my mind whenever I am asked my date of birth. Here I have the memory but I don't trust it, so I don't believe what it tells me. My memory of my date of birth is not a belief but a state distinct from belief which, in Pollock's view, gives me *prima facie* evidence for a belief, evidence which is in this case undermined.

Pollock infers from such examples that even when I have full confidence in my memory, I must distinguish the state of (apparently) remembering that *p* from the state of believing that *p*. Now, I agree that there are phenomena which we may call 'memory impressions', but I have two objections to what Pollock claims about them. First, it is phenomenologically implausible to suppose that such memory impressions are present whenever we consult our memory: in (factual) memory there is nothing like the sensory experience which occurs whether or not we accept it. Second, such memory impressions as there are cannot play the fundamental epistemological role Pollock casts them in. Pollock's cases of memory without belief are best redescribed as cases in which we have a feeling, an impression or a hunch, but no memory – a redescription which makes clear the (non *prima facie*) evidential status of these impressions.[2]

Pressed by the quiz master, I must decide in very little time whether there are more than 120 members of the United Nations. My instant reaction is that there are, and I plump for the answer 'yes'; but I am far from claiming to know that there are more than 120 members. I have no doubt that I am under this impression because of various things I already believe about who is a member of the UN – my response does not strike me either as a pure guess or as an intuition of an *a priori* truth – but I don't think myself able to fix immediately on the right answer to such a precise numerical question.[3] In forming a belief on the matter I must forget about the hunch altogether and perform some sort of rough calculation, calling to mind what I do know about the membership of the UN.

Do I here remember that there are more than 120 members in the UN? My linguistic intuitions are not very clear on this point: perhaps such an impression can properly be called a memory, provided it is generated by beliefs acquired in the past (Radford 1966; Armstrong 1973: Chapter 1; Lehrer 1990: Chapter 2). What matters, though, is not what name we give the impression but whether such an impression should be regarded as providing a *prima facie* reason to form the belief that the impression is correct. I cannot see why it should. The only argument which might be offered on this score is that we have to attribute such a *prima facie* authority to memory impressions if we are to avoid memory scepticism. But there is no need to grant this status to cognitive impressions which are not beliefs in order to get on with our cognitive lives.

The true situation seems to me to be this. Whether my former belief that I was born on New Year's Day, together with the impression which it has left as a residue, constitute evidence in favour of this proposition very much depends on my view of how reliable these beliefs and impressions are. They have no *prima facie* authority for me. It is hard to see how the fact that I once believed something should, in itself, provide me with any reason to believe it now. And it is equally hard to see how such a past belief could acquire a special evidential weight simply by persisting in the form of a current impression. I re-adopt past opinions, since abandoned, just in so far as I have independent grounds for thinking them an accurate guide to the truth.

Memory as belief-preserving

So Pollock's memory impressions have no *prima facie* epistemic authority. But I cannot take such a noncommittal attitude to my present beliefs.[4] If I find myself with the belief that Hitler committed suicide, if I find myself convinced of this point as a result of past cognitive activity, I can't regard this adherence simply as a more or less reliable indicator of what might be the case, or even as a piece of *prima facie* evidence. What memory preserves is belief itself, and to believe that *p* is precisely to have finished inquiring into *p* by forming the view that *p*: it is not to be in possession of a sort of evidence for *p* which, if not outweighed by contrary evidence, will convince one of *p* (Moran 1997: 151).

Awareness of evidence motivates both the formation of belief and its abandonment, but it cannot motivate the maintenance of belief in memory. If I believe that *p* only because I regard my memory of *p* as evidence in *p*'s favour, then whether *p* must be an open question for me which I resolve in the light of my memory of *p*. But if at time *t* it is an open question for me whether *p*, then at time *t* I have no memory belief in *p* and so my memory could hardly resolve that question for me. To remember that *p* is to no longer feel the need of evidence for *p* and so no memory can maintain belief by furnishing evidence for it.

True, I may note that my memory of Hitler's suicide provides me (or others) with evidence that Hitler killed himself. Here, I do not re-open the issue of how Hitler died but merely note a point in favour of a belief I would anyway maintain. This might be in an effort to provide others with grounds for believing what I do. But, as I noted in Chapter 9, the belief itself is seriously in question only if its retention depends on the success of this procedure, and a belief is held only for so long as it is *not* seriously in question.[5] If doubt overwhelms me and forces the abandonment of this belief, I can then use the fact that I previously believed that Hitler committed suicide as inductive evidence in favour of his suicide. Such reflections on what I used to believe might even restore my conviction, but this would be a different belief with a different justification.

I have rejected the idea that memory provides *prima facie* evidence for belief, but I remain sympathetic to the claim that memory has some sort of *prima facie* authority. In the absence of specific grounds for doubt, we are entitled to persist in believing what memory serves up to us, not because memory provides evidence for these beliefs but in another way. What way is that?

The function of memory

I have characterised memory as a faculty for preserving belief and belief as a state in which we feel no need of evidence for the proposition believed. But even if those who remember do not feel impelled to ask why they should believe what they remember, we observers can still pose this question. We can ask how memory preserves the rationality of beliefs if not by providing the believer with continuing evidential support for his belief.

Say I am engaged in a rather long deductive argument. I believe p and q; after some effort I prove that p and q together entail r and further exertions establish that r and another proposition I accept, s, together entail t. Therefore, I come to believe t. Now as I am proving t, I make no effort to hold in mind the proof I discovered for r; neither do I have time to review the proof of r once I have arrived at t. I may even have forgotten it. But since r has been established to my satisfaction, I feel entitled to use r in this and any future argument. What is going on here? I have already dismissed the view that I believe r because my subsequent mental state provides me with some kind of evidence that r is true. Rather my grounds for believing r long after I have proved it are precisely those grounds which led me to believe r in the first place. Provided nothing has happened in the meantime which should make me doubt r, my continued belief in r is rational on just the same grounds as my original belief in it was rational (Burge 1993: 462–5).[6]

The core idea here is that memory is a faculty which preserves the probative and motivational force of evidence beyond the point at which that evidence has been forgotten. It enables current evidence to sustain and justify future belief by perpetuating its belief-fixing influence. When a belief is laid up in memory, it takes with it the probative force of the evidence which led us to adopt that belief in the first place. That is how memory enables us to retain knowledge previously acquired without our being in a position to rehearse the grounds on which we acquired it.

But how is the subject to think of his own epistemic situation once he has forgotten this evidence? What is it like for him when he claims to know via memory that p? He believes that p and like us he thinks that to believe that *p* he must have some reason to think *p* true. Perhaps we, from the outside, can point to his earlier evidence as that which rationalises his current belief, but is not the subject himself uncomfortably endistanced from the grounds for his own beliefs?

In fact, we can't suppose that our subject feels the need of *evidence* to support his continued belief that *p*, for to believe that *p* is precisely to have ceased to feel that need. All that will strike him from his first-person standpoint is that he knows that *p* in a certain way, namely by remembering it. One seems to remember that *p* when one seems to have established that *p* at some point in the past and preserved that knowledge ever since. That is what makes a subject's memory beliefs feel different from those he has just acquired from testimony and other non-memory beliefs.[7]

Though memory does not usually act as a source of evidence for belief, the fact that one seems to remember that *p* is still relevant to one's being justified in believing *p*. If one didn't appear to remember that *p*, if the belief in *p* seemed to have popped into one's head *de nouveaux*, one wouldn't be entitled to defer to one's past self, to evidence one is no longer aware of, for a justification of that belief. To seem to remember that *p* is to be entitled so to defer, provided one has no adequate reason for doubting one's memory.

Memory as rationality preserving

A well-functioning memory preserves the rationality of belief but not by preserving the evidence which prompted the acquisition of the belief. It does this rather by holding the belief in place with a force proportional to the strength of the evidence for it (a force which I call *cognitive inertia*). Given this, the subject will abandon the belief and resume inquiry into the matter just when he receives evidence sufficient to make doubt reasonable. Memory malfunctions where the tenacity of the preserved belief is out of line with, or is not rooted in, the earlier evidential support for it.[8]

There are many ways of fixing beliefs in place which do not preserve the rationality of those beliefs.[9] Say that I am prone to entertain groundless doubts about the fidelity of my partner. Being momentarily free of such jealous suspicions, I decide, perfectly reasonably on the basis of the evidence before me, that my partner is not being unfaithful. But I know full well that I will abandon this conviction at the slightest prompting and fly into a jealous rage, so I decide to pay a visit to the hypnotist in an effort to fix this rational trust in place. Suppose the hypnosis works, and my faith in my partner's fidelity is disturbed only by events which would arouse suspicion in a reasonable person. Does it follow that I have preserved the rationality of my belief, as well as the belief itself, by visiting the hypnotist?[10]

That depends on the answer to a further question: does the efficacy of the hypnosis depend on the strong evidential support I have for the belief?

If so, the hypnosis is an aid to rational retention of the belief. But suppose the hypnosis works just as well regardless of the evidence for my partner's fidelity: here the hypnosis does not preserve the belief's motivation, but rather replaces it. So even if I do have grounds for trust in my partner, and even if the strength of the hypnotically induced belief is proportional to the strength of the evidence I have for their fidelity, in this case that evidence does not justify the belief. The evidence motivates me to consult the hypnotist but it does not *directly* motivate the retention of the belief; so, while it may rationalise the action required to fix this belief in place, it cannot rationalise the belief itself. A true aid to memory works off the probative force of the evidence which justifies the belief: it does not replace it. Visiting the hypnotist may be a perfectly reasonable way of preserving a rational belief without thereby preserving the rationality of the belief.[11]

We can now see the grain of truth in the claim that memory provides *prima facie* evidence for belief. Our memory has a *prima facie* epistemic authority in that we are entitled to persist in believing something remembered provided nothing comes to our notice which should make us desist. But this is because memory preserves the rationality of that belief, not because it gives us (*prima facie*) evidence for the proposition believed.

Epistemic conservatism

An epistemic conservative holds that 'a belief can acquire justification simply by being believed' (Harman 1986: 34). I considered one form of that position when I dismissed the idea that my belief in *p* might be a source of evidence for that very belief. But the conservative need not imagine that the mere fact of belief is evidence for the truth of the proposition believed. What he may think is that my belief in *p* provides me with non-evidential grounds for continuing to believe that *p*. Can such a position be defended and how does it relate to my own view of memory?

According to one sort of epistemic conservative, belief involves a sort of cognitive commitment to a proposition. Consider practical commitments. A person makes promises and signs contracts for all sorts of reasons, but once the commitment is made, he has a reason to do what he has promised, a reason over and above any which might have led him to take on that commitment in the first place. Making a promise is not like visiting the hypnotist in an effort to ensure that one implements a difficult decision when the time comes; rather it is a means of giving yourself an extra *reason* to carry out that decision. To do something simply to keep a promise is a perfectly rational procedure. Now suppose beliefs are epistemic commitments; then wouldn't the fact that one finds oneself committed to a certain proposition provide one with a reason to carry on believing it, a reason which is not evidence for the truth of the proposition believed?

Two points tell against the commitment model of belief.

1 Promises are made to other people, and their social function is to render interpersonal interactions more predictable. But my beliefs are for my own future consumption and only derivatively for other people's. The commitment model needs the idea that one can bind *oneself* with a promise, that one can give oneself an extra reason to ϕ simply by promising oneself that one will ϕ. Now auto-promising might seem an unfamiliar procedure, but several philosophers have argued that taking a decision on future action is like making yourself a promise: it gives you a reason to carry out the decision, a reason independent of the intrinsic desirability of the action decided upon (Raz 1975: 66).[12] If so, perhaps intention formation provides the correct model for belief.

But this view of practical decisions is surely mistaken: if I decide that I will ϕ and it then becomes obvious that ϕ-ing would be a terrible idea, I don't have any reason to do it simply because I decided to do it (Bratman 1987: 23–6; Pink 1996: 125–35). And the analogous view about belief seems equally mistaken. One doesn't make a belief more rational simply by committing it to memory. If a belief is irrational when adopted, it remains just as irrational while laid up in memory.

2 I have accounted for memory's role as a knowledge-retention system by reference to the rationality-preserving character of memory. Unless the epistemic conservative denies that memory is rationality preserving, these peculiar cognitive commitments (and the non-evidential reasons for belief which they generate) are simply not needed to enable memory to perform its epistemic function. It is quite enough to suppose that the past rationality of our beliefs will be reflected in their current normative status. In contrast, the conservative move of awarding each of our beliefs an extra point, as it were, simply for being believed seems both gratuitous and indiscriminate. Theoretical economy and normative intuition each tell against it.

Groundless memory

In reply, the conservative might pose the following question: what if there were no adequate justification for the original acquisition of a memory belief? What if the believer finds herself with a belief which she has no reason to doubt but which is, in fact, ill-grounded? We can't require that she knows why the belief was acquired, as that would defeat the point of memory. Is she entitled to carry on believing provided she has no intimation of this groundlessness? Surely people often are thus entitled, whether or not the belief constitutes knowledge. Yet if all memory does is to preserve beliefs together with their original justifications, how can people be entitled to believe them (Harman 1986: 33–41)?

In the eyes of the epistemic conservative, this is why we need to suppose that the cognitive commitment implicit in belief has a normative weight in excess of the probative force of the evidence which led us to adopt the belief. Even when a vow is irrational, we have some reason to keep it; similarly, might I not be entitled to stick to my (unreasonable) decision that *p* is true until given good reason to abandon it? But, as I'll show, it is unnecessary to postulate epistemic commitments in order to explain why it might be reasonable for me to hold on to a belief that was formed irrationally.

I seem to remember that Hitler committed suicide at the end of the Second World War, so when I read a report in a reliable newspaper saying that an elderly Hitler was spotted in a village in South America some years ago, I conclude that the witness must be either mistaken or else a liar. I don't seriously re-open the issue. Now suppose that at the time I formed the original belief, there was a great deal of uncertainty about Hitler's fate; needing the security of the thought that this evil man was no more, I ignored the evidence that Hitler was still alive and in due course became convinced he was dead. Here, my belief was irrational. This belief is preserved in memory and much later it leads me to infer that the South American witness is misleading us. I have no recollection of how it was arrived at – it has as much claim on me as any other memory. Am I being irrational?

Two-dimensional rationality

As I indicated in Chapter 9, there are really two questions here which it is important to keep apart. The first is 'What reason do I have to suppose that Hitler killed himself?' The answer is 'Very little', and therefore my belief is unjustified. But we could also ask 'Is it reasonable of me to reconsider my belief that Hitler committed suicide?' And the answer to this question might be 'No', however irrational the belief at issue (Foley 1993: 109–12).[13] Note, the believer himself can't even raise the former question until the latter has been settled. To seriously consider whether *p* is true in the light of evidence against *p* is already to have abandoned one's belief in *p*. Therefore, if it is reasonable for me not to reconsider my belief in Hitler's suicide, I can't be irrational in continuing to believe it, though the belief itself might be quite unreasonable.

Why might it be unreasonable of me to re-open the issue of Hitler's fate? Perhaps I don't have time to look into the matter now; it would be difficult to dredge up a fair sample of the relevant evidence, assimilate it, weigh it against the newspaper report, and so forth. And even if I did have time to do all this, the prospects of forming a well-grounded view on that matter might remain slim. Thus there is no point in reconsidering the belief. Needless to say, I will not arrive at this conclusion by deliberation – rather the absence of doubt will be motivated by a tacit appreciation of such considerations. Still, why shouldn't the testimony of the South American lead me to suspend judgement on the point, at least until I can investigate further? Here we come face to face with a phenomenon alluded to in the previous chapter – beliefs have a certain degree of inertia: they resist revision.

The cognitive inertia of belief is a corollary of the rationality-preserving nature of memory. Where belief is rational, the inertial force of the belief is determined by the strength of the reasons which supported its adoption; where the belief is irrational, it is determined by some other factor. Either way, a belief, once acquired, constitutes a psychological obstacle to its own revision: if it didn't, it could never propagate the motivational force of the considerations which led to its formation in the absence of those considerations themselves. So this cognitive inertia, far from being a regrettable lapse, is essential to the rationality-preserving role of memory.

The claim that even rational beliefs have some inertia might seem puzzling. In so far as we are rational, shouldn't we find it easy to rid ourselves of any beliefs we ought to be having doubts about? But my point is precisely that one of the factors we need to consider in deciding whether a subject ought to be having doubts is the strength of his belief. If the belief is strong and the grounds for doubt are relatively weak then it is not rational for him to abandon that belief. And this is so even if the belief's strength is, unbeknown to him, not well-grounded in past evidence. It can be unreasonable to reconsider an irrationally strong belief precisely because of the inertial force behind it.

If, on the other hand, the grounds for doubt are so strong that it is reasonable of our subject to wonder whether p is true, the fact that he used to believe that p should no longer block inquiry; nor should it be a factor in his deliberations about whether p (unless it can be treated as a bit of evidence). The cognitive inertia of belief does not show up in the first-order deliberations of a rational subject precisely because it operates to prevent such deliberation: once deliberation begins, the inertia has disappeared.

My memory decays as time goes on, not just in that I remember less but also because my memory becomes less reliable. Where memory works well, it registers the gradual decline in memory's reliability in an accompanying decline in the cognitive inertia of the retained convictions. The cognitive inertia of the beliefs of a rational person must reflect not only the strength of the original justification for her belief but also the likelihood that both the strength and the content of a justified belief will be correctly preserved in memory. Preserving the rationality of a belief is not just a matter of accurately recording the strength of the original justification – features of the preservation mechanism must be taken into account.

The transfer of epistemic responsibility

Internalists hold that beliefs are subject to reason and that believers are responsible for the rationality of their beliefs. I have argued that a believer is entitled to transfer responsibility for his current beliefs on to his earlier self. A rational belief requires evidence to justify it, but an awareness of that evidence need not accompany the belief it justifies. Provided I was once aware of this evidence, the responsibility for justifying my present belief has been discharged and the connection between rationality and responsibility on which the internalist insists has been preserved.

But if one of my memory beliefs is unjustified, am I always to blame? Obviously, I am to blame if I am not entitled to rely on memory at all in this instance. I am at fault in another way if I rightly lean on my earlier self when my past self can't justify the belief. In the Hitler example just described, my memory is in good working order and the transfer takes place, but my past self is unable to discharge its epistemic responsibilities, and I am to blame for the irrational belief that I (rationally) preserve.

But what if my memory garbles the content of a perfectly reasonable belief and simply fails to link me up with a past self who could bear the epistemic responsibility for the new belief? For example, I commit to memory the justified belief that my car registration ends with 'A', but I end up believing that it begins with 'A'. Am I still at fault because I have an unjustified belief? To say I am at fault seems unfair since my memory's malfunction is something I might remain quite unaware of. But if I am not at fault we seem to have here an unjustified belief for which no one is responsible, finally breaking the internalist connection between justification and responsibility.[14]

Here I rationally preserve a belief whose lack of justification I have no reason to suspect. Learning the truth, I would acknowledge that I had no reason for this belief, that it was groundless. But am I to blame for this? No. This is a case where I, quite rightly, attempted to transfer responsibility for these beliefs on to my earlier self, but the transfer failed: no one is responsible for these beliefs and so no one is to blame. In Chapter 9, I urged internalists to allow responsibility and justification to come apart when no one is capable of taking responsibility for a belief.[15] A person with a mangled memory has an impaired capacity for reasoning; he has no sensitivity to the past reasoning which could justify his current beliefs and so can't be held responsible for their lack of justification.

Memory and control

I have argued that belief retained in memory remains rational without the preservation of the evidence which supports it. On a radical internalist conception of our intellectual responsibilities this looks unacceptable: it is unreasonable to believe something unless one is aware of sufficient evidence in its favour for so long as one believes it. While it might be very convenient for me to be able to hold on to a view which I could justify only at the moment of acquisition, convenience is no excuse: a person cannot bind his future epistemic self by means of his memory and expect to remain fully rational, any more than he can do so by means of a drug or a visit to the hypnotist.

Parallel issues arise in the practical realm. Say I decide to give up smoking. Fearing that I will forget the evils of smoking when offered a cigarette, I take a drug which ensures that I will not abandon this decision, and it instils in me a desire not to smoke commensurate with the evils of smoking but which would work as it does whether or not I am currently aware of these evils. Ingesting this decision drug might be a good way of getting myself to do something which I have decided I should do, but it is not a form of rational self-control. The drug takes the decision about whether to smoke out of my hands and ensures that my subsequent actions are no longer fully rational.

Can we exercise control over our future action while preserving our practical autonomy and integrity? One thing we can do is to give our future selves an incentive to conform to our own past decisions. I might publicly announce my decision, so a serious loss of face would be the result if I ever smoked again. The rationality of my future self is not compromised by this form of self-manipulation: I remain free to decide whether or not to smoke next week. But to act in this way is to treat my future self as I might treat another person: it is to behave as if my current deliberations about whether or not I ought to smoke can have no direct influence over my own future action.

Yet we do think that rational persons can control their future action simply by deciding now what they should then do, that their current appreciation of the relevant considerations can directly motivate future action. Unlike decision drugs, decisions have a rationality-preserving influence on future action (Pink 1996: 93–9). We can exercise control over our future action while preserving our practical autonomy and integrity. Some of the internalist theories of memory reviewed in this chapter can be seen as attempts to model the rationality of belief preservation on the rational subject's control of their own future action.

For example, the evidential model of memory holds that consigning something to memory is a way of giving myself new evidence for p in the future. On this model, it becomes rational for my future self to believe that p because the formation of a rational belief in p has certain effects on my future evidential situation; the fact that I later recall that p is an effect of my current belief and a reason for future belief, just as the public announcement is a consequence of my current decision not to smoke and a reason for future non-smoking. But as an account of how the formation of memories preserves our intellectual integrity this is no more plausible than it is as an account of how intention formation preserves our practical autonomy.

The commitment model of memory is another attempt to find a way in which the believer can bind his future self without forsaking his rational autonomy, without relinquishing control over his beliefs. In the practical arena, when I decide to ϕ I commit myself in advance to ϕ-ing without rendering that action un-free, without depriving myself of control over it.

This is supposed by some to be because deciding is like promising: the fact that I have decided to ϕ in itself gives me reason to ϕ. Given this, I don't need to control myself by making public announcements or whatever. Deciding is a way in which I can give myself new reasons for future action without that sort of self-manipulation. And it is a way which applies to me alone: my decisions bind me and nobody else.

In fact, it is a mistake to model memory's capacity to preserve the rationality of belief on intention's capacity to exercise rational control over future action. I argued in Parts 1 and 2 that we don't control the formation of our beliefs to begin with, so why should we seek to preserve such control over time? In the practical sphere, the maintenance of our integrity as agents may well be a matter of staying in control, but this desire for remote control is out of place in the theoretical realm: the maintenance of our intellectual integrity requires only that memory preserve the rationality of our beliefs. And not only does the parallel between belief and intention distort our treatment of memory, it prevents us seeing how testimony could preserve the rationality of belief.

Descartes and Locke, the founders of the internalist tradition in epistemology, agreed (albeit reluctantly) that we must rely on memory to justify our beliefs. Locke commented:

> I confess, in the opinions men have, and firmly stick to, in the world, their assent is not always from an actual view of the reasons that at first prevailed with them: it being in many cases almost impossible, and in most very hard, even for those who have very admirable memories, to retain all the proofs, which upon a due examination, made them embrace that side of the question. It suffices, that they have once with care and fairness, sifted the matter as far as they could . . . and thus having found on which side the probability appeared to them, after as full and exact an inquiry as they can make, they lay up the conclusion in their memories, as a truth they have discovered; and for the future they remain satisfied with the testimony of their memories, that this is the opinion, that by the proofs they have once seen of it, deserves such a degree of their assent as they afford it.
>
> (Locke 1975: 658)[16]

Here Locke implies that the reasons I had when I formed an opinion can serve to justify my opinion beyond the point at which I cease to be aware of them.

Yet when Locke turns to testimony he roundly rejects the idea that someone else's reasons might justify my beliefs. Locke allows that someone else's testimony sometimes provides me with evidence sufficient to establish the truth of what they assert, given what I know about them (Locke 1975: IV, XVI, Sections 6–11), but he makes no mention of the possibility that the probative force of the reasons *they* have for what they say might justify a belief which *I* acquire from them. Yet if reasons of which I am no longer aware can justify my memory beliefs, why not allow the testimony of another to justify an opinion of mine by reference to the reasons they had for forming their opinion? Why can't testimony preserve the rationality of belief just as memory does?

What lies at the back of Locke's mind here is, I suspect, a parallel with the case of action. There we think of each individual as having direct control over his or her own actions and therefore as having a special responsibility for them which he or she does not have for the actions of other people: each individual's own practical judgement is the final arbiter of what he or she does. Now this conception of practical responsibility can and must be reconciled with the fact that we don't always recall exactly why we are doing something at the moment we come to do it. We take some decisions long before we must implement them in order to avoid having to decide what to do when the moment for action has arrived. This capacity for planning compromises neither our sense of practical control nor our responsibility for our own actions. But to surrender control over our actions to the judgement of another, to do something just because he thinks we ought to do it (and not because we have some independent reason to obey them), would be to evade our responsibilities.[17]

It looks as if the probative force of a practical reason can transcend our awareness of it only intra-personally. My hypothesis is that Locke thought of epistemic reasons (evidence, etc.) as rather like practical reasons in this respect. For him, we have to maintain direct control over our beliefs if we are to discharge our intellectual responsibilities, and we can do this by forming beliefs and laying them up in memory for future consultation, just as we can control our future action by deciding now what we will then do. But in neither case should we surrender control to another. We can shift responsibility for our beliefs on to our earlier selves but not on to another believer.

I have argued that we have no direct control over our beliefs and therefore such control can hardly be transmitted over time by means of a theoretical analogue of the faculty of practical decision making. Our decisions are free, our beliefs are not. Once this is understood, it becomes quite unclear how Locke can allow memory to shift the burden of justification on to his earlier self while denying that testimony can transfer it to another person. A consistent internalist must go all the way.

Chapter 11

The authority of testimony

The motto of the Royal Society – *Nullius in verba* (On no man's word) – sums up the Enlightened attitude to theoretical inquiry. Locke, the Royal Society's philosophical spokesman, penned this and several other diatribes against reliance on second-hand opinion:

> For, I think, we may as rationally hope to see with other men's eyes as to know by other men's understandings. So much as we ourselves consider and comprehend of truth and reason, so much we possess of real and true knowledge. The floating of other men's opinions in our brains makes us not one jot the more knowing, though they happen to be true. . . . In the Sciences every one has so much as he really knows and comprehends: what he believes only and takes upon trust are but shreds; which however well in the whole piece make no considerable addition to his stock who gathers them. Such borrowed wealth, like fairy-money, though it were gold in the hand from which he received it, will be but leaves and dust when it comes to use.
>
> (Locke 1975: 101)

Kant and Hegel regarded Locke's demand for intellectual self-reliance as definitive of the Enlightenment and of modernity, respectively (Kant 1983; Hegel 1990: 131–2).

Seen through Enlightened eyes, medieval culture was based on an acceptance of the word of certain authors: to think was to construe their texts and thereby discern the truth. Interpretations might vary, but one's final view was an interpretation of the text in question. To the modern mind, such deference involves a surrender of rational autonomy, an abdication of intellectual responsibility on the part of the individual thinker. To believe we need reasons, and those reasons must be in the possession of the individual believer. No one can shuffle off their intellectual responsibilities on to someone else, however distinguished; they must, to use Hegel's word, 'authenticate' each belief for themselves.

In Chapter 10, I queried one aspect of this ideal of intellectual responsibility. Memory must be able to transmit the justification provided by our
original reasons for holding the belief without preserving a knowledge of
what those reasons are, otherwise our cognitive lives would grind to a halt.
Rational belief is indeed motivated by the subject's awareness of good
reasons for that belief, in adherence to certain epistemic norms, but this
awareness need not be co-terminal with the belief it justifies: the demands
of rationality are less strenuous than that.

In this chapter, I want to propose a further liberalisation: we should treat
testimony as preserving the rationality of the beliefs it transmits, much as
memory does. If we can find the justification for our current beliefs in evidence of which we are no longer aware, why not locate it also in the thoughts
of others, in evidence of which we are unaware but they are, or were once,
apprised? As I'll show, such dependence on others is indispensable to our
intellectual lives and so must be consistent with our intellectual responsibilities. The more we can relax the over-strenuous conception of our intellectual
responsibilities bequeathed to us by the Enlightenment, the less tempted we
shall be to follow the externalist and renounce them altogether.

Two models of testimony

The reductionist model

Philosophers influenced by the individualistic ideals of the Enlightenment
tend to adopt what, in Chapter 9, I called a 'reductionist' view of testimony.
They see our reliance on testimony as based on a form of inductive inference
from the data provided by the words of others. Now those writing about
testimony tend to treat Hume as the classic representative of reductionism.
This is perfectly understandable. Unlike Descartes, Locke and Kant, Hume
was not sanctimonious about our reliance on testimony. He regarded second-
hand opinion as a ubiquitous and unavoidable feature of human life, and
sought to ground it in a form of induction. But Hume was able to keep a
clear head on the matter precisely because he didn't share the Enlightenment's ideal of intellectual responsibility. And if we take Hume as a paradigm
of reductionist thinking, we risk missing what made testimony problematic in
the first place.

Hume claimed that reliance on testimony is a form of inductive inference
from the statements of people to the things and events their statements concern. But he didn't say this with a view to laying a foundation for testimony
which would satisfy the radical internalist. On the contrary, he thought our
inductive inferences were not governed by reason at all. A reduction of
testimonial to inductive knowledge was attractive to Hume because he
wanted to provide an economical account of the workings of the human
mind, one which invoked a small number of basic principles (of association).

But I take it that those internalists who now discuss Hume's reduction have a different aim in view. They are more sanguine than Hume about the justifiability of induction and they regard Hume's proposal as a way of meeting the intellectual responsibilities imposed on us by the Enlightenment without renouncing our reliance on testimony.[1]

Nevertheless, Hume's work contains the crispest statement of reductionism. He begins by noting that 'there is no species of reasoning more common, more useful, and even necessary to human life, than that which is derived from the testimony of men, and the reports of eye witnesses and spectators' (1975: 111). But this acknowledgement of the importance of testimony does not mean he thinks it fundamental:

> [O]ur assurance in any argument of this kind is derived from no other principle than our observation of the veracity of human testimony, and of the usual conformity of facts to the reports of witnesses.
>
> (Hume 1975: 111)

> The reason why we place any credit in witnesses and historians, is not derived from any *connexion*, which we perceive *a priori*, between testimony and reality, but because we are accustomed to find a conformity between them.
>
> (Hume 1975: 113)

For Hume, the statements of other people are just like the clicks of a Geiger counter, or black clouds in the sky; they acquire their evidential significance from the (inductive) grounds we have for treating them as reliable indicators of radiation and rain, respectively. For such reductionists, there is nothing epistemically special about a rational source of knowledge: a reliable informant has exactly the same epistemic authority as a dependable cipher.

What is testimony?

This picture of testimony has the virtue of simplicity, but it makes a mystery of the fact that my statements transmit knowledge only of that to which I testify. Say that I start to complain of poverty. You might believe what I say and treat me as short of money. On the other hand, you might think this moaning a rather bad guide to my financial state or even as good evidence that I am in fact wealthy; then my words will establish exactly the opposite of what they testify to. But this conclusion, unlike the first, cannot be a piece of knowledge by testimony, however inductively well-grounded it may be. You might learn that I am rich from my words but you didn't learn it *from me*, you didn't learn it by accepting what I said, and so it does not count as testimonial knowledge (Anscombe 1981: 116; Coady 1992: 45–6).

The observation that testimony transmits knowledge only of facts testified to may sound like a linguistic triviality which a reductionist can perfectly well concede while maintaining that our reliance upon testimony is based upon inductive evidence of its reliability. But this would be to miss the deeper point. A linguistic assertion has a sort of meaning which the state of a gauge or a cloud lacks. Statements express beliefs with a certain content, and unlike instruments or clouds, those beliefs are subject to reason. To treat someone as a source of testimony is to treat him as a believer, as a person who adopts convictions for reasons which are more or less appropriate to the content of those convictions and then attempts to convey what he knows in speech.

Consider someone who asserts, as a result of post-hypnotic suggestion, that a certain woman was murdered. Perhaps this woman was indeed murdered, the hypnotist knew this fact and installed this belief in his patient as a way of bringing the murder to light without showing his hand. Suppose I am aware that the hypnotist knows why the woman died and has primed his patient to tell me. Then I am in a position to learn from the patient's words that the woman was murdered. But this is not a case of knowledge by testimony, at least not by the testimony of the patient. The patient has no reason to believe that the woman was murdered – his opinion on the matter is worthless, and I know it. I treat his words not as an expression of a belief with a certain content, held for reasons which have some probative force for me, but rather as a symptom of a certain fact. I learn something from his words but nothing from him.

Suppose now that I know nothing of the hypnosis and treat the hypnotist's patient as a source of testimony about the woman's death. Here the patient's words are a reliable guide to the truth but they do not give me knowledge of the murder. Why not? To treat the patient's words as testimony about the death is to defer to his reasons for belief on the matter. But the patient has no reason to believe the woman was murdered. Therefore I have no reason to believe the woman was murdered, and so I don't know that she was murdered. True, the hypnotist knows, but he can't transmit testimonial knowledge to me *via* his patient; that is not a way of preserving the rationality of the belief as it passes from one person to the next because one link in the chain is an irrational (hypnotically induced) conviction. In contrast, ordinary testimony, the spread of knowledge by sincere assertion expressing well-grounded belief, is a rationality-preserving form of belief transmission, or so I'll argue.

Is reliance on testimony fundamental?

The reductionist's worry about this proposal may be stated as follows: I can't simply assume that every witness has good reason for saying what he or she says; I must have some evidence for this assumption, and only then can I give the witness any credence; I must have some (ultimately non-testimonial) grounds for thinking that the witnesses I credit are rational, sincere and not liable to error before I can treat any utterance of theirs as evidence for the state of affairs which would make it true. For a reductionist, the authority of others' testimony ultimately depends not on the reasons *they* have for what they say but rather on the reasons *I* have for crediting them.

Several authors have recently argued that it is impossible to reconstruct our epistemic position from the materials provided by the reductionist. Almost all our knowledge of the world beyond the current state of our immediate environment is based on the testimony of others. How, they wonder, could we concoct a justification for such reliance without implicitly leaning on testimony at some stage? How else are we to come to know of the laws of nature (including the psychological laws governing the reliability of testimony) or the dispositional facts (like the honesty and sobriety of individual informants) which the reductionist invokes (Coady 1992: Chapter 4; Dummett 1992: 420–5; Plantinga 1993b: 77–82).

The argument for the indispensability of memory which I gave in Chapter 10 established that no rational being with finite intellectual capabilities could arrive at our view of the world without relying on his memory *ab initio*. So far as I can see, testimony is not indispensable in the same way: a socially isolated human being with no opportunity to learn from others might well arrive at a fairly complex set of beliefs about his immediate environment by means of perception, memory and induction alone. Nevertheless, a strong case can be made for treating reliance on testimony as fundamental. For this socially isolated creature would have few, if any, of the historical and scientific beliefs which we all take for granted and his conception of his own history and of the wider world would be grossly impoverished.

A radical internalist might insist that we who do live with and learn from other people should reconstruct our current epistemic position by methodically investigating all the sources of testimony which are available to us. Perception, memory and induction could be used to confirm that our informants are both reliable and trustworthy. I don't think one can rule out this Cartesian project *a priori*, but that is about all there is to be said in its favour. Our beliefs about these sources of information (newspapers, books, teachers and experts) are usually based on testimony, and it is unobvious how we might eliminate this reliance by means of investigations feasible within the lifetime of a normal human being. But suppose such a project could in fact be executed. Would that show that we ought to undertake it?

As things are, we start off by absorbing what our parents say about the world with no question whatsoever; then we rely on what our teachers and school books tell us with only a few queries; and finally we accept what the media announce with even less scepticism than is warranted. We feel fully entitled to the rich panoply of beliefs which they gives us. Anyone who proposed that we reconstruct our epistemic position from the meagre resources of perception, memory and induction alone would be laughed off. So even if reductionism about testimony would not destroy our mental lives entirely, it is radically revisionary of the norms we use to evaluate beliefs actually derived from testimony.

Of course, Enlightened thinkers have objections of principle to such ungrounded reliance on second-hand opinion, and these must be considered before the matter can be finally resolved. Given how hard it is to construct a realistic theory of human knowledge which does not grant testimony *prima facie* authority, once I can clear these objections out of the way I will have done enough to establish the point. In fact, most of the work required to undermine these objections has already been undertaken: I just need to apply it to testimony. My earlier inquiries into belief, reflection, control and memory show that a reductionist view of testimony is not compulsory and so theoretical necessity decides the question against the reductionist.

A non-reductionist model

There is an alternative picture of knowledge by testimony (see Burge 1993 and 1997). Suppose that when I believe what Jones tells me my belief inherits whatever rationality Jones' belief had. I don't mean by this that Jones tells me his reasons; rather, the probative force of his reasons is preserved across the testimonial transaction, so that upon hearing him tell me something he knows I am in a position to know it also, without needing to know the reasons which convinced Jones of the point. Jones will go to the trouble of saying why he believes what he does only if I am liable to be sceptical: he will give me his reasons only if doing so is required to make me believe him. Otherwise he won't bother, confident that my belief inherits the rational standing and epistemic status of his own. If we are dealing with a chain of testimony, Jones might not have anything much to say in favour of his belief, other than to acknowledge his dependence on the person from whom he acquired it. Here, the members of the chain inherit whatever non-testimonial reasons the first member of the chain had for believing what the rest know only by testimony.

The reductionist implicitly denies that I can inherit Jones' reasons for believing what he believes simply by believing what he says. On the contrary, my convictions must be rationalised by the considerations available to me: I must weigh Jones' words in the light of my knowledge of him and his surroundings before I can form any view of their worth. My past experience of Jones' veracity and expertise may entitle me to have faith in what he says without looking into exactly why he says it. Thus, Jones' reasons for what he says, though unknown to me, may bear indirectly on my reasons for believing him, but only *via* my beliefs about his character and abilities. For the reductionist, the alternative is an irrational credulity which simply accepts that p when Jones says that p and which shifts the responsibility for justifying this belief on to Jones.

Evidently the non-reductionist picture of testimony collides with an Enlightened view of our intellectual responsibilities, but it does enable us to explain why knowledge by testimony can only be knowledge of the fact testified to and can come only from someone with good reasons for his or her belief. In the eyes of the non-reductionist, testimony transmits knowledge of p by transmitting the probative force of reasons for belief in p from one party to another. Where Jones lacks any reason to believe that p, others cannot acquire knowledge of p simply by believing what Jones says. Of course, they might infer things from Jones' utterances – that p is true, that p is false or even something quite independent of p – but this inference will not be a case of knowledge by testimony because it will not be supported by the very reasons (if any) which support Jones' utterance.

Testimony is not evidence

Acceptance of the non-reductionist picture of testimony is possible only once we have removed one very natural misconstrual of it. One might respond to the failure of reductionism by insisting that testimony as to p, like sensory experience as of p, is a source of evidence *prima facie* sufficient for belief in p (Reid 1997: 190–202). In Chapter 9 I wondered whether there is any reason to treat testimony as a source of *prima facie* evidence for p which does not apply equally to any apparently reliable indicator of p. Without an answer to this question, the suggestion that we give testimony a special evidential status seems unmotivated.

But can we really avoid treating testimony as evidence of some sort for the proposition testified to? When I learn from one of my colleagues that John F. Kennedy has died, I don't witness his death; rather I see and hear my colleague engaging in a certain activity, the activity of telling me that he is dead. It is very tempting to regard this perceptual experience as my evidence (or at least as an essential part of my evidence) for thinking that he is dead. But this concession is fatal to the non-reductionist.

Say Jones knows that Kennedy has just died and is informing Smith of the fact. Now, on my non-reductionist model of this transaction, provided all goes well Smith will end up believing that Kennedy is dead for exactly the reasons Jones does. But, my opponent will ask, how can this be? Smith must perceive Jones as performing a certain speech-act with the intention of transmitting a bit of knowledge before he can learn about Kennedy's death from Jones. This perception is something that has no place among Jones' reasons for believing that Kennedy is dead. Anything which throws doubt on the fact that Jones is intending to transmit a piece of knowledge will threaten the rationality of Smith's belief in Kennedy's death without thereby undermining the standing of Jones' conviction. So it looks as if

Smith doesn't simply inherit Jones' reasons for thinking Kennedy dead; he needs extra reasons of his own. But now we seem to have fallen back on the reductionist thought that Smith's trust in Jones is based on a tacit inference from Jones' words and Smith's beliefs about him.

To maintain our non-reductionist position, we must insist that, though my acquisition of testimonial knowledge nearly always involves an experience of a source (and thus presupposes the reliability of my sense organs), such experiences are no part of my reason for believing the proposition in question. My reasons are just the same as those of my source. This may sound like a counsel of despair but, as I noted in Chapter 10, there is an exactly parallel point to be made about memory knowledge (Burge 1993: 466, 476–81). Memory knowledge of p does not involve my treating the fact that I remember that p as evidence for p. True, that belief must have been preserved in memory in some reliable fashion (otherwise one's reasons for acquiring the belief that p will not rationalise one's current belief in p). Nevertheless the proposition that one's belief was preserved in this reliable fashion is no part of one's justification for believing that p: it is simply a condition that must obtain for one's original justification to have been preserved in memory.

Similarly, my experience of someone else's assertion of p can be essential to the mechanism which ensures that my belief in p is justified without itself being part of my justification. True, Smith's knowledge of Kennedy's death requires not just that Jones believes for good reason that Kennedy is dead; Smith must have come to believe that Kennedy is dead because he (correctly) took Jones to be seeking to inform him of Kennedy's death. Without this, the rationality of Jones' belief will not have been transmitted to Smith. But it doesn't follow that this experience of Jones' is among Smith's reasons for believing that Kennedy is dead. We can see this by asking what happens in a case where the transmission mechanism breaks down.

Suppose Smith mishears Jones' utterance, and so acquires the belief that his friend Kenney is dead. Here, I would argue, the belief lacks any justification. In particular, it is not justified by Smith's sensory experience. Smith is trying to tap into Jones' reasons for this belief; he is not attempting to base a belief on his experience of Jones' utterance. Due to the misunderstanding, Smith fails to tap into Jones' reasons and therefore fails to get hold of any justification for his belief. And, if he discovered his misapprehension, Smith would admit that there had never been any reason to believe that Kenney is dead.

But is it really plausible to say that Smith is being irrational in holding this belief? Perhaps he has no reason whatsoever to mistrust his hearing, in which case was it not reasonable for him to believe what he thought he heard? Recalling a lesson from Chapter 9, we must carefully distinguish two questions here:

(a) 'Is the belief Smith acquires by testimony rational?'
(b) 'Is it rational of Smith to acquire this belief from testimony?'

Question (a) is decided by evaluating the reasons possessed by the source of the testimony – and where the belief is a product of a misunderstanding there are no such reasons. Question (b) is settled by looking at what Smith, the recipient, knows, and it may well be that he is entitled to acquire this unjustified belief because of what he thought he heard.

To believe something on the basis of testimony is to put yourself in the power of others, not just in respect of whether you have knowledge but equally in respect of the rationality of your belief. Everyone will agree that you can know only if your informant knows, but I feel no less dependent on my informant for evidence for the things I believe. If I have been deceived, it is perfectly natural to admit that there was no reason to believe what I did. True, I may observe that I had no reason to doubt my informant's word, that I was entitled to depend on them; but to say that is not to deny my dependence.

Rational lying

In testimony, an essential part of the process of knowledge acquisition is the assertion, the testifying. Now assertion is an action, and like all actions it is to be assessed for rationality by reference to the norms of practical rather than of theoretical reason. And we all know that it is often rational to lie or mislead others. Suppose Jo tells Flo something. Shouldn't it be a question for Flo whether Jo wants to tell the truth at all, or at least is sufficiently concerned about what she says to be a reliable informant? There is no tension between regarding Jo as a rational believer and supposing that Jo is lying, or being careless in what she says about something that does not matter to her. To treat Jo as a source of testimony is indeed to treat her as a rational believer and not as a mere cipher, but the *activities* of a rational believer (including assertion) are governed by the norms of practical reason. Why should there be any *a priori* bias in favour of supposing that Jo is going to tell the truth conscientiously when the norms of practical reason dictate no such bias?[2]

Here the problem arises not because the transmission of testimony involves an action; what causes the trouble is that the occurrence of this action is being treated as part of Flo's justification for the acquired belief. Once we realise that Flo's perception of this event as a certain speech-act is no part of her justification for the belief acquired but is rather an essential element in the causal process underlying the transmission of its justification, the problem disappears. Flo need no more worry about whether Jo is lying than about the reliability of any other aspect of the mechanism underlying the testimonial transaction. Jo's justification for p is transmitted to Flo provided the theoretical rationality of this belief in p is preserved through every link of the chain from Jo to Flo.

If Jo is right to lie and Flo is right to believe her then we have a case in which there is no reason for Flo's belief, even though neither Flo nor Jo are in the wrong. There is nothing strange about this. We have just considered an example where the rationality of a belief is not preserved, yet neither party is at fault: that in which one party misunderstands what the other is saying. As Chapters 9 and 10 made clear, where one party tries but fails (through no fault of his or her own) to transfer responsibility to another, irrational belief may result without anyone being to blame. But the present case is more complex. Here it is not just that the mechanism failed: there was an intentional deception. Jo seemed to accept epistemic responsibility and then failed to discharge it. Doesn't it follow that Jo must be to blame? Yet we have conceded that Jo's beliefs and actions may be entirely reasonable.

In fact, I think the two cases – lying and misunderstanding – are analogous. When Jo deceives Flo, she does not accept epistemic responsibility for the belief induced, she merely appears to do so. When Smith mishears Jones, Jones appears to accept exactly the same responsibility. The only difference is that the speaker intentionally creates this impression in the former but not in the latter case. Since Jo intentionally creates this impression, we can ask whether she was at fault, but this is a strictly practical matter. So far as epistemic norms go, the situation is just as if Jo had said something which (quite unintentionally) gave rise to a misunderstanding: Flo is entitled to defer to Jo for a justification of her belief, but the transfer of epistemic responsibility never took place because of a malfunction in the transmission mechanism. Neither party intended to provide that belief with a justification and neither is responsible for its absence.

Interpersonal cognitive inertia

A psychological question still remains: what exactly is sustaining Smith's impression that he is entitled to believe that Kennedy is dead on Jones' say-so, entitled to take himself to have learnt of his death from Jones? Smith remains unaware of the reasons which motivate Jones' conviction and, we are supposing, Jones' utterance is not motivating the belief by providing evidence for it. So what holds the belief that Kennedy is dead in place as it leaves Jones' mind and enters Smith's? What makes Jones seem convincing? Earlier, I observed that beliefs have a certain cognitive inertia: once you have acquired them, it is often difficult to rid yourself of them, to reopen the issue.[3] In a rational person, the effort needed to overturn a belief reflects the strength of the reasons for its acquisition and it is by means of this cognitive inertia that the rationality of a belief is preserved. Where rationality lapses, cognitive inertia takes on a life of its own.

Now cognitive inertia exists not just within a single person but between different people (Korsgaard 1996a: 132–42; Reid 1997: 190–202). Other things being equal, I am inclined to believe what others believe, and the firmer they seem in their convictions the stronger the belief I acquire from them. Where the norms of theoretical reason hold sway, the strength of my informant's conviction and thus the tenacity of the belief I inherit from them will reflect the strength of their reasons for holding it. But it is quite possible for these things to become detached, in which case the tenacity of the beliefs I acquire from testimony will no longer reflect the probative force of the reasons behind them. Yet it may still be reasonable for me to refrain from reconsidering an acquired belief which has been deeply entrenched in me by someone else, however irrational that belief turns out to be.

All sorts of cues will indicate how strongly my interlocutor holds the relevant belief: his choice of words and tone of voice, of course, but also contextual factors which are mutual knowledge, facts about how important the issue is to us both (whether we are sitting in a saloon bar or a courtroom), about our social role and what it prescribes (whether we are both scientists or just newspaper readers), etc. It is crucial to the causal mechanism which transmits cognitive inertia from one person to another that I register these cues, but, as I have argued, such cues do not serve as evidence for the proposition accepted on testimony. Someone who feels the need of evidence in favour of a piece of testimony just received has not trusted it and so cannot glean testimonial knowledge from it, however great its value to him as inductive evidence. If he forms a belief by treating the testimony as inductive evidence, he will not inherit the belief expressed together with its justification, rather he will form a different belief with a different justification.

Even a sympathetic critic might wonder whether the rationality-preservation model of testimony will have any practical application. Perhaps it is possible in principle to inherit justification from others when there are no grounds for doubt – but won't there always be doubts which need to be addressed with inductive evidence? In fact, ordinary life is full of occasions when there are no sufficient grounds to generate a doubt (Burge 1993: 468–9). But even where doubts are properly engendered, this does not mean that the rationality-preservation model of testimony has no application. Rather, these doubts need to be eliminated before the model can be applied: once they have been eliminated we are entitled to defer to our interlocutor for our justification as before.

I have several times asserted that Smith inherits Jones' justification for the belief that Kennedy is dead. But I don't wish to deny that such epistemic transactions change the normative situation. As a chain of testimony gets longer mistakes are likely, and even the first stage (from experience to testimony) opens up many possibilities of error. Therefore, among rational people the cognitive inertia of a belief will gradually dissipate as it is passed along the line, in due proportion to the reliability of the testimonial mechanism, just as the inertia of a reasonable memory belief declines over time. All I am denying is that the testimonial mechanism provides a new sort of evidence for the belief, one it did not possess originally and which somehow stands in for its original justification.

Intellectual and practical responsibility

I have been expounding and defending a model of testimony which runs contrary to Enlightened thinking about belief. According to that tradition, each of us has a special responsibility for our own beliefs, as for our own actions. Both our thoughts and our actions must live up to certain normative standards, and the rational person is one who strives to ensure that this normative demand is met. Other people cannot take (ultimate) responsibility for my beliefs any more than they can for my actions: it is *my* job to ensure that they come up to the mark, and mine alone. How could this obligation be met by surrendering control over one's beliefs to someone else? The obligation is on me, and it is I who must fulfil it.

This Enlightened conception models epistemic normativity closely on that of practical reason, and someone who accepts my strictures on this picture of belief might still insist on the essential correctness of the associated picture of practical rationality: we surely have some form of autonomy in the practical sphere.[4] Is this autonomy threatened by anything I have said about testimony?

In Chapter 7 I argued that each of us has a sort of control over our own actions which we do not have over other people's. I claimed that this control is exercised by means of reflection, that it is a matter of the influence which my practical judgements have over my own actions. I can determine what I do by means of my own practical judgement in a way that no one else can.[5] But is this thought really consistent with my model of testimony? If we apply the model to such judgements we get the conclusion that my practical judgements, and thus my actions, can be justified by reasons of which I am not aware and never was. How does this fit with the idea that it is I who determines what I ought to do?

A practical judgement is a judgement about what one ought to do, and one can as easily make such judgements about other people as about oneself. Putting myself in your shoes, I can decide, given what I know of your needs and interests, that you ought to take a holiday. Perhaps I know what's good for you better than you do yourself. Can my awareness of how much the benefits of a holiday outweigh the costs of lost work, etc., really make it reasonable for you to go on vacation just because I tell you to and without any consideration by you of the pros and cons? True, you might have inductive evidence of how expert I am in these matters which entitles you to take my word for it, but we can't rely on such non-testimonial evidence always being available, any more than we can in the theoretical sphere. Without such evidence, can *your* judgement that you ought to holiday (like any belief acquired by testimony) be directly supported by *my* appreciation of your reasons for holidaying? If so, my reasons can rationalise your vacationing by rationalising your judgement that you ought to vacation, without your having to know why you should holiday rather than work.

Here we must recall another of the lessons of Chapter 7: practical judgements are not beliefs, are not claims to knowledge, because they are not arrived at in the light of conclusive reasons.[6] I don't think you have a conclusive reason to holiday rather than to work: I just think that, in the light of various (inconclusive) considerations, you ought to vacation. So when I express the view that you ought to vacation, all that judgement can transmit to you are inconclusive reasons for vacationing. Suppose you are disposed to accept this judgement on my authority and defer to me for your reasons. Still, you will be aware that there is no conclusive reason for you to vacation, and that is what makes room for freedom of practical judgement.

The individual's practical freedom consists in what I called the intrinsic authority of practical judgement. If *you* judge that it would be best to work, it cannot be rational for you to vacation, however desirable a vacation may be. In this regard, your practical judgement has a special authority over what you do. *My* judgement has no similar authority over your actions – it is only as good as the reasons for it, and those reasons are inconclusive. That is why you can always countermand my judgement that you should ϕ, override its authority, make it irrational for you to ϕ, simply by judging that you ought not to. My judgement on a practical matter cannot appear to provide you with conclusive grounds for acting, and therefore it leaves room for you to exercise a judgemental veto.

Nothing analogous is true of belief. Where my informant's words convince me, I will regard him as having conclusive grounds for what he says, grounds which leave no room for a judgemental veto from me. This rules out any analogue of the intrinsic authority of practical judgement. Suppose I acquire in this way from my interlocutor the belief that p, and everything is such that the belief inherits the probity of my interlocutor's belief; yet for some perverse reason (perhaps I don't wish p to be true and so imagine I have some grounds for doubting it) I judge that I ought not to believe that p. Suppose this second-order judgement is inefficacious, cognitive inertia does its work and the belief I acquired by testimony persists. Is this first-order belief irrational? Surely not: any irrationality is on the part of my second-order judgement.

Now consider the practical analogue of this situation. Suppose someone who sees my needs more clearly than I do myself tells me to ϕ, and I do indeed ϕ. But at the same time I form the perverse judgement that I ought not to ϕ. Is it rational for me to ϕ? Here, I take it, the answer is 'No'. To ϕ would be to go against my judgement as to what I ought to do, and however bad that judgement might be, surrendering to someone else's (better) judgement without revising my own is a form of irrationality, an abdication of my responsibility for my own deeds. My practical judgements have an intrinsic authority which is the source of my practical freedom.

To sum up, the non-reductionist model of testimonial knowledge I have endorsed does indeed apply to practical judgement, but it poses no threat to our freedom of practical judgement. We retain control over our actions because each individual is the ultimate arbiter of what he or she ought to do. This reconciliation is good news not just for my model of testimony but for the idea of individual practical freedom itself. Such autonomy would be crippling if it prevented us from tapping rational resources other than our own in our practical reasoning: we depend on each other for practical advice quite as much as we do for factual information, and neither dependence can be underwritten by perception, memory and induction.

Conclusion
Epistemology as moral psychology

> I can be immoral and know the truth. I believe this is an idea that, more or less explicitly, was rejected by all previous culture. Before Descartes, one could not be impure, immoral and know the truth. With Descartes, direct evidence is enough.
>
> (Foucault 1997: 279)

It is widely believed that the Enlightenment effected a divorce between epistemic norms and ethical norms. Its epistemic norms may be grounded in natural facts, created by language, or even established by the *diktat* of a divinity, but in any case they are irrelevant to our virtue. If a pre-modern person was wise, he or she was neither evil nor ignorant. But the modern individual can know all there is to know about the mind-independent world (including, perhaps, the moral law) without even aspiring to virtue. Or so we are told.

Yet, turning to the texts, we find both Descartes and Locke using the language of duty, obligation, blame and reward, fault and sin when assessing belief (Locke 1975: 687–8; Descartes 1984: 40–1). Furthermore, we have seen that both philosophers are very concerned to ensure that the preconditions of accountability are present in the epistemic realm. Issues of control and responsibility are never far from their thoughts, nor from those of their critic David Hume. Perhaps Foucault is right to think that an *otherwise* evil man could faithfully adhere to the epistemic norms which Descartes lays down. But, in Descartes' eyes, at least, a man's virtue is (in part) determined by how closely he adheres to those norms.

Given this outlook, the philosophical problems posed by epistemic norms ought to have much in common with those arising from other forms of normative assessment, and this is indeed what was discovered in Parts 1 and 3. The demand for certainty and the sceptical temptation to renounce belief altogether, the difficulties we face in analysing knowledge and connecting it with the justification of belief, the issues arising from our reliance on memory and testimony – all were traceable to certain assumptions about what it is for someone to be responsible for his or her beliefs. And I tackled these same issues by deploying the account of freedom and responsibility outlined in Part 2.

Yet in contemporary debate among epistemologists the notion of responsibility is sidelined. There are active literatures on epistemic responsibility and doxastic voluntarism, but they are not well integrated into the rest of the subject. Flicking through a textbook of contemporary epistemology, one is much more likely to find these issues considered at the back than at the front. If epistemology is linked to wider philosophical concerns it will be with debates in metaphysics and the philosophy of language rather than moral psychology. Many such works mention various conceptions of truth and meaning, the dispute between metaphysical realists and anti-realists, the notion of objectivity, theories of mental representation and intentional content and so forth, while largely neglecting the issues which have been central both to my reading of the Enlightenment debate and to my treatment of the issues it raised.

We can see the consequences of this neglect by noting (albeit too briefly) two popular responses to scepticism. One line of thought links scepticism with metaphysical realism, with the view that the world is radically independent of our minds. On this view, we can frustrate the sceptic by simply rejecting the realism which he assumes. Now there are many different conceptions of realism, and as many different forms which this diagnosis might take, but they all face at least one *prima facie* difficulty. As Chapter 4 made clear, the Cartesian sceptic need only point out that we could always gather more evidence, that there are always possible sources of error which we leave unchecked, in order to get his argument going. Any plausible metaphysics must acknowledge this fact, whether it accounts itself realist or anti-realist. So any plausible metaphysics is vulnerable to Cartesian scepticism.

Take phenomenalism, the view that statements about physical objects are true simply in virtue of facts about experience, actual and potential: it is true that there is a barn before me if and only if it is true that I would have barn-like experiences under suitable conditions. Phenomenalism would normally be accounted a form of metaphysical idealism, and some philosophers did embrace it as a defence against scepticism. But any viable form of phenomenalism will have to make room for the notion of perceptual error and for the indefinite diversity of sources of such error. That is what phenomenalists do when they trace perceptual error to (perfectly reasonable) inductive inferences which we make from actual to hypothetical experiences: given our past experience of barns, our current barn-like experience may deceive us about what we would experience if we had an experience as of going round the back of it. But once rational error is admitted, how is the Cartesian sceptic to be resisted? He can simply ask us to explain why we don't always wait for more actual experiences to come in before drawing the necessary conclusions about hypothetical experiences.

Rather than dealing with the sceptic by making the world more *mind*-dependent, some recent writers try to frustrate him by making our states of mind more *world*-dependent. This second anti-sceptical strategy has been pursued by 'semantic externalists'. Again, this doctrine takes various forms but, at least as a resource against the Cartesian sceptic, they all leave something to be desired. Semantic externalists offer us an *a priori* guarantee that most of our beliefs are true. Some think that truth must predominate because we must be charitable in the way we interpret other people if we are to make any sense of what they say and do. Others think truth must predominate because mental states acquire their content from reliable causal interactions with the states of the world they represent. Either way, ordinary error needs to be allowed for, and once that is done the sceptic has his foot in the door.

Suppose we accept the *a priori* guarantee that most of our beliefs are true. Take any particular belief of mine. There is no guarantee that this belief is true. Indeed, I am well aware of any number of ways in which it might be false, given the evidence I have for it. Yet I feel entitled to ignore most of these possible sources of error. 'Why so?' asks the sceptic, a question he can repeat when confronted with almost any of our beliefs. Semantic externalism cannot answer him unless it rules out error altogether, and that it cannot do.

Of course, these remarks rest on a certain reading of the sceptic's argumentation, one which I defended in Chapter 4 (see also Owens 2000). Several writers have identified a different, post-Cartesian, form of scepticism, invented by Kant (Stroud 1983; Burnyeat 1997b: 121–3). This focuses not on the pursuit of certainty but rather on the question: do our experiences represent a mind-independent world at all? The thought is that while ordinary illusion does not support a negative answer to this question, the sceptical hypotheses of massive error do, and so these hypotheses must be shown to be incoherent. The resources of metaphysics and/or the philosophy of language are brought to bear to secure this result. I cannot here expound, let alone assess, this hugely influential line of thought. All I insist on is that some other response must be made to Cartesian scepticism.

Even those philosophers who agree with my diagnosis of scepticism tend to overlook its rationale. Equating epistemology with the attempt to provide knowledge with indubitable foundations and seeing no reason to embark on this taxing project, they recommend that we walk away from it. This is to miss the real concerns about control over and responsibility for belief which drive the pursuit of certainty. Such concerns have a life of their own outside epistemology and can't be avoided by just closing it down: what is distinctive about epistemology is simply that it raises these questions about belief.

There is one debate in contemporary epistemology which stays close to the heart of this matter, that between internalists and externalists about epistemic justification. Adopting an externalist view of justification would indeed frustrate the Cartesian sceptic. Yet even here, the discussion has tended to lose its bearings. Internalism is usually thought to involve a demand for awareness of reasons, while externalists are meant to hold that justification is determined by factors of which we are not aware. But, as will have been evident from Part 3, I think this a very inadequate characterisation of the debate. The internalist must concede that justification is determined by factors of which subjects are not aware; but the internalist should also insist, against the externalist, that justification involves awareness of reasons.

A subliminal recognition of these facts has brought to the fore hybrid notions of justification, mixing 'internal' and 'external' elements, notions without any clear theoretical rationale. Unless we realise that what animates internalism is a concern with epistemic responsibility, and unless the internalist's demand is formulated in such a way as to register this deeper motivation, the debate will end in a fudge. And there *is* a real debate here: it is the very debate which Hume conducted with his predecessors, Descartes and Locke.

Notes

Introduction

1 One might read Hume as saying that we can be held responsible to such quasi-biological norms, at least in the only sense in which we can be held responsible for anything, namely by being a suitable object of some attitude of disapprobation if we violate them. But this weak sense of 'responsibility' (and the notion of rationality that goes with it) would not be of any interest to his opponents. See Chapter 8 (pp. 121–3).
2 See McDowell (1994: 4–5) and Burge (1998: 251–2).
3 Plantinga (1993a: p. 24) tells us that while the internalist does not think one can believe at will, he is committed to 'a doxastic voluntarism of some sort'.
4 Goldman (1980) attributes a regulative notion of justification to the internalist and argues that this leads to scepticism.
5 Goldman (1988) qualifies this view somewhat.

Part I: Belief and reason

I Reflection and rationality

1 Frankfurt (1971) argues that the instrument of reflective control is a second-order desire, a desire to act on one desire rather than another.
2 Plantinga (1993a: 15–22) attributes such a line of thought to all epistemic internalists.
3 Goldman (1980: 31) wrongly attributes to the internalist the view that we are infallible about our reasons.
4 Burge emphasises that our knowledge of *other* minds need not be observational or inferential but the first-person–third-person asymmetry with regard to the possibility of brute error remains. See Burge 1998: 262–70.
5 Burge (1996) links the first-person–third-person asymmetry of control and responsibility with the epistemic asymmetry, while Burge (1998: 250–2) states that our evaluations of our own mental states must be capable of having an immediate motivational impact on them.
6 See also Pettit and Smith 1996: 433–6.
7 In considering whether logic lays down 'laws of thought', Frege remarks that 'if we call them laws of thought, or better laws of judgement, we must not forget we are concerned here with laws which, like the principles of morals or the laws of the

state, prescribe how we are to act, and do not, like the laws of nature, define the actual course of events' (Beaney 1997: 246–7).

8 Brandom (1994: 18–20) calls this view 'regulism', and attributes it to Kant.

2 Motivating belief

1 Perhaps I do make some estimate of the likely evidential import of the article before deciding not to read it, but still I forsake the extra evidence which I would gather from actually perusing it, and no purely evidential considerations could explain why I do that.

2 See Chapter 9 (pp. 142–5).

3 Several philosophers (e.g. Bratman 1999a) have distinguished belief from something called 'acceptance'. They might argue that while my examples show that what we *accept* for purposes of practical deliberation and action is indeed influenced by pragmatic considerations, this doesn't indicate that *belief* is so determined. But anyone who thinks my examples simply can't be read as cases of belief formation should provide their own examples of belief formation and tell us how to explain the formation of those beliefs by evidence alone.

4 See Appendix to Part 1.

5 It is a mistake to think that beliefs are governed by both epistemic and practical norms. For example, BonJour (1985: 6–7) says that I may be justified in believing something because prudence (or morality) indicates that I should believe it. Thus BonJour is led to distinguish epistemic norms from other non-epistemic norms governing the formation of belief. I see no need for this. True, prudence (or morality) might justify actions intended to induce a belief, but nothing follows about how justified the belief induced is. Might one instead distinguish the issue of whether a belief is justified – an issue to which epistemic norms alone are relevant – from the question of whether a subject is justified in having that belief? One might but, as I shall argue in Chapter 8, whether we blame the subject is determined as much by the rationality of their beliefs as by anything else about them. Where a subject is obliged to induce an irrational belief, it may be hard to know what to make of them overall.

6 James 1956: 23–5 and Velleman 1989: Chapter 5.

7 For example, Pollock 1995: 64 and Burnyeat 1997a: 44–5. The same is not true of action: one can simply decide to ϕ because one needs to do something, even if the case for not ϕ-ing is just as strong (Pink 1996: 123).

8 Adams points out that sometimes it matters more that one believe p where p is true than that one believe not-p where not-p is true. Indeed so, but a belief that one's son is still alive would not be rational in the situation envisaged. Rather, what follows from Adam's observation is that the balance of evidence would need to tip far more in favour of one's son's death before one ceased to be agnostic and accepted his death than it would have to tip in the other direction before it became reasonable to believe that he was still alive. See Adams 1995: 87.

9 Some writers claim that epistemic norms tell us when beliefs are *permissible*, not when they are required (Pollock 1986: 7). They may say this with a view to defending the idea that epistemic norms are purely evidential, while allowing that prudential considerations are needed to determine which beliefs we actually should form.

10 It is important to realise that the sort of control in question here is reflective control and not subjection to the will, otherwise the contrast between belief formation and intention formation on which I am insisting will be lost. For example,

O'Shaughnessy (1980: 297–303) argues that one has no more control over whether one takes a certain decision than over whether one forms a certain belief. He observes, perfectly correctly, that one can't take a decision as to whether to ϕ simply because one is commanded to take such a decision, any more than one can form a belief about p simply because one is commanded to make up one's mind on whether p. But all this establishes is that the will is not subject to the will and is (like belief) not under our control in *that* sense. Reflective control exists where one can make up one's mind because one *judges* that one ought to, rather than because one *wills* that one ought to. See Chapter 5.

3 Knowledge and conclusive grounds

1 Goldman (1978) argues that it is insufficient for perceptual knowledge of the presence of a barn before me that there be a barn here which I am perceiving and take myself to be perceiving. Suppose there are many realistic barn facades in the area which I can't discriminate from real barns: surely then I can't learn there is a barn before me by perception alone, even if the barn before me is a perfectly genuine one? True, but it doesn't follow that perception that p is insufficient for knowledge of p. Rather, we must distinguish a veridical perceptual experience *of* a barn (which may not yield knowledge) from perception *that* a barn is before me (which is a way of knowing about the barn). Perception *that* there is a barn before me requires a complex combination of circumstances over and above my perception *of* a barn.
2 See Chapter 9 (pp. 139–40).
3 Williamson (1995: 540–3) argues that we should not expect such an analysis.
4 This issue will arise for those externalists who seek to analyse knowledge in terms of subjunctive conditionals in the form of a question about which possible worlds they consider to be relevant to the truth of their subjunctive conditionals.
5 Harman doesn't take this condition to be sufficient for knowledge and adds an externalist component to his analysis which I here ignore.
6 See Chapter 5 (pp. 82–5).

4 Scepticism, certainty and control

1 Descartes 1984: 11; 1984: 16 and 1984: 243.
2 A demand that is reiterated at the start of the *Second Meditation* (Descartes 1984: 16).
3 I now think that this reading of Descartes is not quite right. For a more nuanced interpretation of the *First Meditation* see Owens (2000).
4 See my Conclusion (pp. 178–9) for further discussion of this sort of response to scepticism.
5 Williams (1978: 51–8) argues that Descartes introduces the dreaming hypothesis in order to establish the universal possibility of illusion, while with the evil demon hypothesis Descartes goes further and establishes the possibility of universal illusion. Williams also notes that, for his sceptical purposes, Descartes needs error only to be possible in each case of knowledge based on experience, he needs only the universal possibility of illusion; Descartes' scepticism does not require the more radical possibility that every experience should be illusory, the possibility of universal illusion. Williams concludes that we can't deal with Cartesian scepticism simply by demonstrating that universal illusion is impossible. I endorse Williams' reading of the *First Meditation* except where he implies that Descartes

needs the possibility of dreaming in order to demonstrate that all perceptual knowledge is fallible.

6 'And since God does not wish to deceive me, he surely did not give me the kind of faculty which would ever enable me to go wrong while using it correctly' (ibid.: 37–8).

7 See Chapter 2 (p. 30).

8 I say a little more about these norms in Chapter 9 (pp. 135–8).

9 See also Hookway 1990: 143–5 and 1994: 213–15.

Part 2: Freedom and responsibility

5 Freedom and the will

1 Davidson (1980: 99–102) suggests that to form an intention to ϕ is to make an unconditional or 'all-out' judgement that ϕ-ing would be desirable. This is reminiscent of Cudworth's view that the will is 'the last practical judgement' (1996: 170). But one could intentionally not-ϕ without ceasing to judge that one should ϕ and intentionally ϕ while judging that one shouldn't. So the intention to ϕ cannot be identified with the practical judgement that one should ϕ.

2 See Chapter 7 (pp. 111–12) where I endorse this view and conclude that practical judgement is not a form of belief.

3 This question arises for Pink's account of these matters (1996: 192–200).

4 At this point Pink (1996: Chapters 7–9) distinguishes what he calls 'means–ends justifiability' from 'subjection to the will'. According to him, we have direct control over our decisions as well as our (first-order) activities because they are means–ends justifiable, not because they are subject to the will.

5 *Pace* Plantinga 1993a: 24.

6 O'Shaughnessy (1980: 297–9) carefully disentangles various active and inactive elements in the process of belief formation.

7 Harman (1980: 168) makes no great play of the distinction between belief and full acceptance.

8 See Chapter 9 (p. 144). There I point out that higher order doubts about a belief of mine might motivate inquiry without thereby destroying the belief.

9 Montmarquet (1993: 79–81) insists that belief is not subject to the will and Kornblith (1983: 24) denies that believing is a 'voluntary action'.

6 Locke on freedom

1 I have found the following to be particularly helpful guides to Locke's text: Passmore (1986); Schouls (1992: Chapter 5); Darwall (1995: Chapter 6) and Wolterstorff (1996: 60–118). None of them read Locke in quite the way I do, but I have taken important things from each of them.

2 See Chapter 1 (p. 17).

3 Locke (1975: IV, XIV). Locke retained this antediluvian notion of knowledge (*scientia*), but he departed from Descartes and his medieval predecessors in his pessimism about the narrow scope of *scientia*. For Locke, most of what we take ourselves to know is really opinion (Wolterstorff 1996: 218–26).

4 Here I am, for the moment, ignoring an important fact, namely that assent is, for Locke, a matter of degree. See Chapter 9 (p. 144).

5 In the *Fourth Meditation*, Descartes follows Aquinas on this point; see Chapter 4 (p. 58). Spinoza (1982, II: 49; Scolium: 99) denies that we have any epistemic liberty of indifference.

6 See Chapter 2 (p. 30).

7 Locke expanded and transformed the chapter 'Of Power' in the second edition of the *Essay*.

8 Vienne (1991) suggests that Locke derived this conception of freedom from Malebranche (1992: Discourse III). On the other hand, Darwall (1995: 172–5) argues that once Molyneux had persuaded Locke there was something amiss with his first edition's account of freedom, Locke borrowed from Cudworth to repair the damage (see Cudworth 1996: 178–82).

9 It is not entirely clear from Locke's text whether this necessity is a rational neces- sity or something stronger. Sometimes he seems to think it possible (though irrational) for us to act (i.e. to will) against our final practical judgement, some- times not: compare sections 35 and 44 on the one hand with section 48 on the other. Darwall (1995: 160) argues that Locke (following Cudworth) distinguished 'a merely intellectual belief about which act would be best and a genuinely prac- tical judgement with the same content'.

10 In what follows, I ignore an important aspect of Hume's view, namely his concep- tion of passion as non-representational. Both Locke and Hume draw a distinction between practical judgements (what Hume calls 'reason') on the one hand and 'passion' or 'desire' on the other. But while Hume insists that passions are brute impulses which cause but cannot really rationalise action, Locke expresses no such view of the nature of 'desire' or 'uneasiness'. He thinks we can influence our desires by reflecting on how much good there is in the object desired (Locke 1975: 262–3), an inexplicable fact on the 'blind impulse' view (Hume 1978: 416– 17).

11 Pink (1996: 200–6) argues convincingly that whether you take a decision at all is no more subject to your will than is the particular decision you take.

12 This phrase occurs frequently in Locke 1996, e.g. p. 186.

13 See note 5.

14 Chapter 2 (p. 34).

15 Velleman (1992: 470–80) argues that the source of our control over action is a desire to act in accordance with our judgement of what we ought to do.

16 Some such view can, I think, be found in both Cudworth (1996: 178) and Butler (1983: 29 and 37–8).

17 Aquinas uses this Aristotelian metaphor repeatedly: e.g. see Aquinas (1984: 82–3).

7 A theory of freedom

1 Kant (1948: 61) considers a similar example.

2 See Chapter 1 (pp. 20–1).

3 It is said that Kant held this view. For a helpful discussion, see Korsgaard (1996b).

4 See Chapter 11 (pp. 174–6).

5 Holton (1999) distinguishes weakness of will from *akrasia* and argues that the ordinary notion of weakness of will applies only to cases in which we unreason- ably revise, or fail to implement, our intentions. I accept Holton's distinction but I doubt that it is so clearly marked in ordinary language.

6 Compare Aquinas' view (1983: 182–6) that while an erring conscience binds, an erroneous conscience does not excuse.

7 Kant (1956: 29–30) argues that we know that we are free because we know we are always capable of conforming our actions to our practical (specifically our moral) judgements, regardless of our other inclinations. Where inclination proposes an action, we test the proposal by asking whether we could will the maxim of acting on this inclination as a universal law. If not, a rational subject must veto the action and a rational subject can make that veto effective.

8 Pettit and Smith (1996: 448–9) do not distinguish this sort of case from the more difficult case in which I believe in the person's guilt even though I think I ought to believe in her innocence. Here I am in the situation of believing p but thinking I ought to believe not-p. This looks like a state of mind which I might express either by saying something of the form 'I believe that p but not-p' (namely 'I believe she is guilty even though she is not') or else by saying something of the form 'p but I do not believe that p' (namely 'She is innocent but I do not believe it'). Now there is something extremely paradoxical about both of these remarks, even though each of them might turn out to be true. So if these paradoxical sentences are needed to express my view of my own mental situation, perhaps this should make me wonder whether I could adopt such a view of my mental situation and thus be in that state of mind at all. Fortunately, the claim that higher order belief lacks intrinsic authority over our first-order beliefs can be illustrated without reference to such examples.

9 I might think you ought to believe something which I myself do not believe (or ought not to believe something which I do) because I know that the reasons available to you are different from those available to me. Here there need be no error on either part. The error comes in only when your belief differs from what I think *you* ought to believe.

10 See Chapter 9 (pp. 142–3).

11 This fact perhaps explains why some philosophers equate the will with practical judgement. For example, see Kant (1948: 76).

8 The scope of responsibility

1 Scanlon is an exception. As we saw in Chapter 1, he holds that we are responsible only for those of our attitudes and acts which are 'judgement-sensitive', i.e. under our reflective control, so he endorses the juridical theory of responsibility. But he asserts that desires and feelings are subject to moral criticism, even though they are not under our 'voluntary control', precisely because they are judgement-sensitive. See Scanlon (1998: 267–77).

2 For recent statements of the idea that blame, etc., presupposes control, see Gibbard (1990: 293–300) and Audi (1997).

3 Rawls (1972: 444–5) distinguishes natural shame from moral shame. See also Morris (1987: 220–32).

4 See Adams (1985: 11–14) for an incisive critique of this idea. My line of attack is different but complementary.

5 Needless to say, Kant expresses similar sentiments (e.g. 1948: 118).

6 There are writers who take dangerous character to be the true object of punishment. For a critical discussion of their views, see Duff (1996: Chapter 7).

7 See Chapter 5 (p. 80).

8 Mill (1961: Sections III and V) argues that the very notion of right and wrong implies the presence of sanctions. He divides the moral 'sanctions' into two classes: external (blame, etc.) and internal (guilt, etc.).

9 Williams (1995: 16) thinks blame a fraud precisely because he doubts that male-factors have the reasons which blame attributes to them.

10 It is a real question how this works. I have argued that many of the attitudes for which people are blamed are not under their reflective control; we shouldn't expect blame to remove irrational belief, say, simply by convincing the believer of its irrationality. Indeed, there is more to blaming someone than merely expressing the view that they are in the wrong, and that more may be what is needed for blame to exercise a non-judgmental influence over their attitudes.

11 For a statement of (extreme) retributivism, see Kant (1996: 105).

12 Since the function of punishment is not, for the retributivist, the provision of a practical incentive, he might invoke the account of freedom I offered in Chapter 7 to circumscribe the boundaries of punishment. On that view, intention formation is a free act, one for which we bear that special responsibility which, in the eyes of the retributivist, marks a suitable target for punishment. So decisions and intentions may fall within the scope of criminal law as much as do deeds, even though (as we saw in Chapter 5) the will is not subject to the will. This is something Hobbes explicitly denies: 'the style of law is *do this*, or *do not this*; or *if thou do this, thou shall suffer this*; but no law runs thus, *will this*, or *will not this*, or *if thou has a will to this, thou shalt suffer this*' (Hobbes 1839b: 181). For discussion of whether intentions actually do fall within the scope of the criminal law, see Morris (1976) and Husak (1996: 86–90).

Part 3: Memory and testimony

9 Knowledge and its preservation

1 For a statement of radical internalism, see Foster (1985: 106–16).

2 This question also arises for those (e.g. Reid 1997: 190–202) who treat testimony as a form of 'acquired perception'.

3 A similar point may be made about intentions. Even if my decision to holiday in South Africa rather than France was an irrational one, having now forgotten why I took that decision it may not be rational for me to abandon it and reconsider the whole issue.

4 Something like this line of thought is present in the work of several philosophers. McDowell (1998b: 427–43), for example, suggests that we distinguish the question of whether a belief is a responsible one from the question of whether we have any reason for it, and implies that victims of hallucination who have no reason to doubt their senses have no reason to believe what they do, despite their evident doxastic probity. See also McDowell (1998c: 404–8) and Bach (1985: 251–3).

5 See Chapter 3 (pp. 43–5) and Chapter 4 (pp. 61–5). I suspect that Burge and I would part company at this point. Burgess (1993: 478 and 1997: 28) does seem to think that we are entitled to rely on perceptual experience only if perception is actually reliable (whether or not the subject has any reason to doubt its reliability). See also the distinction he draws between justification and entitlement (Burge 1993: 458–9).

6 Chapter 2 (p. 34).

7 Once again, the same is true of decisions and intentions: some are more tenacious than others, and this has nothing to do with the content of the intentions – with whether they are conditional intentions or not (Bach 1984: 48–50).

8 Wolterstorff (1996: 77–8) argues that when Locke speaks of 'degrees of assent', he means what I mean by tenacity of belief and not what the Bayesians mean by level of confidence. For a different reading of Locke, see Foley (1993: 140–1).

10 The authority of memory

1 Pollock is criticising Malcolm (1963).
2 I was helped to see this by Michael Martin.
3 I might be hesitating because I am trying to decide whether I already believe that the UN has 120 members, i.e. whether I remember this. This would be a rather different sort of case.
4 Nor, as I show in Chapter 11, can I adopt this general attitude to the current beliefs of other people.
5 Chapter 9 (pp. 142–3).
6 My discussion is much indebted to Burge's article though, as I noted in Chapter 9, note 5, Burge would not endorse my internalist assumptions.
7 Pollock observes that there is a *phenomenological* difference between remembering that something happened to you in the past and believing that it happened on the basis of testimony. He infers that even factual memory must have an experiential element, an element which would still be present in the absence of belief (1974: 51). But it is clear from what I have just said that we can highlight the distinctive feature of memory beliefs without endorsing Pollock's view.
8 Much more needs to be said about when exactly beliefs should be abandoned or retained. Consider a couple of questions raised in conversation by Josh Wood. Suppose I have a belief and adequate support for it to start off with, but then evidence mounts up against it which ought to lead me to query it. Irrationally I don't query it, but then the countervailing evidence is shown to be fraudulent. Do I end up with a rational belief? I would think not. Obviously the evidence which is holding the belief in place is being given more than its proper weight if the belief is impervious to rational reconsideration. Alternatively, suppose I start off with an inadequately supported belief, but that evidence comes along which fully justifies it, evidence which I note with satisfaction. Does this make my belief rational? That depends on whether this new evidence becomes the basis for my belief or not, something we can discover by asking what would happen if this new evidence were to disappear. If I would then stick to my guns, then my belief is irrational all along since it is held regardless of the adequacy of the evidence for it.
9 It is a familiar point that not all strategies for acquiring true beliefs are rational methods of belief formation (Firth 1981: 149–56). The same is true of belief retention.
10 For a practical parallel, see below (pp. 159–60).
11 Alternatively, perhaps I realise that I ought to form the belief that *p* but can't bring myself to do it: neurotic doubts keep crowding in. Hypnosis which removes the neurotic basis for the doubts would be an aid to rational belief preservation, but Hypnosis which simply implants the belief without working off the probative force of evidence available to the subject would not.
12 Adler (1996) applies this idea to beliefs. Van Fraassen (1984) endorses the commitment model of belief for rather different reasons.
13 Foley notes a parallel with practical decision making: see Bratman (1987: Chapter 5).
14 I thank Michael Huemer for pressing this important objection.

15 Chapter 9 (pp. 140–2).
16 Locke's reluctance is evident in other passages. See e.g. 1975: 533–4. Descartes (1985: 218–20) shares Locke's concern about memory, though he makes the same concession (ibid.: 15).
17 See Chapter 11 (pp. 174–6).

11 The authority of testimony

1 Locke himself seems to think such a *rapprochement* possible. See Locke (1975: IV, XV, 4–6 and IV, XVI, 6–11).
2 Burge (1993: 474–5) raises this difficulty and wonders whether he has the resources to deal with it.
3 Chapter 10 (p. 158).
4 Brandom (1994: 474–5) sees a big difference between the theoretical and the practical here: while I can defer to others when justifying belief, action requires an inferential justification.
5 Chapter 7 (p. 105).
6 Chapter 7 (pp. 111–12).

Bibliography

Adams, R. (1985) 'Involuntary Sins', *Philosophical Review* 94: 3–31.
—— (1995) 'Moral Faith', *Journal of Philosophy* 92: 75–95.
Adler, J. (1996) 'An Overlooked Argument for Epistemic Conservatism', in *Analysis* 56: 80–4.
Alston, W. (1998) 'The Deontological Conception of Epistemic Justification', in Tomberlin (ed.) (1988).
Anscombe, E. (1981) 'Authority in Morals', in *Ethics, Politics and Religion*, Oxford: Basil Blackwell.
Aquinas, T. (1983) *Treatise on Happiness*, trans. J. Oesterle, Notre Dame: University of Notre Dame Press.
—— (1984) *Treatise on Virtue* trans. J. Oesterle, Notre Dame: University of Notre Dame Press.
Aristotle (1925) *Nicomachean Ethics* trans. D. Ross, Oxford: Oxford University Press.
Armstrong, D. (1973) *Belief, Truth and Knowledge*, Cambridge: Cambridge University Press.
Audi, R. (1990) 'Weakness of Will and Rational Action', *Australasian Journal of Philosophy* 68: 270–81.
—— (1997) 'Responsible Action and Virtuous Character', in *Moral Knowledge and Ethical Character*, Oxford: Oxford University Press.
Bach, K. (1984) 'Default Reasoning', *Pacific Philosophical Quarterly* 65: 37–54.
—— (1985) 'A Rationale for Reliabilism', *The Monist* 68: 246–63.
Beaney, M. (1997) *The Frege Reader*, Oxford: Basil Blackwell.
BonJour, L. (1985) *The Structure of Empirical Knowledge*, Cambridge, MA: Harvard University Press.
—— (1998) *In Defense of Pure Reason*, Cambridge: Cambridge University Press.
Brandom, R. (1994) *Making It Explicit*, Cambridge, MA: Harvard University Press.
Bratman, M. (1987) *Intentions, Plans and Practical Reasoning*, Cambridge, MA: Harvard University Press.
—— (1999a) 'Practical Reasoning and Acceptance in a Context', in *Faces of Intention*, Cambridge: Cambridge University Press.
—— (1999b) 'Responsibility and Planning', in Bratman (1999a).
Burge, T. (1993) 'Content Preservation', *Philosophical Review* 102: 457–88.
—— (1996) 'Our Entitlement to Self-Knowledge', *Proceedings of the Aristotelian Society* 96: 91–116.

—— (1997) 'Interlocution, Perception and Memory', *Philosophical Studies* 86: 21–47.
—— (1998) 'Reason and the First Person', in C. Wright, B. Smith and C. McDonald (eds) *Knowing Our Own Minds*, Oxford: Oxford University Press.
Burnyeat, M. (ed.) (1983) *The Skeptical Tradition* London: University of California Press.
—— (1997a) 'Can the Sceptic Live His Skepticism?', in M. Burnyeat and M. Frede (eds) *The Original Sceptics,* Indianapolis, IN: Hackett.
—— (1997b) 'The Sceptic in His Place and Time', in Burnyeat and Frede (1997).
Butler, S. (1983) *Five Sermons*, ed. S. Darwell, Indianapolis, IN: Hackett.
Chisholm, R. (1977) *A Theory of Knowledge* (2nd edn), Englewood Cliffs, NJ: Prentice-Hall.
Christensen, D. and Kornblith, H. (1997) 'Testimony, Memory and the Limits of the *A Priori*', *Philosophical Studies* 86: 1–20.
Clark, T. (1972) 'The Legacy of Scepticism', *Journal of Philosophy* 69: 754–69.
Clifford, W. (1879) 'The Ethics of Belief', in *Lectures and Essays*, London: Macmillan.
Coady, A. (1992) *Testimony*, Oxford: Oxford University Press.
Craig, E. (1990) *Knowledge and the State of Nature*, Oxford: Oxford University Press.
Cudworth, R. (1996) *Treatise Concerning Eternal and Immutable Morality*, ed. S. Hutton, Cambridge: Cambridge University Press.
Darwall, S. (1995) *The British Moralists and the Internal 'Ought'*, Cambridge: Cambridge University Press.
Davidson, D. (1980) 'Intending', in *Essays on Actions and Events*, Oxford: Oxford University Press.
Dennett, D. (1991) 'Two Contrasts: Folk Craft Versus Folk Science, and Belief Versus Opinion', in J. Greenwood (ed.), *The Future of Folk Psychology*, Cambridge: Cambridge University Press.
Descartes, R. (1984) *The Philosophical Writings of Descartes Volume II*, trans. J. Cottingham, R. Stoothoff and D. Murdoch, Cambridge: Cambridge University Press.
—— (1985) *The Philosophical Writings of Descartes :Volume I*, trans. J. Cottingham, R. Stoothoff and D. Murdoch, Cambridge: Cambridge University Press.
De Sousa, R. (1980) 'The Rationality of Emotions', in A. Rorty (ed.), *Explaining Emotions*, London: University of California Press.
Dretske, F. (1971) 'Reasons, Knowledge and Probability' *Philosophy of Science* 38: 216–20.
—— (1978) 'Conclusive Reasons', in Pappas and Swain (eds) (1978).
Duff, A. (1996) *Criminal Attempts*, Oxford: Oxford University Press.
Dummett, M. (1992) 'Memory and Testimony', in *The Seas of Language*, Oxford: Oxford University Press.
Firth, R. (1981) 'Epistemic Merit, Intrinsic and Instrumental', *Proceedings of the American Philosophical Association* 55: 5–23.
Foley, R. (1993) *Working without a Net*, Oxford: Oxford University Press.
Foster, J. (1985) *A. J. Ayer*, London: Routledge.
Foucault, M. (1997) 'On the Genealogy of Ethics', in his *Ethics*, London: Penguin.
Frankfurt, H. (1971) 'Freedom of the Will and the Concept of a Person', *Journal of Philosophy* 68: 5–20.

French, P., Uehling, T. and Wettstein, H. (eds) (1980) *Midwest Studies in Philosophy*, Volume V, Minneapolis, MN: University of Minnesota Press.

Evans, G. (1982) *The Varieties of Reference*, Oxford: Oxford University Press.

Gettier, E. (1963) 'Is Justified True Belief Knowledge', *Analysis* 23: 212–13.

Gibbard, A. (1990) *Wise Choices, Apt Feelings*, Oxford: Oxford University Press.

Goldman, A. (1978) 'Discrimination and Perceptual Knowledge', in Pappas and Swain (eds) (1978).

—— (1979) 'What Is Justified Belief?', in G. Pappas (ed.), *Justification and Knowledge*, Dordrecht: Reidel.

—— (1980) 'The Internalist Conception of Justification', in French *et al.* (eds) (1980).

—— (1986) *Epistemology and Cognition*, Cambridge, MA: Harvard University Press.

—— (1988) 'Strong and Weak Justification', in Tomberlin (ed.) (1988).

Harman G. (1973) *Thought*, Princeton, NJ: Princeton University Press.

—— (1980) 'Reasoning and Evidence One Does Not Possess', in French *et al.* (eds) (1980).

—— (1986) *Change in View*, Cambridge, MA: MIT Press.

Heal, J. (1990) 'Pragmatism and Choosing to Believe', in A. Malachowski (ed.), *Reading Rorty*, Oxford: Basil Blackwell.

Hegel, G. W. F. (1990) *Lectures on the Philosophy of History: Volume III*, ed. R. F. Brown, Berkeley: University of California Press.

Heil, J. (1984) 'Doxastic Incontinence', *Mind* 93: 56–70.

Hobbes, T. (1839a) *Discourse of Liberty and Necessity*, in *The English Works of Thomas Hobbes: Volume IV*, ed. W. Molesworth, London: J. Bohn.

—— (1839b) *The English Works of Thomas Hobbes: Volume V*, ed. W. Molesworth, London: J. Bohn.

Holton, R. (1999) 'Intention and Weakness of Will', *Journal of Philosophy* 96: 241–62.

Hookway, C. (1990) *Scepticism*, London: Routledge.

—— (1994) 'Cognitive Virtues and Epistemic Evaluations', *International Journal of Philosophical Studies* 2: 213–27.

Hume, D. (1975) *An Enquiry Concerning Human Understanding*, ed. L. Selby-Bigge, Oxford: Oxford University Press.

—— (1978) *A Treatise of Human Nature*, ed. L. Selby-Bigge, Oxford: Oxford University Press.

Husak, D. (1996) 'Does Criminal Liability Require an Act?', in R. Duff (ed.), *Philosophy and the Criminal Law*, Cambridge: Cambridge University Press.

James, W. (1950) *The Principles of Psychology: Volume Two*, New York: Dover.

—— (1956) *The Will to Believe*, New York: Dover.

Jeffrey, R. (1992) *Probability and the Art of Judgement*, Cambridge: Cambridge University Press.

Kant, I. (1948) *Groundwork of the Metaphysic of Morals*, trans. H. Paton, London: Hutchinson.

—— (1956) *Critique of Practical Reason*, trans. L. White Beck, Indianapolis, IN: Bobbs-Merrill.

—— (1983) 'What Is Enlightenment?', in *Perpetual Peace and Other Essays*, Indianapolis, IN: Hackett.

—— (1996) *The Metaphysics of Morals*, trans. M. Gregor, Cambridge: Cambridge University Press.

Kaplan, M. (1985) 'It's Not What You Know that Counts', *Journal of Philosophy* 82: 350–63.

—— (1991) 'Epistemology on Holiday', *Journal of Philosophy* 88: 132–54.

Kavka, G. (1983) 'The Toxin Puzzle', *Analysis* 43: 33–6.

Kent, B. (1996) *Virtues of the Will*, Washington, DC: Catholic University of America Press.

Kornblith, H. (1983) 'Justified Belief and Epistemically Responsible Action', *Philosophical Review* 93: 33–48.

Korsgaard, C. (1996a) *The Sources of Normativity*, Cambridge: Cambridge University Press.

—— (1996b) 'Morality as Freedom', in *Creating the Kingdom of Ends*, Cambridge: Cambridge University Press.

Lehrer, K. (1990) *Theory of Knowledge*, London: Routledge.

Leibniz, G. (1981) *New Essays on Human Understanding*, ed. P. Remnant and J. Bennett, Cambridge: Cambridge University Press.

Locke, J. (1965) 'A Letter Concerning Toleration', in M. Cranston (ed.), *Locke on Politics, Religion and Education*, New York: Collier.

—— (1975) *An Essay Concerning Human Understanding*, ed. P. Nidditch, Oxford: Oxford University Press.

—— (1996) *Of the Conduct of the Understanding*, ed. R. Grant and N. Tarcov, Indianapolis, IN: Hackett.

McDowell, J. (1994) *Mind and World*, Cambridge, MA: Harvard University Press.

—— (1998a) 'Having the World in View: Lecture One', *Journal of Philosophy* 95: 431–50.

—— (1998b) 'Knowledge by Hearsay', in *Meaning, Knowledge and Reality*, Cambridge, MA: Harvard University Press.

—— (1998c) 'Knowledge and the Internal', in *Meaning, Knowledge and Reality*, Cambridge, MA: Harvard University Press.

McGinn, C. (1982) *The Character of Mind*, Oxford: Oxford University Press.

McIntyre, A. (1990) 'Is Akratic Action Always Irrational?', in O. Flanagan and A. Rorty (eds), *Identity, Character and Morality*, Cambridge, Mass: MIT Press.

Malcolm, N. (1963) 'A Definition of Factual Memory', in his *Knowledge and Certainty*, Englewood Cliffs, NJ: Prentice-Hall.

Malebranche, N. (1992) *Treatise on Nature and Grace*, trans. P. Riley, Oxford: Oxford University Press.

Meinong, A. (1973) 'Toward an Epistemological Assessment of Memory', in (ed.) R. Chisholm and S. Schwartz *Empirical Knowledge*, Englewood Cliffs, NJ: Prentice Hall .

Mill, J. (1961) *Utilitarianism*, ed. M. Lerner, New York: Bantam.

Montmarquet, J. (1993) *Epistemic Virtue and Doxastic Responsibility*, Lanham, MD: Rowman & Littlefield.

Moran, R. (1997) 'Self-Knowledge: Discovery, Resolution and Undoing', *European Journal of Philosophy* 5: 141–61.

Morris, H. (1976) 'Punishment For Thoughts', in *On Guilt and Innocence*, Berkeley: University of California Press.

—— (1987) 'Non-Moral Guilt', in F. Shoeman (ed.), *Responsibility, Character and the Emotions*, Cambridge: Cambridge University Press.

Nagel, T. (1986) *The View From Nowhere*, Oxford: Oxford University Press.

Nozick, R. (1993) *The Nature of Rationality*, Princeton, NJ: Princeton University Press.

O'Shaughnessy, B. (1980) *The Will: Volume Two*, Cambridge: Cambridge University Press.

Owens, D. (1996) 'A Lockean Theory of Memory Experience', *Philosophy and Phenomenological Research*, 54: 319–32.

—— (2000) 'Scepticisms', *Proceedings of the Aristotelian Society* (Supplementary volume LXXIV).

Pappas, G. and Swain, M. (1978) *Essays on Knowledge and Justification*, Ithaca, NY: Cornell University Press.

Passmore, J. (1986) 'Locke and the Ethics of Belief', in A. Kenny (ed.), *Rationalism, Empiricism and Idealism*, Oxford: Oxford University Press.

Pettit, P. and Smith, M. (1996) 'Freedom in Belief and Desire', *Journal of Philosophy* 93: 433–6.

Peacocke, C. (1986) *Thoughts: An Essay on Content*, Oxford: Basil Blackwell.

Pink, T. (1996) *The Psychology of Freedom*, Cambridge: Cambridge University Press.

Plantinga, A. (1993a) *Warrant: The Current Debate*, Oxford: Oxford University Press.

—— (1993b) *Warrant and Proper Function*, Oxford: Oxford University Press.

Pollock, J. (1974) *Knowledge and Justification*, Princeton, NJ: Princeton University Press.

—— (1986) *Contemporary Theories of Knowledge*, London: Hutchinson.

—— (1995) *Cognitive Carpentry*, Cambridge, MA: MIT Press.

Radford, C. (1966) 'Knowledge – By Examples', *Analysis* 27: 1–11.

Rawls, J. (1972) *A Theory of Justice*, Oxford: Oxford University Press.

Raz, J. (1975) *Practical Reason and Norms*, London: Hutchinson.

Reid, T. (1997) *Inquiry into the Human Mind*, (ed.) D. Brookes, Edinburgh: Edinburgh University Press.

Scanlon, T. (1998) *What We Owe to Each Other*, Cambridge, MA: Harvard University Press.

Schouls, P. (1992) *Reasoned Freedom: John Locke and Enlightenment*, Ithaca, NY: Cornell University Press.

Shoemaker, S. (1988) 'On Knowing One's Own Mind', in Tomberlin (ed.) (1988).

Sidgwick, H. (1981) *The Methods of Ethics*, Indianapolis, IN: Hackett.

Spinoza, B. (1982) *Ethics*, ed. F. Feldman, Indianapolis, IN: Hackett.

Stroud, B. (1983) 'Kant and Scepticism', in M. Burnyeat (ed.) (1983).

—— (1989) 'Understanding Human Knowledge in General', in M. Clay and K. Lehrer (ed.), *Knowledge and Scepticism*, Boulder, CO: Westview.

Tomberlin, J. (ed.) (1988) *Philosophical Perspectives 2: Epistemology*, Reseda, California: Ridgeview Publishing Company.

Unger, P. (1975) *Ignorance*, Oxford: Oxford University Press.

Van Cleve, J.(1979) 'Foundationalism, Epistemic Principles and the Cartesian Circle', *Philosophical Review* 88: 55–91.

Van Fraassen, B. (1984) 'Belief and the Will', *Journal of Philosophy* 81: 235–56.

Velleman, J. (1989) *Practical Reflection*, Princeton, NJ: Princeton University Press.

—— (1992) 'What Happens When Someone Acts?', *Mind* 101: 461–81.

Vienne, J. (1991) 'Malebranche and Locke', in S. Brown (ed.), *Nicholas Malebranche,* Maastricht van Gorcum: Assen.

Wallace, J. (1978) *Virtues and Vices,* Ithaca, NY: Cornell University Press.

Williams, B. (1973a) 'Deciding to Believe', in *Problems of the Self,* Cambridge: Cambridge University Press.

—— (1973b) 'Ethical Consistency', in his *Problems of the Self,* Cambridge: Cambridge University Press.

—— (1978) *Descartes,* London: Penguin.

—— (1983) 'Descartes's Use of Scepticism', in M. Burnyeat (ed.) (1983).

—— (1995) 'How Free Does the Will Need to Be?', in *Making Sense of Humanity,* Cambridge: Cambridge University Press.

Williams, M. (1996) *Unnatural Doubts,* Princeton, NJ: Princeton University Press.

Williamson, T. (1995) 'Is Knowing a State of Mind?', *Mind* 104: 533–65.

Wolterstoff, N. (1996) *John Locke and the Ethics of Belief,* Cambridge: Cambridge University Press.

Zagzebski, L. (1994) 'The Inescapability of Gettier Problems', *Philosophical Quarterly* 44: 65–73.

—— (1996) *Virtues of the Mind,* Cambridge: Cambridge University Press.

Index